ANCIENT CHINA
221 BCE - 1644 AD

EMPERORS TO PHILOSOPHERS & WALLS TO MASTERPIECES

4 BOOKS IN 1

BOOK 1
EMPERORS OF THE SILK ROAD: ANCIENT CHINA'S DYNASTIC SAGA (221 BCE - 220 CE)

BOOK 2
CONFUCIANISM: THE MORAL COMPASS OF ANCIENT CHINA (551 BCE - 479 BCE)

BOOK 3
THE GREAT WALL: ENGINEERING MARVEL OF ANCIENT CHINA (7TH CENTURY BC - 17TH CENTURY AD)

BOOK 4
MING DYNASTY TREASURES: ART AND CULTURE IN ANCIENT CHINA (1368 - 1644)

BY A.J. KINGSTON

*Copyright © 2023 by A. J. Kingston
All rights reserved. No part of this book may be reproduced or transmitted in any form or by any means, electronic or mechanical, including photocopying, recording, or by any information storage and retrieval system, without permission in writing from the publisher.*

*Published by A. J. Kingston
Library of Congress Cataloging-in-Publication Data
ISBN 978-1-83938-477-6
Cover design by Rizzo*

Disclaimer

The contents of this book are based on extensive research and the best available historical sources. However, the author and publisher make no claims, promises, or guarantees about the accuracy, completeness, or adequacy of the information contained herein. The information in this book is provided on an "as is" basis, and the author and publisher disclaim any and all liability for any errors, omissions, or inaccuracies in the information or for any actions taken in reliance on such information.

The opinions and views expressed in this book are those of the author and do not necessarily reflect the official policy or position of any organization or individual mentioned in this book. Any reference to specific people, places, or events is intended only to provide historical context and is not intended to defame or malign any group, individual, or entity.

The information in this book is intended for educational and entertainment purposes only. It is not intended to be a substitute for professional advice or judgment. Readers are encouraged to conduct their own research and to seek professional advice where appropriate.

Every effort has been made to obtain necessary permissions and acknowledgments for all images and other copyrighted material used in this book. Any errors or omissions in this regard are unintentional, and the author and publisher will correct them in future editions.

Join Our Productivity Group and Access your Bonus

If you're passionate about history books and want to connect with others who share your love of the subject, joining our Facebook group (search for "History Books by A.J.Kingston") can be a great way to do so. By joining a group dedicated to history books, you'll have the opportunity to connect with like-minded individuals, share your thoughts and ideas, and even discover new books that you might not have come across otherwise. You can also access your FREE BONUS once you joined our Facebook group called "History Books by A.J.Kingston".

One of the biggest advantages of joining our Facebook group is the sense of community it provides. You'll be able to interact with other history book enthusiasts, ask questions, and share your own knowledge and expertise. This can be especially valuable if you're a student or someone who is just starting to explore the world of history books.

If you love audiobooks, then joining our YouTube channel that offers free audiobooks on a weekly basis can be a great way to stay entertained and engaged. By subscribing to our channel, you'll have access to a range of audiobooks across different genres, all for free. Not only this is a great opportunity to enjoy some new audiobooks, but it's also a chance to discover new authors and titles that you might not have come across otherwise.

Lastly, don't forget to follow us on Facebook and YouTube by searching for A.J. Kingston.

TABLE OF CONTENTS – BOOK 1 - EMPERORS OF THE SILK ROAD: ANCIENT CHINA'S DYNASTIC SAGA (221 BCE - 220 CE)

Introduction 6
Chapter 1: The Birth of the Qin Dynasty 9
Chapter 2: Qin Shi Huang: The First Emperor 17
Chapter 3: The Great Wall and Imperial Expansion 21
Chapter 4: Han Dynasty: A Golden Era 30
Chapter 5: Silk Road: Gateway to the West 39
Chapter 6: The Han-Sino Nomadic Encounter 49
Chapter 7: Dynastic Challenges and Rebellions 57
Chapter 8: Wu Zetian: China's Only Empress 66
Chapter 9: End of an Era: The Fall of the Han 74
Chapter 10: Legacy of the Silk Road: Han Dynasty's Lasting Influence 83

TABLE OF CONTENTS – BOOK 2 - CONFUCIANISM: THE MORAL COMPASS OF ANCIENT CHINA (551 BCE - 479 BCE)

Chapter 1: The World of Ancient China (551 BCE) 93
Chapter 2: Confucius: Life and Early Influences (551 - 539 BCE) 101
Chapter 3: Formation of Confucian Philosophy (532 - 517 BCE) 108
Chapter 4: The Analects: Core Teachings of Confucius (512 - 479 BCE) 118
Chapter 5: The Five Relationships and Moral Conduct (505 - 484 BCE) 127
Chapter 6: Confucianism's Impact on Education and Governance (490 - 475 BCE) 136
Chapter 7: Challenges and Critiques of Confucianism (475 - 479 BCE) 145
Chapter 8: The Legacy of Confucianism in Ancient China 154
Chapter 9: Confucianism Beyond China: Global Influence 162
Chapter 10: Confucianism in the Modern World 170

TABLE OF CONTENTS – BOOK 3 - THE GREAT WALL: ENGINEERING MARVEL OF ANCIENT CHINA (7TH CENTURY BC - 17TH CENTURY AD)

Chapter 1: The Origins of a Defensive Vision (7th Century BC) 180
Chapter 2: The Warring States Period and Early Defensive Structures (475 - 221 BC) .. 188
Chapter 3: Qin Dynasty: The Birth of the Great Wall (221 - 206 BC) 197
Chapter 4: The Han Dynasty and Expanding the Frontier (206 BC - 220 AD) 205
Chapter 5: The Silk Road Connection and Economic Impact (221 - 589 AD) 213
Chapter 6: Turmoil and Unification during the Sui and Tang Dynasties (589 - 907 AD) 221
Chapter 7: The Ming Dynasty: The Great Wall's Golden Age (1368 - 1644 AD) 226
Chapter 8: Life on the Frontier: Soldiers and Communities 233
Chapter 9: Challenges and Invasions: The Wall in Conflict 239
Chapter 10: The Great Wall's Enduring Legacy 244

TABLE OF CONTENTS – BOOK 4 - MING DYNASTY TREASURES: ART AND CULTURE IN ANCIENT CHINA (1368 - 1644)

Chapter 1: The Rise of the Ming Dynasty (1368) 251
Chapter 2: Imperial Patronage of the Arts (1368 - 1398) 257
Chapter 3: Porcelain and Ceramics: The Ming Blue and White (1400s) 262
Chapter 4: Literature and Poetry: The Ming's Scholarly Pursuits (1400s) 267
Chapter 5: Ming Imperial Gardens and Architecture (1400s) 272
Chapter 6: Silk, Textiles, and Fashion (1400s - 1500s) 276
Chapter 7: Ming Artisans and Craftsmanship (1500s) 280
Chapter 8: Cultural Exchanges and Foreign Diplomacy (1500s - 1600s) 284
Chapter 9: Decline and the Arrival of the Qing Dynasty (1600s - 1644) 288
Chapter 10: The Ming Dynasty's Enduring Cultural Legacy 292
Conclusion 298
About A. J. Kingston 300

Introduction

In the vast expanse of history, there exists a civilization that spans millennia, a civilization whose influence reverberates through the annals of time—Ancient China. From the mighty emperors who forged dynasties to the profound philosophers who shaped ethical codes, from the monumental engineering marvels to the exquisite artistic treasures, Ancient China's legacy is a tapestry woven with threads of brilliance and innovation.

In the pages of this remarkable book bundle, we invite you to embark on a captivating journey through the heart of Ancient China. Across four distinct volumes, we delve deep into the epochs that define this remarkable civilization, from its emergence in the Qin Dynasty to its zenith during the Ming Dynasty, and finally, to the twilight years of the Ming Dynasty.

Book 1 - Emperors of the Silk Road: Ancient China's Dynastic Saga (221 BCE - 220 CE): Here, we unveil the epic dynastic saga of Ancient China, from the visionary Qin Shi Huang's unification of warring states to the golden era of the Han Dynasty. Witness the rise and fall of emperors, the expansion of territories, and the intricate dance of power and diplomacy along the Silk Road.

Book 2 - Confucianism: The Moral Compass of Ancient China (551 BCE - 479 BCE): Enter the realm of philosophy and ethics as we explore the teachings of Confucius, the sage whose moral compass guided generations. Discover the profound impact of Confucianism on Chinese culture, governance, and the intricate web of human relationships.

Book 3 - The Great Wall: Engineering Marvel of Ancient China (7th Century BC - 17th Century AD): Journey through time and explore one of the world's most iconic engineering feats—the Great Wall of China. Trace its evolution from early defensive structures to the monumental wonder that spans centuries, offering insights into the challenges faced by its builders and the significance of its existence.

Book 4 - Ming Dynasty Treasures: Art and Culture in Ancient China (1368 - 1644): Immerse yourself in the opulent world of the Ming Dynasty, where art, culture, and craftsmanship thrived. Witness the creation of exquisite blue and white porcelain, stroll through magnificent imperial gardens, and delve into a cultural renaissance that continues to captivate hearts.

These four volumes come together to create a comprehensive exploration of Ancient China, where emperors, philosophers, engineers, and artists collectively crafted a civilization that transcends time. This is a civilization that left an indelible mark on the world, a civilization whose stories are as grand as its dynasties, as profound as its philosophies, as enduring as its walls, and as captivating as its masterpieces.

Join us on this extraordinary odyssey through Ancient China, where history and culture intertwine to form an epic narrative that has shaped the course of humanity. As we turn the pages of this bundle, we invite you to traverse the Silk Road, ponder the wisdom of sages, stand in awe of architectural wonders, and immerse yourself in the artistry of a bygone era. Welcome to Ancient China—a journey through time and imagination that awaits your discovery.

**BOOK 1
EMPERORS OF THE SILK ROAD
ANCIENT CHINA'S DYNASTIC SAGA
(221 BCE - 220 CE)
BY A.J. KINGSTON**

Chapter 1: The Birth of the Qin Dynasty

The rise of the Qin state in ancient China represents a pivotal moment in the country's history, as it laid the foundation for the establishment of the first Chinese imperial dynasty, the Qin Dynasty. This remarkable ascent began in the turbulent period known as the Warring States era, a time characterized by incessant warfare, political fragmentation, and social upheaval. The Qin state, led by visionary leaders and fueled by military prowess and innovative reforms, emerged as a dominant power in this chaotic landscape.

At the outset of the Warring States period, the region that would later become the Qin state was relatively minor compared to the powerful states of Qi, Chu, Yan, Zhao, Wei, and Han. The Qin people resided in the western part of what is now China, an area marked by rugged terrain and a harsh climate. These geographical challenges initially placed the Qin state at a disadvantage, as its resources and agricultural capabilities were limited compared to its more prosperous neighbors.

However, it was during this adversity that the Qin state began to develop its military might and political acumen. Qin rulers recognized the need for a strong and disciplined army to survive in the highly competitive environment of the Warring States. They implemented a series of military reforms that would eventually become the hallmark of the Qin military.

One of the key figures in the rise of the Qin state was Duke Xiao of Qin, who reigned from 361 BCE to 338 BCE. Duke Xiao implemented significant changes in the state's military organization and strategy. He promoted the use of infantry over chariots, a shift that allowed for greater mobility and adaptability on the battlefield. This reform laid the foundation for the formidable Qin infantry, which played a crucial role in the state's military successes.

In addition to military reforms, the Qin state also adopted administrative innovations that contributed to its rise. Shang Yang, a renowned legalist philosopher and statesman, served as an advisor to Duke Xiao and later to King Huiwen of Qin. Shang Yang's policies, collectively known as the "Shang Yang reforms," aimed to strengthen the central authority of the state and promote the welfare of its citizens. These reforms included the implementation of a strict legal code that applied to all citizens, regardless of social status. This code helped to establish a more equitable society and discouraged corruption among officials. Shang Yang also introduced a system of land allocation based on merit rather than hereditary privilege, which further strengthened the state and its agricultural productivity.

The rise of the Qin state also benefited from its strategic location. Situated in the western part of China, it had access to valuable resources, including metallurgical materials and salt, which were crucial for both military and economic purposes. Controlling these resources allowed the Qin state to develop a strong economy and maintain a well-equipped military.

The Qin state's military successes were not confined to its borders. It expanded its territory through conquests and alliances, gradually absorbing neighboring states. One of its most notable achievements was the annexation of the state of Shu, located to the southwest. This expansion solidified the Qin state's control over crucial western regions.

The culmination of the Qin state's rise came with the leadership of King Zheng, who later became known as Qin Shi Huang, the First Emperor of Qin. Ascending to the throne in 246 BCE, Qin Shi Huang embarked on a mission to unify China under his rule. His vision was not merely about territorial conquest; he aimed to establish a centralized and autocratic system of governance.

Under Qin Shi Huang's rule, the state undertook several monumental projects, the most famous of which was the construction of the Great Wall of China. While earlier walls existed in various states, it was Qin Shi Huang who initiated the ambitious project of connecting and extending these walls into a single defensive barrier. This monumental undertaking showcased the Qin state's engineering and organizational prowess.

Qin Shi Huang's rule was also characterized by a series of reforms that standardized currency, writing, and measurements throughout the newly unified empire. This standardization helped to facilitate trade, communication, and governance, creating a more cohesive and efficient state.

However, the First Emperor's rule was not without controversy. His authoritarian policies and harsh measures, such as the suppression of dissent and the burning of books, provoked resistance and resentment among some segments of society. Nonetheless, his legacy as a unifier of China cannot be denied.

In 221 BCE, after years of military campaigns and consolidation, Qin Shi Huang proclaimed himself the First Emperor of the Qin Dynasty. This marked the beginning of China's imperial era, as the Qin Dynasty became the first dynasty to unite China under a single centralized government. The establishment of a unified Chinese empire was a monumental achievement, and it laid the groundwork for the subsequent dynasties that would shape China's history for centuries to come.

In summary, the rise of the Qin state was a complex and multifaceted process that involved military prowess, innovative reforms, and strategic leadership. It transformed a relatively minor state into a dominant power in ancient China and paved the way for the establishment of the first Chinese imperial dynasty, the Qin Dynasty. This period of history, marked by the rise of the Qin state, represents a crucial chapter in China's long and rich cultural heritage.

The Qin Unification Campaigns, also known as the Qin's Wars of Unification, were a series of military campaigns undertaken by the Qin state during the Warring States period of ancient China. These campaigns, which spanned over several decades, culminated in the unification of China under the rule of Qin Shi Huang, the First Emperor of the Qin Dynasty. The successful conclusion of these campaigns marked a pivotal moment in Chinese history, as it laid the foundation for the first centralized imperial dynasty in China. The Warring States period (475 - 221 BCE) was characterized by political fragmentation, incessant warfare, and social upheaval as numerous states vied for supremacy and territorial control. During this turbulent era, the Qin state, located in the western part of China, emerged as a dominant power, thanks to its innovative military reforms, strong leadership, and strategic vision.

The Qin Unification Campaigns were initiated by Duke Xiao of Qin, who ruled from 361 BCE to 338 BCE. Duke Xiao implemented significant changes in the state's military organization and strategy, setting the stage for future conquests. Under his leadership, the Qin state began to develop a disciplined and formidable infantry, which replaced the traditional reliance on chariots in warfare.

One of the early targets of the Qin Unification Campaigns was the state of Shu, located to the southwest of Qin. In 316 BCE, Qin forces launched a successful campaign against Shu, annexing its territory and expanding Qin's western borders.

This marked the beginning of Qin's territorial expansion efforts.

The most famous and significant campaign of the Qin Unification Campaigns was the conquest of the state of Zhao. In 260 BCE, the Qin general Bai Qi led a successful invasion of Zhao, which resulted in the capture of its capital, Handan, in 236 BCE. This victory marked a turning point in the campaigns and demonstrated the military prowess of the Qin state.

The conquest of Yan and Qi followed, further expanding Qin's territory and influence. By 221 BCE, Qin Shi Huang had ascended to the throne, and under his leadership, the Qin Unification Campaigns continued with the ultimate goal of unifying all of China.

One of the most remarkable aspects of these campaigns was the innovative use of military strategies and tactics. The Qin state employed strategies such as encirclement, siege warfare, and psychological warfare to gain the upper hand in battles. The use of siege engines and the standardization of weapons and equipment across the Qin army also contributed to their military success.

However, the campaigns were not without challenges and hardships. The Qin state faced strong opposition from other powerful states, such as Chu and Han, which put up fierce resistance. The battles were often brutal and protracted, with significant loss of life on both sides.

The unification of China was finally achieved in 221 BCE when Qin Shi Huang proclaimed himself the First Emperor of the Qin Dynasty. He implemented a centralized system of government, standardized writing, measurements, and currency, and initiated monumental construction projects, including the Great Wall of China. The Qin Dynasty's establishment marked the end of the Warring States period and the beginning of China's imperial era.

While the Qin Unification Campaigns were successful in uniting China under a single ruler, they also left a lasting legacy of centralized power and bureaucracy that would influence the subsequent dynasties in Chinese history. The campaigns played a crucial role in shaping the political and cultural landscape of ancient China, leaving an indelible mark on the nation's history.

The formation of the Qin Dynasty, one of the most significant dynasties in Chinese history, represents a pivotal period characterized by political consolidation, the unification of warring states, and the establishment of a centralized imperial government. This era, marked by the rise of Qin Shi Huang, the First Emperor, saw the culmination of efforts that began with the Qin state's military campaigns and reforms during the Warring States period.
The Qin Dynasty was founded by Qin Shi Huang, originally known as Ying Zheng, who ascended to the throne in 246 BCE at the age of 13. His reign marked the realization of a long-cherished vision: the unification of China under a single central authority. This vision had eluded previous rulers and states for centuries during the Warring States period.
One of the key factors contributing to the formation of the Qin Dynasty was the successful outcome of the Qin Unification Campaigns, which were launched in earlier decades. These military campaigns, carried out by Qin generals and strategists, aimed to conquer rival states and expand Qin territory. The campaigns were marked by both innovative military tactics and ruthless determination.
The conquest of states such as Zhao, Yan, and Qi, as well as the annexation of Shu to the southwest, significantly expanded Qin's territory and influence. Each victory brought the Qin state closer to its goal of unifying all of China. However, it was the annexation of the state of Chu in 223

BCE that solidified Qin's dominance, as Chu was one of the most powerful and formidable states at the time.

In 221 BCE, with the conquest of the state of Qi, Ying Zheng declared himself the First Emperor of Qin, taking the name Qin Shi Huang. This declaration marked the official establishment of the Qin Dynasty and the beginning of a new era in Chinese history. Qin Shi Huang's title, "Huangdi," means "Imperial Sovereign," signifying his intention to rule over all of China as its first emperor.

The formation of the Qin Dynasty was not solely a military achievement. Qin Shi Huang implemented a series of sweeping political, administrative, and cultural reforms aimed at centralizing power and establishing a unified system of governance. These reforms were intended to strengthen the authority of the central government and eliminate regional autonomy.

One of the most significant reforms introduced by Qin Shi Huang was the standardization of various aspects of Chinese society. This included standardizing the writing system, currency, weights and measures, and the width of cart axles. These reforms contributed to the integration and cohesion of the newly unified empire.

Another major reform was the division of the empire into administrative units called commanderies and counties. These administrative divisions allowed for greater control and oversight of the vast territory. Qin Shi Huang appointed loyal officials to govern these units, further centralizing power in the hands of the central government.

In addition to political and administrative reforms, the First Emperor implemented a policy of book burning in an attempt to suppress dissenting thought and centralize ideological control. While this policy aimed to eliminate perceived threats to the regime, it also resulted in the loss of valuable historical and cultural texts.

The construction of the Great Wall of China also began during the Qin Dynasty. Initially, various sections of defensive walls existed in different states. Qin Shi Huang ordered the connection and extension of these walls to form a continuous barrier. This ambitious project was not only a defensive measure but also a symbol of the dynasty's unification and imperial authority.

Despite the accomplishments of the Qin Dynasty, it was also marked by authoritarianism, harsh legalism, and forced labor, which generated resentment among the populace. Qin Shi Huang's rule was characterized by a highly centralized government with strict control over all aspects of life.

The Qin Dynasty's existence was relatively short-lived, spanning only 15 years, from 221 BCE to 206 BCE, when it was succeeded by the Han Dynasty. However, its legacy as the first centralized imperial dynasty in Chinese history and its contributions to the formation of a unified China are enduring and foundational aspects of Chinese civilization.

Chapter 2: Qin Shi Huang: The First Emperor

Qin Shi Huang, the First Emperor of China and the driving force behind the formation of the Qin Dynasty, had a fascinating and tumultuous early life that set the stage for his remarkable reign and historical legacy. Born in 259 BCE as Ying Zheng, he was the son of King Zhuangxiang of Qin and Queen Zhao. His upbringing was marked by political intrigue, palace intrigue, and a precarious royal succession.

At the time of Ying Zheng's birth, the Qin state was one of several powerful states in ancient China, and it was engaged in the tumultuous Warring States period (475 - 221 BCE). During this era, the various Chinese states were locked in continuous warfare, vying for supremacy and territorial control. The state of Qin, located in the western part of China, was known for its military strength and innovative reforms, which would eventually pave the way for Ying Zheng's ascent to the throne.

Ying Zheng's early life was overshadowed by a bitter and complex struggle for power within the royal court. His father, King Zhuangxiang, died when Ying Zheng was just nine years old, leaving a power vacuum in the Qin state. Queen Zhao, Ying Zheng's mother, sought to consolidate power on behalf of her son but faced opposition from other factions within the court.

During this time, political maneuvering and power struggles were rampant. Queen Zhao's efforts to secure her son's position as the heir apparent were met with resistance from influential court officials and rival factions. These factions sought to undermine her authority and promote their own interests, leading to a tumultuous and uncertain environment for young Ying Zheng.

Amid this turmoil, a pivotal figure emerged in Ying Zheng's life—Lu Buwei, a merchant, and a trusted court advisor. Lu Buwei played a crucial role in supporting Queen Zhao's efforts to secure Ying Zheng's future as the rightful heir to the Qin throne. He orchestrated a plan to place Ying Zheng on the throne by circumventing potential rivals and internal opposition.

As part of this plan, Lu Buwei arranged for Ying Zheng to be married to Lady Zhao, a concubine who had strong ties to the influential merchant class and could provide support for Ying Zheng's claim to the throne. This strategic marriage further solidified Ying Zheng's position within the Qin court.

In 246 BCE, at the age of 13, Ying Zheng officially ascended to the throne as King of Qin following a series of political maneuvers orchestrated by Lu Buwei. His reign was marked by a regency led by Lu Buwei and other influential advisors due to his youth. During this period, the state continued its efforts to expand its territory through military campaigns and strategic alliances.

Despite the challenges and intrigues of his early life, Ying Zheng's ascent to the throne marked the beginning of a transformative era in Chinese history. As he matured and solidified his power, he would eventually declare himself the First Emperor of the Qin Dynasty and embark on a mission to unify all of China under his rule. His early life's experiences, marked by political maneuvering and the quest for legitimacy, played a significant role in shaping his determination to achieve this ambitious goal and establish a centralized imperial dynasty.

The consolidation of power during the early years of Qin Shi Huang's reign as the First Emperor of the Qin Dynasty was a complex and significant process that shaped the trajectory of his rule and laid the foundation for the unification of China. This period was marked by both political maneuvering and the implementation of policies aimed at centralizing authority and strengthening the imperial state.

Upon ascending to the throne in 246 BCE, at the age of 13, Ying Zheng—later known as Qin Shi Huang—faced the challenges of youth and inexperience. As a result, a regency was established to provide guidance and stability during his early years as king. Lu Buwei, an influential court advisor, played a pivotal role in this regency, acting as a de facto regent and overseeing the affairs of the state.

One of the key objectives during this period was to consolidate the authority of the central government and eliminate potential threats to the young king's rule. To achieve this, several important steps were taken:

Maintaining Lu Buwei's Influence: Lu Buwei, a skilled statesman and strategist, continued to exert significant influence within the court. His support and guidance were instrumental in preserving the stability of the Qin state during the transition of power.

Reforms and Standardization: Qin Shi Huang and his advisors initiated a series of reforms aimed at standardizing various aspects of governance and society. These reforms included the standardization of writing scripts, weights and measures, currency, and laws. By standardizing these elements, the central government gained greater control and oversight.

Centralization of Power: Efforts were made to centralize political power in the hands of the monarch and his advisors. The feudal system that had characterized earlier periods of Chinese history was gradually dismantled, and regional autonomy was curtailed. Local aristocratic elites were disempowered in favor of appointed officials loyal to the central government.

Construction Projects: Qin Shi Huang initiated several monumental construction projects during this period, including the construction of the Great Wall of China. These projects not only served as symbols of imperial authority but also provided employment opportunities for the population, reducing potential sources of unrest.

Cultural Policies: The early years of the Qin Dynasty were marked by a policy of book burning aimed at suppressing dissenting thought and centralizing ideological control. While controversial, this policy was part of a broader effort to exert control over intellectual and cultural spheres.

Reign of Law: Legalist principles, which emphasized the role of strict laws and harsh punishments in maintaining social order, played a significant role in the governance of the Qin state. Legalist ideas influenced the formulation of the Qin legal code and the administration of justice.

Territorial Expansion: The state continued its military campaigns and territorial expansion efforts, solidifying its control over newly acquired regions and incorporating them into the unified state. The consolidation of power during this period was not without challenges and controversies. The centralization of authority often came at the expense of regional autonomy and the interests of local elites. Harsh measures, such as the burning of books and the suppression of dissent, generated opposition and resentment among certain segments of the population. Nonetheless, these policies and reforms played a crucial role in setting the stage for the unification of China under a single centralized government. Qin Shi Huang's determination to establish a unified empire and his willingness to implement bold and far-reaching measures were instrumental in achieving this ambitious goal. The consolidation of power during these formative years of the Qin Dynasty marked a critical chapter in Chinese history, ultimately shaping the course of the nation's governance and culture for centuries to come.

Chapter 3: The Great Wall and Imperial Expansion

The legacy of Qin Shi Huang, the First Emperor of the Qin Dynasty, is a multifaceted and complex one that has left an indelible mark on Chinese history and culture. His rule, marked by the unification of China and the establishment of a centralized imperial government, has enduring significance, but it is also a subject of controversies and debates.

One of the most enduring and positive aspects of Qin Shi Huang's legacy is his role in unifying China. Prior to his ascent to power, China was a fragmented land, with various states vying for supremacy and control. The Warring States period was characterized by incessant warfare, political instability, and social upheaval. Qin Shi Huang's vision of a unified empire was realized through military conquests and the imposition of a centralized government.

The unification of China under the Qin Dynasty marked the end of the Warring States period and the beginning of the imperial era. This transformation was a pivotal moment in Chinese history, setting the stage for the subsequent dynasties that would rule over a unified China. The Qin Dynasty's administrative innovations and standardization efforts also contributed to the development of a cohesive and enduring Chinese state.

Qin Shi Huang's legacy is closely associated with the construction of the Great Wall of China, one of the most iconic architectural marvels in history. While earlier walls existed in various states, it was during his reign that the ambitious project of connecting and extending these walls into a single defensive barrier was initiated. The Great Wall served not only as a formidable defensive structure but also as a symbol of imperial authority and unity. Its historical and cultural significance is celebrated worldwide.

Another aspect of Qin Shi Huang's legacy is the standardization efforts that aimed to create a unified Chinese identity. These efforts included the standardization of writing scripts, weights and measures, currency, and laws. The standardization of the Chinese writing system, known as "small seal script," laid the foundation for the development of a common written language that continues to be used in modern China.

However, the legacy of Qin Shi Huang is not without its controversies and criticisms. One of the most contentious aspects of his rule was the policy of book burning, known as the "burning of books and burying of scholars." This policy aimed to suppress dissenting thought and centralize ideological control. It led to the destruction of numerous historical and philosophical texts, including works by Confucian scholars.

The burning of books and the suppression of intellectual diversity generated significant opposition and resentment, both during Qin Shi Huang's reign and in subsequent periods of Chinese history. Critics argue that the loss of valuable cultural and historical heritage was a high price to pay for centralized control.

Qin Shi Huang's approach to governance was heavily influenced by Legalist principles, which emphasized the role of strict laws and harsh punishments in maintaining social order. While this approach helped to consolidate power and maintain control, it also led to a regime characterized by authoritarianism and severe penalties for dissent or perceived threats to the state.

The construction of the Great Wall, while celebrated as a symbol of Chinese unity and defense, also had its critics. The labor force used for the wall's construction included conscripted peasants and laborers who faced harsh conditions and suffered greatly during the project. Critics argue that the human cost of the Great Wall's construction was high and that it represents a dark chapter in Chinese history.

Qin Shi Huang's reign and legacy also raise questions about his personal character and leadership style. He was known for his suspicion of betrayal and his ruthlessness in dealing with potential rivals. The use of legalistic principles in governance often resulted in severe punishments for perceived offenses, leading to a climate of fear and distrust.

Despite these controversies, Qin Shi Huang's legacy is a complex one that cannot be reduced to a simple narrative of either heroism or tyranny. His unification of China and the establishment of a centralized government had a profound and lasting impact on Chinese history and culture. The Qin Dynasty's administrative innovations, standardization efforts, and construction projects left an enduring mark on the nation.

In contemporary China, Qin Shi Huang's legacy is a subject of ongoing debate and discussion. Some view him as a visionary leader who played a crucial role in shaping the course of Chinese history, while others emphasize the human costs and authoritarian aspects of his rule. The legacy of Qin Shi Huang serves as a reminder of the complexities of historical figures and the nuanced nature of history itself.

In summary, the legacy of Qin Shi Huang, the First Emperor of the Qin Dynasty, is a multifaceted one that encompasses both achievements and controversies. His role in unifying China, the construction of the Great Wall, and the standardization efforts have enduring significance. However, his policies of book burning, authoritarian governance, and the human cost of his projects are subjects of criticism and debate. Qin Shi Huang's legacy underscores the complexity of historical figures and the enduring impact of their actions on the course of history.

The construction of the Great Wall of China is a monumental and iconic feat of human engineering and labor that has captured the imagination of people around the world for centuries. This remarkable structure is an enduring symbol of China's ancient history, its imperial ambitions, and its determination to defend against external threats. The story of the Great Wall's construction is a tale of innovation, sacrifice, and the enduring legacy of a civilization.

The history of the Great Wall dates back over two millennia, with the earliest walls and fortifications being built during the 7th century BC. These early walls were constructed by various Chinese states as defensive structures to protect their territories from raids and invasions by nomadic tribes and rival states. Over time, these individual walls and fortifications were expanded and interconnected to form what we now know as the Great Wall.

The most famous phase of Great Wall construction took place during the reign of Qin Shi Huang, the First Emperor of the Qin Dynasty, in the 3rd century BC. Qin Shi Huang is known for unifying China and establishing the first centralized imperial government. Recognizing the need for a strong defense against northern nomadic tribes, he ordered the construction of a continuous defensive barrier along the northern borders of his empire.

The construction of the Great Wall during the Qin Dynasty was a massive undertaking that required immense resources and labor. The wall stretched over a vast expanse of rugged terrain, including deserts, mountains, and grasslands. To complete this monumental project, hundreds of thousands of laborers, including conscripted peasants and prisoners of war, were mobilized.

One of the engineering marvels of the Great Wall is its adaptability to the diverse topography of northern China. In areas with more accessible terrain, the wall was built using tamped earth, while in mountainous regions, it was constructed with stone and brick. The Great Wall featured not only walls but also watchtowers, signal towers, and fortresses strategically positioned along its length.

The purpose of the Great Wall extended beyond mere defense. It served as a means of communication, enabling the transmission of signals and messages across vast distances. Beacon towers were constructed at regular intervals along the wall, and signal fires were lit to convey messages rapidly. This system allowed for swift communication and the mobilization of troops in response to threats.

The construction of the Great Wall was a monumental logistical challenge. Materials such as stone, brick, and earth had to be transported to remote and often inhospitable locations. The labor force toiled under challenging conditions, facing harsh weather, rugged terrain, and the constant threat of attacks by nomadic tribes. The construction process was arduous, and countless workers lost their lives during its execution.

Despite the difficulties and hardships, the Great Wall gradually took shape over the centuries, and its completion marked a significant achievement in the history of human engineering. It played a crucial role in safeguarding China's northern borders and served as a physical and symbolic barrier against external threats.

The Great Wall's role in Chinese history extends beyond its military function. It became a symbol of China's unity and determination to defend its territory. It embodied the collective effort of the Chinese people to protect their homeland. The Great Wall also played a vital role in facilitating trade and cultural exchange along the Silk Road, as it provided a secure route for merchants and travelers.

Throughout its long history, the Great Wall underwent periods of expansion, maintenance, and repair under various dynasties. Different dynasties contributed to its construction and renovation, each leaving its mark on this iconic structure. Notable periods of expansion occurred during the Ming Dynasty, when the wall was extended and reinforced to confront new threats.

The Ming Dynasty's contribution to the Great Wall's construction is particularly well-known, and many of the sections of the wall that are popular tourist destinations today date from this era. The Ming Dynasty's efforts in fortifying the wall included the addition of watchtowers, gates, and defensive features designed to enhance its defensive capabilities.

The Great Wall's significance extended beyond China's borders. It became a symbol of China's cultural identity and historical heritage, recognized and admired by people worldwide. Its mystique and grandeur have inspired countless travelers, poets, and scholars over the centuries. It has been the subject of art, literature, and folklore, embodying China's enduring spirit and resilience.

In contemporary times, the Great Wall has been designated as a UNESCO World Heritage Site and is considered one of the most iconic and visited landmarks in the world. It draws millions of tourists annually, eager to explore its ancient ramparts, climb its watchtowers, and marvel at its breathtaking vistas.

The construction of the Great Wall of China is a testament to the ingenuity, determination, and sacrifices of countless individuals throughout history. It stands as a symbol of China's enduring cultural heritage and its commitment to defending its borders. Its legacy transcends time and borders, embodying the spirit of a nation and its unwavering pursuit of unity and protection. The Great Wall continues to inspire awe and wonder, inviting all who visit to contemplate its historical significance and marvel at the human achievement it represents.

The significance of the Great Wall of China transcends its role as a defensive structure and extends into the realms of history, culture, symbolism, and human achievement. This iconic wall, which stretches thousands of miles across northern China, holds a profound place in the hearts and minds of people around the world. Its enduring significance can be understood through various lenses:

Historical Legacy: The Great Wall stands as a tangible testament to China's rich and complex history. Its construction began over two millennia ago, and it has played a pivotal role in various dynasties' efforts to protect their territories from external threats. As such, it embodies the historical narrative of China's struggles, triumphs, and the resilience of its people.

Unification of China: One of the most significant aspects of the Great Wall's historical significance is its association with the unification of China. Qin Shi Huang's construction of the wall during the Qin Dynasty marked a turning point in Chinese history, signaling the end of the Warring States period and the beginning of China's imperial era. It represented a commitment to unity and the centralization of authority.

Symbol of National Unity: The Great Wall is more than just a physical barrier; it symbolizes China's unity as a nation. It embodies the collective effort of the Chinese people to protect their homeland from external threats. This symbolism has endured through centuries and remains a source of pride and patriotism for the Chinese people.

Cultural Icon: The Great Wall is an integral part of China's cultural identity. It has been celebrated in art, literature, music, and folklore. Poets and scholars have drawn inspiration from its grandeur, and it has been depicted in countless paintings and writings. Its presence in Chinese culture reinforces the idea that it is not just a physical structure but a cultural icon.

Symbol of Human Achievement: The construction of the Great Wall is a remarkable feat of human engineering and labor. It reflects the ingenuity and determination of generations of builders who faced formidable challenges, including rugged terrain and harsh weather conditions. Its sheer scale and complexity serve as a testament to human achievement and innovation.

International Symbol: The Great Wall is recognized and admired worldwide as one of the most iconic landmarks in history. It has become a symbol of China and has garnered global admiration for its historical and architectural significance. Tourists from around the world visit the Great Wall, making it a symbol of international fascination and curiosity.

UNESCO World Heritage Site: Many sections of the Great Wall have been designated as UNESCO World Heritage Sites. This official recognition highlights its cultural and historical importance on a global scale and underscores its status as a treasure of humanity.

Tourist Attraction: The Great Wall has a significant economic impact as a major tourist attraction. It draws millions of visitors each year, contributing to the local and national economies. It provides employment opportunities and supports various industries related to tourism.

Symbol of Endurance: The Great Wall has weathered the test of time, standing as a symbol of endurance and resilience. It has survived centuries of exposure to the elements, conflicts, and natural forces. Its enduring presence reflects the enduring spirit of the Chinese people and their ability to persevere through challenges.

In summary, the Great Wall of China is a monument with profound significance that transcends its original purpose as a defensive structure. Its historical, cultural, and symbolic importance is woven into the fabric of China's identity and is recognized and admired worldwide. As a testament to human achievement, it continues to inspire awe and wonder, inviting people to contemplate its historical and cultural significance and marvel at its enduring legacy.

Chapter 4: Han Dynasty: A Golden Era

The founding of the Han Dynasty represents a pivotal moment in Chinese history, marking the transition from the short-lived Qin Dynasty to a new era of stability, prosperity, and cultural development. The Han Dynasty, which endured for over four centuries, played a significant role in shaping the course of Chinese civilization and left an enduring legacy that continues to influence contemporary China.

The rise of the Han Dynasty can be traced back to the aftermath of the Qin Dynasty's collapse. The Qin Dynasty, known for its centralization efforts and the construction of the Great Wall, was characterized by authoritarian rule and harsh governance. The policies of the First Emperor, Qin Shi Huang, including the burning of books and the suppression of dissent, had generated discontent and opposition among the populace.

Amidst the upheaval following the fall of the Qin Dynasty, a new era was ushered in with the emergence of Liu Bang, a commoner and military commander who would become the founder of the Han Dynasty. Liu Bang's rise to power was marked by his ability to garner support from various factions, including peasant uprisings and regional leaders who opposed the harsh policies of the Qin Dynasty.

In 206 BCE, Liu Bang declared himself Emperor Gaozu of Han, marking the official establishment of the Han Dynasty. The founding of the Han Dynasty represented a shift away from the authoritarian rule of the Qin Dynasty and a return to a more traditional style of governance that emphasized Confucian principles and sought to address the concerns of the people.

One of the key principles of the early Han Dynasty was the pursuit of the "Mandate of Heaven," a concept deeply rooted in Chinese political philosophy. It held that the legitimacy of rulers was based on their ability to govern justly and in the best interests of the people. Emperor Gaozu and his successors sought to govern in accordance with this mandate, fostering a sense of legitimacy and moral authority.

The founding of the Han Dynasty marked a period of political and social consolidation. Emperor Gaozu and his advisors implemented a series of reforms aimed at reestablishing order, rebuilding infrastructure, and addressing the grievances of the people. These reforms included the reduction of taxes and the easing of harsh legalist policies that had characterized the Qin Dynasty.

One of the most enduring legacies of the Han Dynasty was its embrace of Confucianism as the guiding ideology of the state. Emperor Wu of Han, who reigned from 141 BCE to 87 BCE, played a pivotal role in promoting Confucianism and elevating it to a position of prominence within the imperial government. Confucian scholars were appointed to key positions, and Confucian principles were integrated into the state's educational and administrative systems.

Emperor Wu's reign also saw significant territorial expansion. The Han Dynasty embarked on military campaigns that extended its control into regions such as southern China, Vietnam, and parts of Central Asia. These campaigns not only expanded the empire but also facilitated cultural exchange and trade along the Silk Road.

The early Han Dynasty was marked by economic growth and prosperity. The development of a stable agricultural system, including the widespread use of the iron plow, contributed to increased agricultural productivity. The construction of roads and canals facilitated trade and transportation, promoting economic development.

The Han Dynasty is also renowned for its advancements in science and technology. During this period, Chinese scholars made significant contributions to fields such as astronomy, mathematics, and medicine. The invention of paper and the refinement of printing techniques greatly influenced the dissemination of knowledge and the development of literature.

One of the most celebrated literary works of the Han Dynasty is the "Records of the Grand Historian" (Shi Ji), written by the historian Sima Qian. This comprehensive historical record covers the history of China from ancient times to the Han Dynasty and remains a valuable source of information about China's past.

The Han Dynasty's legacy extends to the realm of governance and administration. It established a system of bureaucracy that endured for centuries and served as a model for subsequent dynasties. The civil service examination system, which allowed individuals to enter government service based on merit rather than birthright, became a hallmark of Chinese governance and contributed to social mobility.

The later years of the Han Dynasty saw periods of political intrigue and strife. Factionalism within the imperial court, coupled with external pressures such as invasions by nomadic tribes, contributed to instability. The dynasty experienced a series of internal and external challenges, leading to the eventual fragmentation of the Han Empire.

In 220 CE, the Han Dynasty officially came to an end, as the last Han emperor, Emperor Xian, abdicated the throne. This marked the beginning of the Three Kingdoms period, characterized by the division of China into three competing states: Wei, Shu, and Wu. Despite its eventual decline, the

Han Dynasty's influence and legacy continued to shape the political, cultural, and social landscape of China for centuries to come.

In contemporary China, the Han Dynasty is celebrated as a foundational period in the nation's history. Its emphasis on Confucian values, governance reforms, and cultural achievements continue to resonate in modern Chinese society. The legacy of the Han Dynasty serves as a reminder of the enduring impact of historical dynasties on the evolution of China and its rich cultural heritage.

The economic prosperity of the Han Dynasty, often referred to as the "Han Economic Miracle," is a testament to the dynasty's innovative policies, administrative efficiency, and enduring cultural influence. Lasting for over four centuries, the Han Dynasty achieved remarkable economic growth and stability, laying the groundwork for China's subsequent economic development.

Agricultural Advancements: One of the cornerstones of the Han Dynasty's economic prosperity was its commitment to agricultural development. The widespread use of the iron plow, harnessing of draft animals, and irrigation systems significantly increased agricultural productivity. These innovations allowed for more efficient cultivation of land, leading to surplus food production.

Land Reforms: The Han Dynasty implemented land reforms that aimed to redistribute land to peasants and reduce the power of wealthy landowners. By providing land to those who worked it, the government ensured a stable agricultural base and a more equitable distribution of resources.

Taxation System: The Han Dynasty introduced a system of taxation based on the land's fertility, which helped to ensure that the tax burden was distributed fairly. This tax system, known as the "equal-field system," promoted agricultural productivity and reduced the potential for social unrest.

Trade and Commerce: The development of a vast network of roads and canals facilitated trade and commerce within the empire. These transportation infrastructure improvements connected distant regions of China, promoting the exchange of goods and the growth of markets.

Silk Road: The Han Dynasty played a pivotal role in the opening of the Silk Road, a vast network of trade routes that connected China with Central Asia, the Middle East, and Europe. The trade of silk, spices, precious metals, and other commodities along the Silk Road enriched both China and its trading partners.

Monetary System: The Han Dynasty introduced a standardized and regulated coinage system. The use of copper coins as the primary currency facilitated economic transactions and contributed to the growth of a monetary economy.

Merchants and Guilds: The role of merchants in the Han economy expanded significantly. Merchant guilds and associations played a vital role in facilitating trade, protecting the interests of merchants, and promoting economic growth.

Innovation and Invention: The Han Dynasty was a period of significant technological innovation. Inventions such as papermaking, the watermill, and the compass contributed to economic growth and the dissemination of knowledge.

State Monopolies: The government's control over certain industries, including salt and iron production, provided a steady source of revenue and ensured the availability of essential commodities.

Bureaucratic Efficiency: The Han Dynasty's centralized administrative structure and efficient bureaucracy allowed for the effective management of resources, taxation, and governance. This administrative efficiency played a crucial role in economic stability.

Cultural and Intellectual Influence: The enduring cultural influence of Confucianism, which emphasized the importance of social harmony and stability, contributed to a conducive environment for economic prosperity.

Territorial Expansion: The expansion of the Han Dynasty's territory through military campaigns opened up new trade routes, brought in additional tax revenue, and expanded the empire's economic reach.

The economic prosperity of the Han Dynasty had a profound and lasting impact on Chinese society and culture. It contributed to the development of a strong middle class, the growth of cities and urban centers, and the spread of literacy and education. The prosperity also fostered cultural achievements in areas such as art, literature, and philosophy.

The legacy of the Han Dynasty's economic prosperity continues to influence China's economic policies and development strategies today. It serves as a reminder of the enduring importance of stable governance, agricultural innovation, trade, and infrastructure in promoting economic growth and prosperity.

The cultural flourishing of the Han Dynasty represents a golden age in Chinese history, marked by remarkable achievements in art, literature, philosophy, and science. Lasting for over four centuries, the Han Dynasty witnessed a period of intellectual and creative vitality that left an indelible mark on Chinese culture and continues to shape the nation's identity today.

Literature and Philosophy: During the Han Dynasty, literature and philosophy reached new heights. Confucianism, with its emphasis on moral values and social harmony, became the dominant ideology of the state. The Confucian Classics were revered, and Confucian scholars played a central role in the imperial government. Sima Qian's "Records of the Grand Historian" is a classic work of historical literature that remains influential to this day. Additionally, the "Book of Songs" (Shi Jing) preserved ancient Chinese poetry, providing insights into the culture and sentiments of the time.

Poetry and Prose: Poetry was a beloved art form in the Han Dynasty, with poets like Qu Yuan and Li Bai leaving a lasting legacy. Qu Yuan's poems, particularly his "Li Sao" (The Lament), explored themes of patriotism and moral integrity. The "Fu" style of prose, characterized by rich and ornate language, also flourished during this period.

Calligraphy and Writing: Calligraphy, the art of beautiful writing, became a revered form of artistic expression. Chinese calligraphy masters like Wang Xizhi and Wang Xianzhi are celebrated for their exquisite brushwork and unique styles. The development of standard script (kaishu) during the Han Dynasty laid the foundation for the evolution of Chinese writing.

Inventions and Innovations: The Han Dynasty was a period of great innovation and invention. The invention of paper revolutionized writing and communication, making knowledge more accessible. The development of the watermill improved agricultural productivity and industrial processes. Additionally, the compass and seismoscope were important scientific innovations of the time.

Silk and Textiles: The Han Dynasty is synonymous with the Silk Road, a network of trade routes that facilitated the exchange of goods, culture, and ideas between China and the rest of the world. The production of silk and textiles became a major industry, and Chinese silk was highly sought after by traders along the Silk Road.

Art and Sculpture: Han Dynasty art is characterized by its realistic and detailed representations of daily life, nature, and mythology. Jade sculptures, pottery, and bronze vessels exemplify the artistic achievements of the time. The Han Dynasty also saw the development of ceramic glazing techniques that produced vibrant and colorful pottery.

Architecture and Engineering: The construction of grand architectural structures, such as temples, palaces, and tombs, reflected the cultural and artistic prowess of the era. Notable examples include the mausoleum of Emperor Wu of Han and the Wu Liang Shrine, known for its intricate stone carvings and reliefs. The Great Wall of China, though primarily a defensive structure, also exhibited architectural skill and engineering ingenuity.

Music and Dance: Music and dance played an integral role in Han Dynasty culture. Court musicians and dancers entertained the imperial court with elaborate performances. Traditional Chinese musical instruments, such as the guqin and pipa, were refined during this period.

Religion and Beliefs: A rich tapestry of religious beliefs and practices emerged during the Han Dynasty. While Confucianism held sway in official circles, Daoism and Buddhism began to gain followers. These belief systems contributed to the spiritual and philosophical diversity of Chinese culture.

Education and Scholarship: The Han Dynasty fostered a culture of scholarship and intellectual pursuit. The civil service examination system was established, allowing individuals to enter government service based on merit. This system promoted the study of Confucian classics and ensured a highly educated bureaucracy.

Legacy: The cultural flourishing of the Han Dynasty left a profound and enduring legacy. Many of the artistic, literary, and philosophical achievements of this era continue to influence Chinese culture and society. Confucianism remains a fundamental ethical and moral framework in China, and Chinese calligraphy and ink painting are still highly regarded art forms. The Silk Road's historical and cultural significance continues to be explored and celebrated, and Chinese inventions like paper and the compass have had a global impact.

In summary, the cultural flourishing of the Han Dynasty represents a remarkable period of creativity and intellectual vitality in Chinese history. It was a time when art, literature, philosophy, and science flourished, leaving a profound and lasting impact on Chinese culture and civilization. The legacy of this golden age continues to be celebrated and cherished as an integral part of China's rich cultural heritage.

Chapter 5: Silk Road: Gateway to the West

The origins of the Silk Road, a network of trade routes that connected the East and West, are deeply rooted in ancient history and mark a significant chapter in the development of human civilization. This vast and intricate web of routes, spanning thousands of miles, facilitated the exchange of goods, culture, and ideas between the great civilizations of the time, leaving an indelible mark on the course of history.

The Silk Road, though often associated with China, was not the creation of a single nation or ruler but rather the result of centuries of interactions, explorations, and exchanges among various cultures. Its origins can be traced back to multiple factors and developments that unfolded over time.

One of the earliest factors contributing to the formation of the Silk Road was the quest for valuable commodities. As early as the 2nd millennium BCE, Chinese merchants were seeking precious materials such as jade, silk, and bronze. These sought-after goods were not only symbols of wealth and status but also held cultural and religious significance.

China's legendary Silk production was a pivotal driver of early trade routes. The secrets of Sericulture (silkworm cultivation and silk production) were closely guarded by the Chinese for centuries, giving them a virtual monopoly on this highly coveted fabric. The Silk industry played a central role in the initiation of trade contacts beyond China's borders.

During the Western Zhou Dynasty (1046–771 BCE) and the subsequent Eastern Zhou period (770–256 BCE), trade between China and its western neighbors began to intensify. The Silk Road was not a single road but a collection of interconnected routes, and these early exchanges set the stage for the Silk Road's later expansion.

Another significant catalyst for the Silk Road was the establishment of centralized empires. The Qin Dynasty, under the rule of Qin Shi Huang, implemented a system of roads and canals that improved transportation and facilitated trade. However, it was the Han Dynasty (206 BCE–220 CE) that played a pivotal role in the expansion and formalization of trade routes.

Emperor Wu of Han, in particular, is credited with expanding the Silk Road's reach during his reign (141–87 BCE). He launched military campaigns into the western regions, extending China's control and influence along the trade routes. These campaigns not only secured the routes but also fostered cultural exchanges and diplomatic relations.

One of the most famous Silk Road travelers from the West is Zhang Qian, a Chinese diplomat and explorer. He embarked on a mission during the 2nd century BCE to seek alliances with the Yuezhi people and establish connections with various Central Asian tribes. Zhang Qian's travels opened up new trade routes and played a crucial role in expanding the Silk Road.

The Silk Road was not limited to overland routes; it also included maritime routes. The Indian Ocean, often referred to as the "Maritime Silk Road," facilitated the exchange of goods between China, Southeast Asia, India, the Arabian Peninsula, and East Africa. Ancient Chinese texts mention voyages to regions such as India and Southeast Asia, indicating the extent of maritime trade.

One of the pivotal elements of the Silk Road was the interplay of cultures and religions. Along the trade routes, travelers encountered a mosaic of beliefs, languages, and traditions. Buddhism, originating in India, spread along the Silk Road and found a home in China. The transmission of Buddhist texts and art from India to China was a significant cultural exchange.

Similarly, the spread of Christianity, Zoroastrianism, Islam, and other religious and philosophical traditions was facilitated by the Silk Road. The exchange of ideas and beliefs contributed to the rich tapestry of cultures that flourished along these routes.

The Silk Road was not without its challenges and perils. It traversed vast and diverse landscapes, from deserts and mountains to steppes and forests. Travelers faced extreme weather conditions, rugged terrain, and the threat of bandits. Yet, the allure of the Silk Road's treasures and the potential for profit motivated traders, merchants, and explorers to undertake these arduous journeys.

The goods exchanged along the Silk Road extended far beyond silk and precious materials. Chinese exports included ceramics, tea, paper, and technologies such as printing. In return, China received goods such as spices, gems, textiles, glassware, and exotic animals. This exchange of commodities enriched both China and its trading partners.

The decline of the Silk Road began with the fall of the Han Dynasty and the subsequent fragmentation of the Chinese empire. The collapse of the Roman Empire and the rise of maritime trade routes also played a role in diminishing the Silk Road's significance. However, remnants of the Silk Road continued to function throughout the centuries, and its legacy persists in contemporary trade and cultural exchanges.

Today, the Silk Road is celebrated as a symbol of human curiosity, innovation, and cooperation. It exemplifies the profound impact of interconnectedness on the course of history and serves as a reminder of the enduring power of trade, cultural exchange, and exploration in shaping our world. The origins of the Silk Road are a testament to the human drive to connect, discover, and engage with diverse cultures and civilizations, leaving a lasting legacy that continues to shape our global society.

Trade and cultural exchange have been fundamental drivers of human civilization, fostering the exchange of goods, ideas, and customs across diverse cultures and regions. Throughout history, trade routes and networks have crisscrossed continents, facilitating the flow of commodities and knowledge, and leading to cultural enrichment, economic growth, and the formation of global interconnectedness.

Trade and cultural exchange are deeply intertwined, as the movement of goods often goes hand in hand with the transmission of cultural practices, beliefs, and innovations. This exchange has shaped societies, influenced art and architecture, and fostered the spread of languages and religions. Here, we explore the rich tapestry of trade and cultural exchange throughout history.

Ancient Trade Routes: The earliest recorded trade routes date back to ancient times. The Silk Road, connecting East and West, remains one of the most iconic trade routes in history. Originating in China, it extended through Central Asia, the Middle East, and into Europe. Along this route, silk, spices, precious metals, and ideas were exchanged, creating a bridge between civilizations. The Silk Road was not a single road but a complex network of interconnected routes.

Indian Ocean Trade: The Indian Ocean played a central role in maritime trade, serving as a "Maritime Silk Road" connecting the regions surrounding the Indian Ocean basin. This maritime trade route facilitated the exchange of goods, including spices, textiles, gems, and spices, among India, Southeast Asia, the Arabian Peninsula, East Africa, and beyond. It also contributed to the spread of cultures, languages, and religions.

Hanseatic League: During the Middle Ages, the Hanseatic League was a powerful confederation of merchant guilds and trading cities in northern Europe. It dominated trade in the Baltic and North Sea regions, establishing a network of trading posts and alliances. The League played a crucial role in the exchange of goods such as timber, fish, metals, and textiles.

Trans-Saharan Trade: Across the vast Sahara Desert, trans-Saharan trade routes connected North Africa with sub-Saharan Africa. The exchange of goods, including gold, salt, ivory, and textiles, enriched both regions and stimulated cultural interactions. The spread of Islam along these routes influenced the religious and cultural landscape of West Africa.

The Columbian Exchange: The Age of Exploration, marked by Christopher Columbus's voyages to the Americas, initiated a transformative period known as the Columbian Exchange. This global exchange of plants, animals, foods, and cultures between the Old World (Europe, Asia, and Africa) and the New World (the Americas) had profound and far-reaching effects. Crops like maize, potatoes, and tomatoes revolutionized diets, while diseases and livestock had profound demographic consequences.

Silk and Spice Routes: In Southeast Asia, the maritime Silk and Spice Routes connected the Indonesian archipelago with India, China, and the Middle East. Spices, such as cloves, nutmeg, and pepper, were highly sought after and contributed to the growth of empires and the enrichment of cultures. The exchange of textiles, ceramics, and precious metals also thrived in this region.

East African Trade: Along the eastern coast of Africa, the Swahili Coast served as a vibrant hub of trade and cultural exchange. Swahili city-states like Zanzibar, Kilwa, and Mombasa were key players in facilitating the exchange of goods such as ivory, gold, spices, and textiles. The Swahili culture, influenced by Arab, Persian, and African traditions, flourished along these trade routes.

Silk Road Revival: In the modern era, efforts to revive the Silk Road have continued. The Belt and Road Initiative, launched by China in the 21st century, seeks to enhance connectivity and trade across Asia, Europe, and Africa. This ambitious project aims to rekindle the spirit of ancient trade routes and promote economic development and cultural exchange.

Cultural Diffusion and Syncretism: Trade routes have not only facilitated the exchange of physical goods but also the spread of cultural elements. Languages, religions, art, and architecture have been shared and adapted along trade routes. Cultural diffusion and syncretism, the blending of different cultural elements, have led to the creation of vibrant and diverse societies.

Impact on Art and Architecture: Cultural exchange has profoundly influenced art and architecture. The architectural styles of mosques, temples, and cathedrals often reflect the blending of cultural influences from different regions. Artistic traditions have been enriched by exposure to new techniques, materials, and motifs.

Religious Spread: Trade routes have been conduits for the spread of religions. Buddhism, originating in India, was carried along trade routes to East Asia, influencing the cultures of China, Japan, and Korea. Christianity, Islam, and Hinduism also spread through trade and cultural exchange, shaping the spiritual beliefs of diverse communities.

Globalization and Contemporary Trade: In the modern era, globalization has brought trade and cultural exchange to unprecedented levels. Advances in transportation, communication, and technology have interconnected the world's economies and societies. International trade agreements, such as the World Trade Organization, have fostered global economic integration.

The Silk Road, a network of interconnected trade routes that spanned across Asia, Europe, and Africa, left an indelible mark on the world by facilitating a profound exchange of goods, ideas, cultures, and technologies. Its influence on the regions it traversed can be observed in various domains, from economics and politics to culture, religion, and art.

Economic Impact: The Silk Road was the lifeline of commerce in ancient times, fostering economic growth and prosperity for regions involved in the trade network. Goods such as silk, spices, precious metals, textiles, ceramics, and exotic fruits were transported along these routes, stimulating economic development and trade between East and West. The wealth generated from Silk Road trade fueled the growth of powerful empires and helped establish economic centers along the route.

Spread of Knowledge and Innovation: The exchange of ideas and technologies was a hallmark of the Silk Road. Chinese inventions such as papermaking, printing, and gunpowder spread westward, transforming the way information was disseminated and warfare conducted. In return, the East absorbed knowledge from the West, leading to advancements in medicine, astronomy, mathematics, and engineering.

Cultural Cross-Pollination: The Silk Road was a conduit for cultural exchange, facilitating the blending of diverse traditions, beliefs, and artistic styles. It allowed for the movement of people and cultures, leading to the spread of languages, religions, and philosophies. Buddhism, for example, traveled from India to China along these routes, transforming Chinese spirituality and art.

Religious Diffusion: The Silk Road played a pivotal role in the dissemination of religious beliefs. Buddhism, Zoroastrianism, Islam, Christianity, and other faiths spread across continents through trade contacts. Religious texts, art, and iconography found their way to new regions, influencing spiritual practices and beliefs. The religious diversity along the Silk Road enriched the cultural fabric of the participating societies.

Political and Diplomatic Relations: The Silk Road was not solely a commercial venture but also a platform for diplomacy and intercultural exchange. Diplomatic missions were conducted along these routes, fostering political alliances and cooperation. Empires like the Roman Empire and the Han Dynasty established diplomatic ties through these channels, promoting peaceful coexistence.

Artistic and Architectural Influence: The Silk Road left an enduring artistic legacy. Artistic styles, motifs, and techniques were shared across regions, leading to the fusion of artistic traditions. The blending of architectural designs and decorative arts resulted in the creation of distinctive structures, such as the Buddhist cave temples of Dunhuang and the mosques of Central Asia. The art and architecture along the Silk Road bear the imprint of diverse cultural influences.

Language and Literature: The Silk Road facilitated linguistic exchange, contributing to the development of languages and literature. Translations of texts between languages like Sanskrit, Greek, Chinese, and Arabic facilitated the transfer of knowledge and literature. Literary works, travelogues, and historical accounts emerged as a testament to the cultural interactions that took place along these routes.

Influence on Cuisine: Culinary traditions were another dimension of cultural exchange along the Silk Road. Spices, fruits, and culinary techniques moved between regions, influencing the flavors and cooking methods of different cuisines. The Silk Road's influence can still be seen in dishes that incorporate ingredients like saffron, cardamom, and rice.

Urban Development: Cities and settlements along the Silk Road flourished as trade hubs. These urban centers became melting pots of cultures, where diverse communities lived and interacted. The architecture of these cities reflects the multicultural influences, with markets, caravanserais, and religious structures shaping the urban landscape.

Geopolitical Significance: The Silk Road had geopolitical significance, influencing the rise and fall of empires. Control over key segments of the trade routes translated into economic and political power. The Silk Road was a driver of diplomacy and conflict, as states vied for control over strategic points along the routes.

Enduring Legacy: The Silk Road's legacy continues to shape the modern world. Initiatives like China's Belt and Road Initiative seek to revive the spirit of ancient trade routes by promoting infrastructure development, connectivity, and trade among nations. The idea of interconnectedness and the exchange of goods and ideas remains a powerful force in today's globalized world.

Cultural Identity: The Silk Road played a significant role in shaping the cultural identity of regions and nations. It contributed to the formation of hybrid cultures that draw from multiple traditions. For many countries along the Silk Road, the historical legacy of these routes remains a source of pride and a symbol of their rich cultural heritage.

Educational and Academic Pursuits: The study of the Silk Road continues to captivate scholars and researchers across various disciplines. Academic pursuits in archaeology, history, anthropology, art history, and linguistics have shed light on the complexities of the Silk Road's interactions and the enduring impact of these exchanges.

In summary, the Silk Road's influence transcends time and geography. Its historical significance is not confined to the past but continues to shape the present and future. The Silk Road stands as a testament to the power of trade, cultural exchange, and human connectivity in fostering innovation, cultural richness, and understanding among diverse societies.

Chapter 6: The Han-Sino Nomadic Encounter

The nomadic tribes of ancient China were a diverse and dynamic group of people who played a significant role in the history and development of the region. These nomadic societies inhabited the vast grasslands, deserts, and steppes surrounding China, and their interactions with the settled agricultural communities of the Central Plains had far-reaching consequences for the politics, culture, and economy of ancient China.

Xiongnu: One of the most prominent nomadic tribes in ancient China were the Xiongnu. They inhabited the northern and western regions of China and were known for their formidable military prowess. The Xiongnu frequently raided Chinese territories and posed a significant threat to the Chinese states. Their interactions with the Chinese Han Dynasty led to diplomatic efforts and the establishment of the "Heqin" system, which involved the exchange of gifts and marriages to maintain peace along the northern borders.

Xianbei: The Xianbei were another nomadic group who lived in northern China and played a role in the history of the region. They are known for establishing the Northern Wei Dynasty in the 4th century AD, marking a period of nomadic rule over parts of northern China. During their rule, there was a fusion of Chinese and Xianbei cultures, and Buddhism gained prominence in the region.

Rouran Khaganate: The Rouran Khaganate was a confederation of nomadic tribes in the 4th and 5th centuries AD that exerted influence over northern China and Central Asia. They played a significant role in shaping the political landscape of the region and had interactions with various

Chinese dynasties, including the Northern Wei and Northern Zhou.

Turkic Tribes: The Turkic nomadic tribes, including the Göktürks and Uighurs, inhabited the western regions of China and Central Asia. They were known for their skilled horsemanship and their control over key trade routes along the Silk Road. The Turkic tribes established various states and empires, often clashing with Chinese dynasties in border conflicts.

Qiang and Di Tribes: The Qiang and Di tribes inhabited the western and southwestern regions of China, including parts of present-day Sichuan and Tibet. These tribes had a long history of interaction with Chinese civilizations, and they contributed to the ethnic diversity and cultural tapestry of ancient China.

Mongolic Tribes: The Mongolic nomadic tribes, such as the Xianbei, Khitan, and Mongols, lived in the northern and northeastern regions of China. These tribes played a crucial role in the rise of powerful empires, including the Khitan Liao Dynasty and the Mongol Empire, which conquered the entirety of China under the leadership of Genghis Khan and his successors.

Tibetan Nomads: The Tibetan Plateau was home to Tibetan nomadic tribes who herded livestock and practiced a unique form of Buddhism, Tibetan Buddhism. These nomads had a distinct way of life and cultural traditions that continue to influence the region to this day.

Interactions and Conflicts: The interactions between the settled Chinese states and these nomadic tribes were marked by both cooperation and conflict. Chinese dynasties often sought to establish diplomatic relations with neighboring nomadic tribes to secure peace along the borders, which sometimes involved political marriages and tribute payments. However, periodic invasions and conflicts also occurred, as nomadic tribes sought to expand their territories and exert control over Chinese lands.

Cultural Exchange: Despite the challenges and conflicts, there was a significant cultural exchange between the settled Chinese and nomadic tribes. This exchange included the spread of languages, art, technology, and religious beliefs. For example, Buddhism, which originated in India, was transmitted to China through interactions with nomadic tribes along the Silk Road.

Legacy: The legacy of these nomadic tribes in ancient China is a complex one. While they posed challenges to the stability of Chinese states, they also contributed to the cultural diversity and evolution of the region. The interactions between the Chinese and nomadic cultures left an indelible mark on Chinese history, influencing everything from military strategies and language to art and cuisine.

In summary, the nomadic tribes of ancient China were integral to the historical narrative of the region. Their nomadic way of life, military prowess, and cultural exchanges with the Chinese played a significant role in shaping the course of Chinese history and the broader history of Eurasia.

The Xiongnu threat was a significant geopolitical challenge that loomed over the northern borders of ancient China, particularly during the Western Han Dynasty (206 BCE - 9 CE) and the subsequent Eastern Han Dynasty (25 - 220 CE). The Xiongnu were a powerful confederation of nomadic tribes inhabiting the vast steppes and grasslands to the north of China. Their military prowess and frequent incursions into Chinese territories posed a persistent and formidable threat to the stability of the Chinese states.

Geographical Location: The Xiongnu homeland, often referred to as the Xiongnu Confederation, was situated in the region corresponding to modern-day Mongolia and parts of northern China, including Inner Mongolia. The vastness of this territory provided the Xiongnu with strategic advantages, as it allowed them to control key passages and trade routes and to launch raids and invasions deep into Chinese territory.

Military Strength: The Xiongnu were renowned for their formidable military capabilities, particularly their skilled cavalry. They excelled in horseback riding, archery, and hit-and-run tactics, which made them a formidable adversary for the Chinese states. Their mobility and knowledge of the terrain gave them an edge in confrontations with the more sedentary and agriculture-based Chinese armies.

Raids and Incursions: The Xiongnu conducted frequent raids and incursions into the northern regions of China. These raids targeted not only border settlements and villages but also key agricultural areas, trade routes, and cities. The Xiongnu's ability to disrupt trade and agricultural production posed a significant economic and security challenge for the Chinese states.

Diplomatic Efforts: Chinese attempts to deal with the Xiongnu threat were multifaceted. The Western Han Dynasty initially sought to appease the Xiongnu through diplomatic means, using a strategy known as the "Heqin" system. This involved sending princesses from the Han imperial family to marry Xiongnu leaders and the exchange of gifts as a form of tribute. The goal was to maintain a tenuous peace along the northern borders.

Diplomatic Failures: While the Heqin system achieved periods of stability, it was not a sustainable long-term solution. The Xiongnu often demanded more substantial tribute, and the marriages meant to secure peace sometimes ended in kidnappings and hostage situations. The

Xiongnu saw the Han Dynasty as a source of tribute and gifts, and the tensions between the two persisted.

Military Campaigns: In addition to diplomacy, Chinese rulers also launched military campaigns to counter the Xiongnu threat. Emperor Wu of the Western Han Dynasty is particularly known for his aggressive efforts to expand Chinese control into Xiongnu territories. These campaigns, although costly and resource-draining, resulted in the establishment of some Chinese footholds in the north.

Impact on Chinese Society: The Xiongnu threat had a profound impact on Chinese society. It led to increased militarization, the development of defensive fortifications such as the Great Wall, and the need for a well-organized military apparatus. It also prompted shifts in agricultural practices, as regions along the northern borders had to adapt to the threat of raids.

Legacy: While the Xiongnu were eventually subdued by the Northern Wei Dynasty (a nomadic Xianbei state) in the 4th century CE, their impact on Chinese history and culture endured. The memory of the Xiongnu threat remained influential, shaping Chinese military strategies, diplomatic relations, and the construction of defensive structures. The Great Wall of China, which began as a defensive measure against the Xiongnu, stands as a testament to the enduring legacy of this nomadic confederation.

In summary, the Xiongnu threat represented a significant challenge to ancient China, prompting a complex interplay of diplomatic efforts, military campaigns, and defensive measures. Their formidable military capabilities and frequent incursions into Chinese territory left an indelible mark on the history and security concerns of the Chinese states, shaping their approach to external threats for centuries to come.

Diplomacy and conflict with nomadic neighbors were defining features of the political and security landscape of ancient China. The interaction between the sedentary, agrarian Chinese states and the nomadic tribes that inhabited the vast northern and western frontiers was marked by both diplomatic negotiations and military confrontations, and it played a crucial role in shaping the course of Chinese history.

The nomadic tribes, such as the Xiongnu, Xianbei, Rouran, and Turkic peoples, occupied the steppes, grasslands, and deserts surrounding China. Their way of life centered around herding livestock and maintaining a mobile lifestyle. These nomadic groups were known for their equestrian skills, which included horseback riding and archery, and their ability to traverse long distances across challenging terrains. The nomadic lifestyle was inherently different from the settled, agricultural society of the Chinese states in the Central Plains.

The interaction between the Chinese and their nomadic neighbors was complex and multifaceted. Diplomacy played a crucial role in managing relations with these nomadic tribes. Diplomatic efforts aimed to establish peaceful coexistence, secure trade routes, and prevent military conflicts that could devastate border regions. However, diplomacy often existed alongside conflicts, raids, and territorial disputes.

One of the primary diplomatic strategies employed by Chinese dynasties was the use of marriage alliances. This practice, known as the "Heqin" system, involved sending Chinese princesses to marry leaders of nomadic tribes and exchange tribute gifts. The marriages were seen as a means of establishing familial ties and securing peace along the northern borders. However, the effectiveness of the Heqin system was mixed, as it sometimes led to the kidnapping of Chinese princesses or increased demands for tribute from nomadic leaders.

Emperor Wu of the Western Han Dynasty (reigned 141-87 BCE) is notable for his ambitious military campaigns against the Xiongnu, a prominent nomadic confederation in northern China. These campaigns aimed to establish Chinese control over key territories and trade routes and reduce the Xiongnu threat. While they achieved some short-term successes, they were costly in terms of resources and lives, and they did not eliminate the Xiongnu threat entirely.

The interactions between the Chinese states and their nomadic neighbors were further complicated by the changing political landscape among the nomadic tribes. Nomadic confederations often underwent internal shifts in leadership and alliances, making it challenging for Chinese dynasties to maintain stable relations. Nomadic tribes sometimes allied with Chinese dynasties against other nomadic threats or engaged in power struggles with each other.

Religion and culture were also significant aspects of diplomacy and interaction. Buddhism, originating in India, spread along the Silk Road and found adherents among both the Chinese and nomadic tribes. The transmission of religious texts, art, and iconography played a role in fostering cultural exchanges and diplomatic ties. Additionally, the Silk Road itself, which facilitated trade and cultural exchange, played a vital role in shaping diplomatic relations.

While diplomacy was a preferred approach to managing relations with nomadic neighbors, conflicts and military confrontations were not uncommon. The nomadic tribes, with their mobile cavalry forces, often posed a military threat to the settled Chinese states. Defensive fortifications, such as the Great Wall of China, were constructed to deter and defend against incursions and raids by nomadic groups. These fortifications served as physical barriers and as symbols of Chinese resolve in the face of external threats.

One of the enduring legacies of the interactions between China and its nomadic neighbors was the impact on Chinese society and culture. The memory of nomadic threats influenced Chinese military strategies and the construction of defensive structures, such as the Great Wall. Additionally, the Silk Road, which emerged as a result of trade interactions with nomadic tribes, contributed to the exchange of goods, ideas, and technologies between East and West, leaving a lasting imprint on Chinese culture and civilization.

In summary, diplomacy and conflict with nomadic neighbors were integral aspects of ancient China's foreign relations. The interactions between the Chinese states and nomadic tribes were marked by a delicate balance of diplomacy, military campaigns, and cultural exchanges. These interactions left a lasting impact on Chinese history, influencing military strategies, diplomatic approaches, and cultural developments that continue to shape China's identity and its relations with neighboring regions.

Chapter 7: Dynastic Challenges and Rebellions

The Yellow Turban Rebellion was a pivotal event in ancient China's history, marking a period of widespread social unrest, rebellion, and political upheaval during the late Eastern Han Dynasty (circa 184 - 205 CE). This rebellion was named after the distinctive yellow turbans worn by the insurgents and was characterized by a combination of socio-economic grievances, religious beliefs, and opposition to the ruling dynasty. It had far-reaching consequences for China's political landscape and laid the foundation for the eventual collapse of the Han Dynasty.

The origins of the Yellow Turban Rebellion can be traced to the deteriorating conditions in Eastern Han Dynasty China. The empire was plagued by a series of internal and external challenges, including corruption, land redistribution issues, famine, and flooding. These hardships created a climate of discontent among the populace, particularly among the peasants, who bore the brunt of these difficulties.

Central to the rebellion's ideology were the religious and mystical beliefs of the Yellow Turban rebels. Led by charismatic figures who claimed to possess supernatural powers and divine mandates, the rebels drew upon Daoist and millenarian concepts. They believed that by wearing yellow scarves or turbans, they could harness spiritual energies and gain protection from the heavens.

The Yellow Turbans advocated a radical vision for society. They called for the overthrow of the Han Dynasty, the division of land among the common people, the abolition of private property, and the establishment of a utopian society based on communal principles. Their message resonated with many who were suffering from economic hardships and social inequalities.

The rebellion erupted in the early 180s CE, with multiple uprisings occurring simultaneously across various regions of China. The Yellow Turbans organized themselves into regional units, each led by a charismatic figure who claimed divine authority. Among the most prominent leaders were Zhang Jiao, Zhang Bao, and Zhang Liang, who were collectively known as the "Three Zhangs."

The rebellion's initial success was partly attributed to the weakened state of the Eastern Han Dynasty. The central government was grappling with internal factionalism, corruption, and a lack of effective leadership. As the Yellow Turbans gained momentum, they captured cities and territories, posing a serious threat to the imperial authority.

In response to the rebellion, the Han government under Emperor Ling (reigned 168-189 CE) mobilized its forces to suppress the uprising. However, the imperial forces faced numerous challenges, including logistical difficulties, the vast geographical extent of the rebellion, and the rebels' guerrilla tactics. The conflict dragged on for several years, with neither side gaining a decisive advantage.

One of the key developments during the Yellow Turban Rebellion was the emergence of regional warlords who took advantage of the chaos to further their own ambitions. These warlords, often called "proto-warlords" or "local magnates," began to consolidate power and establish semi-autonomous fiefdoms. This fragmentation of central authority weakened the Eastern Han Dynasty's ability to quell the rebellion effectively.

As the rebellion continued, the Eastern Han Dynasty adopted a two-pronged approach to address the crisis. On one hand, they initiated military campaigns to suppress the Yellow Turban insurgents. On the other hand, they introduced reforms aimed at addressing some of the socio-economic grievances that had fueled the rebellion. These measures included the reduction of land taxes and the establishment of granaries to alleviate food shortages.

The most significant military campaign against the Yellow Turbans was led by the general Cao Cao. Cao Cao achieved several notable victories against the insurgents and played a crucial role in containing the rebellion's spread. Other notable generals, such as Liu Bei and Sun Jian, also rose to prominence during this period.

Gradually, the Eastern Han Dynasty managed to regain control of many regions that had been under Yellow Turban control. However, the rebellion had lasting effects on the dynasty. It exacerbated the fragmentation of power, as warlords continued to assert their independence and challenge the central authority. The rebellion also contributed to the decline of the imperial bureaucracy and the rise of regionalism.

Ultimately, the Yellow Turban Rebellion did not result in the immediate collapse of the Eastern Han Dynasty. However, it set in motion a series of events that would eventually lead to the fall of the dynasty and the onset of the Three Kingdoms period (220 - 280 CE), characterized by the division of China into three major rival states: Wei, Shu, and Wu.

In summary, the Yellow Turban Rebellion was a significant episode in ancient Chinese history, marked by a confluence of socio-economic grievances, religious fervor, and opposition to the ruling dynasty. It reflected the challenges faced by the Eastern Han Dynasty and the emergence of regional warlords who would shape the future of China. While the rebellion itself was ultimately suppressed, its legacy reverberated through the subsequent period of turmoil and division known as the Three Kingdoms era.

Wang Mang's Xin Dynasty stands as a unique and controversial chapter in the history of ancient China. This short-lived dynasty, which lasted from 9 CE to 23 CE, marked a significant departure from the established Han Dynasty and introduced a series of radical reforms and innovations. Wang Mang, the founder of the Xin Dynasty, sought to address the socioeconomic disparities and inefficiencies of the Han Dynasty, but his rule was marked by controversy, rebellion, and ultimately, his downfall.

Wang Mang, a member of the influential Wang clan, had served in various high-ranking positions during the Western Han Dynasty. However, it was his role as the regent for the child emperor, Liu Ying, that catapulted him to power. In 9 CE, Wang Mang seized the throne and proclaimed the establishment of the Xin Dynasty, effectively ending the Western Han Dynasty.

One of the defining features of Wang Mang's Xin Dynasty was his commitment to implementing radical reforms. Wang Mang believed that the socioeconomic problems plaguing China during the late Western Han Dynasty required a complete overhaul of the existing systems. His reforms, collectively known as the "New Policies," were aimed at redistributing land, wealth, and power to address social inequalities.

Land reform was a central component of Wang Mang's agenda. He sought to break up large estates and redistribute land to peasants, with the goal of reducing landlessness and tenant farming. While this reform was intended to benefit the common people, it faced resistance from landowners and often led to social unrest.

Wang Mang also introduced a new system of coinage known as the "Taiping Wuzhu." This standardized currency aimed to combat inflation and stabilize the economy. However, the sudden change in the currency system created confusion and economic disruptions.

Another significant reform was the introduction of the "equal-field system," which aimed to regulate land ownership and taxation. Under this system, land was distributed based on family size and the ability to cultivate it. However, implementing such a system on a vast scale proved challenging, and it faced opposition from powerful landowning elites.

Wang Mang's Xin Dynasty also saw attempts to regulate and control trade and commerce. He established state monopolies on certain industries, including iron production and salt mining, in an effort to generate revenue for the government. While these efforts were intended to strengthen the state, they often resulted in inefficiencies and corruption.

The Xin Dynasty also introduced a new calendar, known as the "Dazhong Calendar," and a revised legal code. These changes were part of Wang Mang's broader efforts to reorganize and centralize the administrative structure of the state.

Wang Mang's rule, however, was not without opposition. His radical reforms, land redistribution policies, and the upheaval they caused fueled discontent among various segments of society. Peasant uprisings, such as the Red Eyebrow Rebellion, erupted in response to the perceived failures and injustices of Wang Mang's policies. These rebellions sought to challenge his rule and restore the Han Dynasty.

Furthermore, natural disasters, such as floods and famines, compounded the challenges faced by Wang Mang's regime. These calamities exacerbated food shortages and further strained the government's resources.

The opposition to Wang Mang's rule culminated in the rise of regional warlords and rebel leaders who sought to overthrow him. Among these figures was Liu Xuan, who declared himself the emperor of the Han Dynasty's Gengshi Emperor. The Gengshi Emperor garnered support from various factions and initiated military campaigns to challenge Wang Mang's authority.

In 23 CE, after years of internal strife and external pressures, Wang Mang's Xin Dynasty collapsed. He was captured and executed, marking the end of his ambitious but divisive rule. The Han Dynasty was briefly restored under the Gengshi Emperor, but it was short-lived, and China entered a period of further fragmentation and conflict.

The Xin Dynasty, despite its relatively short duration and ultimate failure, left a lasting legacy in Chinese history. Wang Mang's reform efforts, while controversial and often poorly executed, addressed some of the deep-rooted issues of social inequality and land distribution. Elements of his reforms, such as the equal-field system, would resurface in later dynasties as China grappled with similar challenges.

The Xin Dynasty also serves as a cautionary tale about the complexities of implementing radical reforms and the potential for social and political upheaval when attempting to reshape the foundations of society. Wang Mang's rule underscores the delicate balance required to address societal disparities without alienating powerful interest groups or triggering widespread unrest.

In summary, Wang Mang's Xin Dynasty represents a period of significant reform and upheaval in ancient China. His ambitious but controversial policies aimed at addressing socioeconomic disparities had far-reaching consequences, both in the short term and as a source of inspiration and caution in subsequent dynasties. Wang Mang's reign serves as a testament to the challenges and complexities of governance and reform in the context of a vast and diverse empire.

The War of the Eight Princes, a tumultuous and tragic period in Chinese history, unfolded during the Jin Dynasty (266 - 420 CE) and left an indelible mark on the fate of the dynasty and the lives of its people. This civil conflict, which erupted in the 4th century CE, saw the imperial family divided into factions, vying for power, and ultimately contributing to the decline of the Jin Dynasty.

The roots of the War of the Eight Princes can be traced back to the weakening of the central Jin Dynasty's authority and the rise of regional governors and military commanders known as "wu-hu." These regional powers, often led by powerful warlords, gained significant autonomy and influence over their territories, eroding the central government's control.

The triggering event for the war was the death of Emperor Hui of Jin in 290 CE. His demise set off a succession crisis, as his son, Emperor Huai, was a child at the time. Various factions within the imperial family and the powerful warlords seized the opportunity to advance their interests and vie for control of the throne.

The conflict is named after the eight key princes who played prominent roles in the struggle for power:

Sima Wei: Sima Wei was one of the leading figures in the early stages of the conflict. He was initially named regent for the young Emperor Huai but later declared himself emperor, becoming known as Emperor Huai of Jin. His reign, however, was marked by political instability and a struggle for dominance.

Sima Yong: Sima Yong, another influential prince, sought to challenge Sima Wei's rule. He gathered support from regional warlords and initiated military campaigns against Sima Wei's faction, leading to further fragmentation of the empire.

Sima Liang: Sima Liang was a prince who, for a time, acted as a stabilizing force within the Jin Dynasty. He advocated for reconciliation and sought to mediate conflicts between the rival princes. His efforts aimed to restore unity to the fractured empire.

Sima Lun: Sima Lun, known for his ambition, orchestrated a coup against Sima Wei and declared himself emperor. His reign marked a period of centralized power, but it was short-lived, as he faced opposition from other princes.

Sima Jiong: Sima Jiong, a prince with aspirations to ascend to the throne, engaged in a power struggle with Sima Lun. His actions contributed to the ongoing turmoil and further divided the imperial family.

Sima Yue: Sima Yue, a prominent prince and military leader, played a significant role in the conflict. He commanded a formidable army and sought to expand his territorial holdings. Sima Yue's actions added to the complexity of the war.

Sima Ai: Sima Ai, like many of the other princes, had aspirations of becoming emperor. He formed alliances with various warlords and joined the fray in the struggle for supremacy.

Sima Ying: Sima Ying was another prince who joined the ranks of contenders for the throne. His involvement in the conflict further exacerbated the chaos and instability.

The War of the Eight Princes was marked by shifting alliances, betrayals, and military campaigns that ravaged the land and caused immense suffering to the population. The constant power struggles among the princes led to a lack of effective governance, economic hardship, and social disintegration.

During this turbulent period, regional warlords and military commanders played a decisive role in determining the outcome of the conflict. They often switched allegiances, aligning themselves with the prince they believed could best serve their interests or provide stability to their territories. The manipulation of these regional powers by the competing princes added layers of complexity to the war.

One of the enduring tragedies of the conflict was the toll it took on the civilian population. The people of the Jin Dynasty endured the ravages of war, including violence, famine, and displacement. Their lives were disrupted, and they suffered from the political maneuvering of the princes and warlords.

Ultimately, the War of the Eight Princes resulted in the fragmentation of the Jin Dynasty into several rival states, with each prince or warlord controlling a portion of the empire. The once-unified dynasty was irreparably weakened, and its decline continued in the subsequent years. In 317 CE, the Jin Dynasty was divided into the Eastern Jin Dynasty (317 - 420 CE) and the Western Jin Dynasty (265 - 316 CE), further contributing to its disintegration.

The War of the Eight Princes stands as a tragic episode in Chinese history, marked by political strife, power struggles, and the suffering of the people. It exemplifies the challenges faced by dynasties as they grappled with internal divisions and the rise of regional warlords. The conflict had far-reaching consequences for the Jin Dynasty and, ultimately, for the course of Chinese history as a whole.

Chapter 8: Wu Zetian: China's Only Empress

The rise to power of Wu Zetian, China's only empress in history, is a remarkable and often controversial chapter in ancient Chinese history. Her ascent to the throne challenged traditional gender roles and the established order, and her rule had a significant impact on the Tang Dynasty and the broader history of China.

Wu Zetian, born Wu Zhao, came from a well-educated and aristocratic family during the Tang Dynasty (618 - 907 CE). Her early life was marked by talent and ambition, which eventually caught the attention of Emperor Taizong, the second emperor of the Tang Dynasty. She entered the palace as a concubine of Emperor Taizong and quickly distinguished herself for her intelligence and political acumen.

Wu Zhao's life took a pivotal turn after the death of Emperor Taizong in 649 CE. She was sent to a Buddhist nunnery in accordance with the traditional practice of retiring consorts and concubines after the emperor's death. However, Wu Zhao maintained her political ambitions and did not accept her fate as a recluse.

One of the key factors in Wu Zhao's rise to power was her relationship with Emperor Gaozong, the son of Emperor Taizong, who succeeded his father as the third emperor of the Tang Dynasty. While in the nunnery, Wu Zhao cultivated a close relationship with Emperor Gaozong, who visited her frequently. Her political influence began to grow as she provided counsel to the emperor and actively participated in political discussions.

Wu Zhao's journey to the throne was marked by a series of strategic moves. Her opportunity to become empress consort came in 655 CE when she gave birth to a son, Li Hong, who was designated as the crown prince. As empress consort, she gained further influence over Emperor Gaozong and the court.

However, Wu Zhao's path to power faced a significant obstacle: the rivalry with Empress Wang, the first empress consort of Emperor Gaozong. Empress Wang was a powerful figure in her own right, and their competition for influence within the court was intense. In 660 CE, Empress Wang was accused of practicing witchcraft and was subsequently deposed and demoted. This event cleared the way for Wu Zhao to become the empress, solidifying her position as the highest-ranking woman in the empire.

Emperor Gaozong's reign was marked by a series of debilitating illnesses that gradually weakened his ability to govern effectively. During this time, Wu Zhao's role in the government continued to expand. She assumed more responsibilities in state affairs, including the management of administrative matters and appointments.

In 675 CE, Emperor Gaozong passed away, leaving the throne to their son, Emperor Zhongzong. However, Emperor Zhongzong's reign was marked by political instability and conflict within the court. Wu Zhao took advantage of these divisions and orchestrated a palace coup in 690 CE. She had Emperor Zhongzong demoted and placed under house arrest. Wu Zhao then assumed the throne, becoming the first and only female emperor in Chinese history.

As Emperor Wu of Zhou, she ruled China from 690 to 705 CE, establishing the Zhou Dynasty as a short-lived but transformative era in Chinese history. Her reign was characterized by a series of reforms and policies that aimed to strengthen central control, curb the power of the aristocracy, and promote Confucianism. She implemented a merit-based system for selecting government officials, which was seen as a departure from traditional aristocratic appointments.

Emperor Wu's rule also had a significant impact on gender relations and the status of women in Chinese society. She promoted women to key government positions and encouraged their education. Her reign was characterized by greater gender equality than in previous dynasties.

Despite her achievements, Wu Zetian's rule was not without controversy and opposition. Her ascent to power and consolidation of authority faced resistance from rival factions and critics who viewed her rule as illegitimate. Additionally, her reign was marked by political intrigues and purges of officials perceived as threats.

In 705 CE, Emperor Wu of Zhou was deposed, marking the end of her reign. Her death followed shortly after in 705 CE, and the Tang Dynasty was restored under Emperor Zhongzong's son.

Wu Zetian's legacy is complex and multifaceted. She remains a figure of historical fascination and debate, celebrated by some as a trailblazer who challenged gender norms and promoted governance reforms, while criticized by others for her ruthless pursuit of power and political intrigues. Her rise to the throne and the legacy of her rule continue to be subjects of historical analysis and discussion in China and beyond.

Wu Zetian's reform and rule as China's only empress were marked by a combination of political, administrative, and social changes that left a lasting impact on the Tang Dynasty and Chinese history. Her reign, which began in 690 CE and continued until 705 CE, introduced a series of transformative measures aimed at consolidating her authority, strengthening the central government, and promoting Confucianism.

Administrative Reforms: One of the key aspects of Wu Zetian's rule was her commitment to reforming the administrative apparatus of the Tang Dynasty. She established a merit-based system for selecting government officials, known as the "zhaoling" system, which emphasized qualifications and performance rather than aristocratic lineage. This marked a significant departure from the traditional practice of appointing officials based on their social status. The zhaoling system allowed individuals from diverse backgrounds to serve in government positions, which contributed to greater efficiency and competence in administration.

Centralization of Power: Wu Zetian sought to centralize power within the imperial court and diminish the influence of the aristocracy. She took steps to reduce the power of regional governors and military commanders, known as "jiedushi," who had gained significant autonomy during the Tang Dynasty. Her efforts aimed to strengthen the authority of the central government and enhance the emperor's control over the provinces.

Promotion of Confucianism: Wu Zetian was a proponent of Confucianism and actively promoted its principles as a means of legitimizing her rule. She encouraged the study of Confucian texts, held Confucian rituals, and appointed Confucian scholars to key positions within her government. Her support for Confucianism was in contrast to some of the previous dynasties, which had favored other philosophical and religious traditions.

Gender Equality: Wu Zetian's rule was notable for its relatively progressive stance on gender equality. She appointed women to key government positions and encouraged their education. Her reign saw the rise of female officials and scholars who played important roles in government and cultural life. While her promotion of women's rights was not without limits, it represented a departure from the patriarchal norms of the time.

Public Works and Infrastructure: Wu Zetian's reign witnessed significant investments in public works and infrastructure. She initiated projects to repair and expand the Grand Canal, which facilitated transportation and trade within the empire. Additionally, she oversaw the construction of major Buddhist temples and monuments, leaving a lasting cultural and architectural legacy.

Military Campaigns: Wu Zetian's rule was not without military conflicts. She engaged in campaigns against neighboring states and nomadic tribes, seeking to expand the empire's territory and secure its borders. These military endeavors aimed to consolidate her rule and protect the realm from external threats.

Literary Patronage: Wu Zetian was a patron of literature and the arts. Her court attracted poets, scholars, and artists, leading to a flourishing of cultural production during her reign. Her patronage contributed to the development of Chinese poetry and literature.

While Wu Zetian's reforms and rule were characterized by ambition and innovation, they were also marked by controversy and opposition. Critics viewed her rule as illegitimate, and her consolidation of power led to political intrigue and purges of officials perceived as threats. Her promotion of Buddhism, at the expense of other religious traditions, also drew criticism.

After her deposition in 705 CE, Wu Zetian's legacy continued to influence subsequent generations. Her impact on gender relations, governance reforms, and cultural patronage left a lasting imprint on Chinese history. She remains a subject of historical fascination and debate, celebrated by some as a pioneering ruler who challenged societal norms and criticized by others for her authoritarian methods. Wu Zetian's reign stands as a testament to the complexities of power, reform, and gender in the context of ancient China.

The legacy of Empress Wu Zetian, the only female emperor in Chinese history, is a subject of enduring fascination and debate. Her rule, which spanned from 690 to 705 CE during the Tang Dynasty, left a profound impact on China's political, social, and cultural landscape. Empress Wu's legacy is complex, with her achievements and controversies continuing to shape the narrative of her reign and her place in history.

Gender Equality and Empowerment of Women: One of the most notable aspects of Empress Wu's legacy is her role in promoting gender equality and empowering women in Chinese society. Her reign saw the appointment of women to key government positions, including high-ranking officials and military commanders. This departure from traditional gender roles was a significant departure from the norms of her time and has had a lasting influence on perceptions of women's capabilities and roles in governance.

Administrative Reforms: Empress Wu's legacy also includes her administrative reforms, particularly the establishment of the "zhaoling" system, a merit-based system for selecting government officials. This system emphasized qualifications and performance over aristocratic lineage, contributing to greater competence and efficiency in government. While this system was later abandoned after her reign, it left a lasting impression on Chinese administrative practices.

Centralization of Power: Empress Wu's efforts to centralize power and diminish the influence of regional governors and military commanders had a lasting impact on the structure of the Chinese government. Her attempts to strengthen the authority of the central government influenced subsequent dynasties and their approaches to governance.

Promotion of Confucianism: Empress Wu's support for Confucianism during her reign had a significant impact on the philosophical and ideological landscape of China. She actively promoted the study of Confucian texts, held Confucian rituals, and appointed Confucian scholars to key positions in her government. This elevation of Confucianism as a state ideology influenced later dynasties and their adoption of Confucian principles.

Cultural Patronage: Empress Wu was a patron of literature, poetry, and the arts. Her court attracted poets, scholars, and artists, leading to a flourishing of cultural production during her reign. Her patronage contributed to the development of Chinese poetry and literature, leaving a lasting cultural legacy.

Public Works and Infrastructure: Empress Wu's investments in public works and infrastructure had a tangible impact on the empire. Her initiatives included repairing and expanding the Grand Canal, a vital transportation route, and overseeing the construction of significant Buddhist temples and monuments. These projects contributed to the empire's economic and cultural development.

Military Campaigns: While Empress Wu's military campaigns aimed to secure the empire's borders and consolidate her rule, they also had a lasting impact on the empire's territorial boundaries. The territories gained during her reign influenced the geopolitical landscape of subsequent dynasties.

Criticism and Controversy: Empress Wu's legacy is also marked by controversy and criticism. Her ascent to power was accompanied by political intrigue and purges of officials who opposed her rule. Her authoritarian methods and consolidation of power drew criticism from those who viewed her rule as illegitimate.

Impact on Successive Dynasties: The influence of Empress Wu's reign extended beyond the Tang Dynasty. Her gender-neutral policies and promotion of women in government challenged traditional norms and influenced later dynasties' approaches to governance. The enduring debate about her rule and her gender continues to shape discussions of women's roles in Chinese history and leadership.

Historical Interpretations: Empress Wu's legacy has been subject to differing historical interpretations. Some view her as a trailblazing ruler who challenged gender norms and promoted governance reforms, while others emphasize her ruthless pursuit of power and political intrigues. These varying perspectives reflect the complexities of her reign and its historical significance.

In summary, the legacy of Empress Wu Zetian is multifaceted, reflecting both her achievements and controversies during her rule. Her promotion of gender equality, administrative reforms, and cultural patronage have left a lasting impact on Chinese history and society. While her rule remains a subject of historical debate and discussion, there is no doubt that her reign marked a pivotal moment in the history of China, challenging established norms and leaving an indelible imprint on the nation's historical narrative.

Chapter 9: End of an Era: The Fall of the Han

The decline of the Eastern Han Dynasty marked a tumultuous period in Chinese history, characterized by political instability, social upheaval, and economic challenges. This decline, which occurred from the late 2nd century CE to the early 3rd century CE, eventually led to the fragmentation of the dynasty and the onset of the Three Kingdoms period. Several interconnected factors contributed to the decline of the Eastern Han Dynasty and the ensuing chaos.

1. Court Intrigue and Factionalism: The Eastern Han Dynasty was plagued by court intrigue and factionalism among eunuchs, imperial relatives, and influential officials. These power struggles frequently paralyzed the government and undermined the authority of the emperor. Eunuchs, in particular, gained significant influence and were often involved in political machinations that hindered effective governance.

2. Weak Leadership: The later Eastern Han emperors were characterized by weak leadership and were often manipulated by court factions. Many of them were young or inexperienced, making them susceptible to the influence of powerful eunuchs and officials. This weak central authority exacerbated political instability.

3. Economic Decline: Economic challenges played a significant role in the decline of the Eastern Han Dynasty. The state's revenues were insufficient to support its vast bureaucracy and military, leading to fiscal crises and a heavy tax burden on the peasantry. Corruption and exploitation further exacerbated economic woes, leading to widespread poverty and discontent.

4. Yellow Turban Rebellion: The Yellow Turban Rebellion, which began in 184 CE, was a massive uprising led by peasants and fueled by socioeconomic grievances. The rebellion symbolized the widespread discontent with the ruling elite and the economic hardships faced by the common people. While the rebellion was eventually suppressed, it highlighted the deep-rooted issues facing the dynasty.

5. Warlords and Regionalism: The Eastern Han Dynasty saw the rise of powerful regional warlords who commanded their own armies and controlled significant territories. These warlords, known as "jiedushi," operated with a high degree of autonomy, further weakening the central government's authority. Their loyalty often lay with their own interests rather than the emperor.

6. Natural Disasters: The Eastern Han Dynasty also faced a series of natural disasters, including floods, droughts, and famines. These calamities led to food shortages, displacement of the population, and further economic strain on the empire.

7. External Threats: Beyond internal challenges, external threats posed a significant danger to the Eastern Han Dynasty. The nomadic Xiongnu and Xianbei tribes were recurrent threats to the northern borders. The dynasty's inability to effectively counter these threats contributed to a sense of vulnerability.

8. Cultural and Intellectual Shifts: Cultural and intellectual changes were underway during the Eastern Han Dynasty. The spread of Daoism and Buddhism introduced new belief systems that challenged Confucianism, which had traditionally played a central role in Chinese governance. These shifts in thought contributed to a sense of cultural change and uncertainty.

9. Fragmentation: As the central government's authority eroded, the Eastern Han Dynasty fragmented into a collection of regional kingdoms and territories controlled by warlords. This fragmentation set the stage for the Three Kingdoms period, during which several states vied for dominance.

In the midst of these challenges, several attempts were made to reform and revitalize the Eastern Han Dynasty. Prominent officials such as Wang Mang and He Jin sought to address some of the dynasty's issues through political and administrative reforms. However, these efforts often faced opposition and were not successful in stemming the overall decline.

Ultimately, the decline of the Eastern Han Dynasty culminated in the year 220 CE when Emperor Xian abdicated the throne, marking the official end of the dynasty. The subsequent period, known as the Three Kingdoms, saw the emergence of three powerful states—Wei, Shu, and Wu—each vying for control of China. This period of division and conflict continued until the reunification of China under the Jin Dynasty.

The decline of the Eastern Han Dynasty serves as a cautionary tale about the challenges of governing a vast and diverse empire. It highlights the importance of effective leadership, fiscal responsibility, and the ability to adapt to changing circumstances. The legacy of the Eastern Han Dynasty, while marked by decline and turmoil, also includes important cultural and intellectual developments that shaped the course of Chinese history in subsequent dynasties.

The Three Kingdoms Period, a pivotal era in Chinese history, emerged from the decline of the Eastern Han Dynasty and the fragmentation of China into several powerful states. This period, which lasted from 220 CE to 280 CE, was marked by political intrigue, military conflict, and the rise and fall of three prominent states: Wei, Shu, and Wu. The Three Kingdoms Period is a captivating chapter in Chinese history, filled with complex characters, strategic maneuvers, and enduring cultural legacies.

Context of the Three Kingdoms Period: The decline of the Eastern Han Dynasty, characterized by weak leadership, internal strife, and economic challenges, set the stage for the fragmentation of China. Regional warlords, known as "jiedushi," had gained considerable power and autonomy, controlling vast territories. The central government's authority was eroding, and this power vacuum contributed to the emergence of the Three Kingdoms.

The Three Kingdoms:

Wei: Cao Wei, led by Cao Cao and later his descendants, was one of the three major states that emerged during this period. Cao Cao, a brilliant military strategist, initially served the Eastern Han court and played a pivotal role in suppressing the Yellow Turban Rebellion. He later established his own state, Wei, and was known for his ambition to reunify China. Despite his authoritarian rule, Cao Cao was also a patron of culture and education.

Shu: Shu Han, led by Liu Bei, was another of the three kingdoms. Liu Bei, a charismatic leader, was known for his commitment to Confucian ideals and his sense of benevolence. He formed an alliance with other notable figures, such as Guan Yu and Zhang Fei, and established Shu as a state with a focus on virtuous governance. The state of Shu represented a noble and righteous cause during this period.

Wu: Wu, led by Sun Quan, was the third major state. Sun Quan, a skilled strategist, founded Wu and established a strong naval presence. Wu was known for its maritime activities, including its battles on the Yangtze River. The state was characterized by its pragmatism and adaptability, often forging alliances with different powers to maintain its position.

Military Conflicts: The Three Kingdoms Period was marked by numerous military conflicts and battles, some of which have become legendary in Chinese history. The Battle of Red Cliffs, fought in 208 CE, is one of the most famous battles of this era. It saw the allied forces of Liu Bei and Sun Quan defeat Cao Cao's fleet in a strategic showdown. This battle had a significant impact on the balance of power among the three states.

Cultural and Literary Contributions: Despite the tumultuous nature of the period, the Three Kingdoms Period was also a time of cultural flourishing. Scholars and writers produced important literary works, such as the "Romance of the Three Kingdoms" by Luo Guanzhong. This epic novel, based on historical events and characters, has become a classic of Chinese literature and is still widely read and studied today.

Political Alliances and Betrayals: The period was characterized by intricate political alliances and betrayals among the three kingdoms and their leaders. Alliances were formed and dissolved as each state sought to gain an advantage. For instance, the alliance between Shu and Wu at the Battle of Red Cliffs was instrumental in their victory over Cao Cao, but it eventually dissolved as they pursued their own interests.

Legacy and Historical Significance: The Three Kingdoms Period has had a lasting impact on Chinese culture, literature, and historical consciousness. The characters and events of this era continue to be celebrated in literature, theater, and popular culture. The strategies and tactics employed by military commanders during this period are studied in military academies around the world.

End of the Three Kingdoms Period: The Three Kingdoms Period came to an end when the state of Jin emerged as a powerful contender. Sima Yan, the ruler of Jin, conquered the three kingdoms one by one, unifying China in 280 CE. This marked the end of the era of division and the beginning of the Jin Dynasty.

In summary, the Three Kingdoms Period stands as a testament to the resilience, ambition, and complexity of the human experience during times of upheaval. It was a time of extraordinary leaders, legendary battles, and enduring cultural contributions. The legacy of this period continues to captivate the imagination of people around the world, serving as a rich source of historical, literary, and cultural inspiration.

Cao Cao, a central figure during the tumultuous Three Kingdoms Period in ancient China, played a pivotal role in shaping the destiny of the Wei Dynasty. Known for his strategic brilliance, political acumen, and controversial legacy, Cao Cao's leadership left an indelible mark on Chinese history.

Cao Cao's Rise to Power: Cao Cao was born in 155 CE during the Eastern Han Dynasty, a period marked by political turmoil and regional fragmentation. He came from a privileged background, hailing from a family of landowners and officials. Cao Cao's early years were marked by his military exploits, particularly in suppressing the Yellow Turban Rebellion, a massive peasant uprising that threatened the Eastern Han Dynasty.

Cao Cao's military successes and political ambitions propelled him to prominence. He established a power base in the northern region of China, known as the Central Plain, where he gained the loyalty of both civilian administrators and military officers. As he expanded his influence, Cao Cao found himself in a position to challenge the authority of the Eastern Han court.

The Establishment of Wei: Cao Cao's ambitions ultimately led him to break with the Eastern Han Dynasty, setting the stage for the establishment of the state of Wei. In 196 CE, he seized control of the Han capital, Xu Chang, and effectively took command of the central government. While he nominally served the Han Dynasty, his authority was de facto, and he governed as a regional warlord.

Cao Cao's control over the central government allowed him to implement important administrative and political reforms. He established the "zhaoling" system, a merit-based approach to appointing officials based on competence rather than social status. This system aimed to improve governance and enhance the efficiency of the state.

Cao Cao's Military Campaigns: One of Cao Cao's defining characteristics was his military prowess. He was a master tactician and strategist, known for his innovative approaches to warfare. He conducted numerous campaigns to expand his territories and consolidate his rule.

One of the most significant battles of Cao Cao's career was the Battle of Red Cliffs in 208 CE. Fought against the combined forces of the southern warlords Sun Quan and Liu Bei, this battle saw Cao Cao's fleet decisively defeated. The battle had a profound impact on the balance of power during the Three Kingdoms Period, as it prevented Cao Cao from further expanding his influence southward.

Political Ambitions and Controversies: Cao Cao's political ambitions were clear: he sought to reunify China under his rule. He saw himself as a champion of order and sought to restore stability to the empire, which had been plagued by decades of conflict and fragmentation. However, his authoritarian rule and centralization of power also generated controversy and opposition.

Cao Cao's consolidation of authority and the prominence of eunuchs in his administration drew criticism. His rule was characterized by strict control and a focus on centralization, which often clashed with the interests of regional warlords and the imperial court.

Cultural Patronage: Despite his image as a military leader and statesman, Cao Cao was also known for his cultural patronage. He supported the arts, literature, and scholarship during his rule. Cao Cao was a poet himself and is remembered for his contributions to Chinese literature. His verses are considered classics of Chinese poetry, reflecting themes of war, governance, and personal reflection.

Cao Cao's Poems: One of Cao Cao's most famous poems is the "Short Song Style," in which he expresses his regrets and reflections on life. The poem reflects his introspective side and reveals the complexity of his character. In it, he writes:

"I remember my early years, as in a dream; In the beginning, I was troubled and unknown. Now, since I've learned to accept what comes, I am a bit more peaceful."

This poem showcases Cao Cao's introspective nature and his ability to reflect on his life and experiences.

Legacy and the Wei Dynasty: Cao Cao passed away in 220 CE, leaving his legacy to be carried forward by his descendants. His son, Cao Pi, officially declared the establishment of the Wei Dynasty and proclaimed himself emperor, effectively ending the Eastern Han Dynasty. The Wei Dynasty would continue to play a significant role in the political landscape of the Three Kingdoms Period.

Cao Cao's legacy remains complex and multifaceted. He is remembered as a military genius, a poet, and a central figure during a pivotal period in Chinese history. His rule, characterized by centralization and authoritarianism, continues to be a subject of historical analysis and debate. While some view him as a ruthless warlord, others see him as a pragmatic leader who sought to restore order to a fractured empire.

In Chinese culture, Cao Cao's name is often invoked to refer to a person who is clever and resourceful. His historical significance extends beyond his own time, as his actions and legacy have left an enduring imprint on the Chinese historical narrative and the collective memory of the Chinese people.

Chapter 10: Legacy of the Silk Road: Han Dynasty's Lasting Influence

Cultural exchanges and innovations have played a profound role in shaping the course of human history, fostering the cross-pollination of ideas, technologies, and artistic expressions across different societies and civilizations. These exchanges have not only enriched the cultural tapestry of humanity but have also contributed to the advancement of knowledge, science, and art.

Silk Road: A Path of Exchange: One of the most iconic conduits for cultural exchange was the Silk Road, an ancient network of trade routes that connected the East and West, spanning from China to the Mediterranean. The Silk Road facilitated the movement of goods, including silk, spices, precious metals, and textiles, but it also served as a highway of ideas, religions, and innovations.

Spread of Knowledge and Philosophy: The Silk Road was instrumental in the spread of knowledge, philosophy, and religious beliefs. For instance, the transmission of Buddhist teachings from India to East Asia occurred along this route. Buddhist monks and scholars carried scriptures, art, and architectural styles as they journeyed, leaving an indelible impact on the cultures of China, Japan, Korea, and beyond.

Technological Exchanges: Cultural exchanges were not limited to ideas and beliefs but also extended to technology. The Silk Road facilitated the exchange of agricultural practices, metallurgy, and engineering innovations. For example, the introduction of papermaking technology from China to the Islamic world revolutionized the way knowledge was recorded and disseminated. It eventually found its way to Europe, transforming the production of books and manuscripts.

Artistic Influences: Artistic styles and techniques were also exchanged along these routes. The interaction between Eastern and Western artistic traditions led to a fusion of styles, seen in the synthesis of Greco-Buddhist art. This unique artistic tradition combined Greek realism with Buddhist themes and was prominent in regions like Gandhara, which is now part of modern-day Pakistan and Afghanistan.

Scientific Progress: Cultural exchanges also fueled scientific progress. The sharing of mathematical knowledge, including Indian numerals and the concept of zero, had a transformative impact on mathematical and scientific developments. These mathematical innovations laid the foundation for modern mathematics and were integral to the scientific achievements of the Islamic Golden Age and the European Renaissance.

Language and Literature: Language and literature were deeply influenced by cultural exchanges. The translation of texts between languages allowed for the dissemination of literary works, scientific treatises, and philosophical writings. For example, the translation of Greek texts into Arabic during the Islamic Golden Age played a critical role in preserving and advancing knowledge.

Diverse Religious Traditions: Religious diversity was another hallmark of cultural exchanges. Along the Silk Road, diverse religious traditions coexisted and interacted. Buddhism, Zoroastrianism, Christianity, Islam, and various forms of indigenous spirituality found adherents and influenced one another's beliefs and practices. This religious diversity contributed to a rich tapestry of beliefs and rituals.

Innovations in Medicine: Medical knowledge also benefited from cross-cultural exchanges. The movement of medical texts, herbal remedies, and surgical techniques helped expand the understanding of the human body and its ailments. Chinese contributions to medicine, such as acupuncture, made their way to other parts of the world, while Islamic scholars preserved and expanded upon Greek and Roman medical knowledge.

Culinary Traditions: Cultural exchanges extended to culinary traditions, leading to the introduction of new ingredients and cooking techniques. Spices, herbs, and cooking methods traversed the Silk Road, influencing the cuisines of various regions. This exchange of culinary knowledge enriched the flavors and diversity of food in different cultures.

Cultural Preservation: Cultural exchanges not only fostered innovation but also played a role in preserving cultural heritage. Manuscripts, artworks, and artifacts were transported along trade routes, helping to safeguard the cultural achievements of different societies. Many ancient texts and artworks would have been lost to history were it not for these exchanges.

Challenges and Conflicts: While cultural exchanges brought about significant benefits, they were not without challenges and conflicts. Trade disputes, territorial rivalries, and cultural misunderstandings occasionally led to tensions and conflicts along the Silk Road. However, these challenges were often outweighed by the positive aspects of exchange.

In summary, cultural exchanges and innovations have been instrumental in shaping the course of human history. The Silk Road and other trade routes served as conduits for the exchange of ideas, technologies, and artistic expressions, fostering a rich and interconnected global civilization. These exchanges have not only enriched individual cultures but have also contributed to the collective heritage of humanity, shaping the world we know today. Cultural exchange continues to be a powerful force, promoting understanding, cooperation, and progress in our interconnected world.

The trade in silk and spices stands as one of the most iconic and enduring chapters in the history of commerce. Spanning centuries and bridging continents, this exchange of valuable goods has not only shaped global trade but has also left an indelible mark on cultures, societies, and economies across the world.

The Silk Road: The Silk Road, a network of trade routes connecting the East and West, was the primary conduit for the exchange of silk and spices. This ancient network, which traversed vast expanses of Asia, the Middle East, and Europe, facilitated not only the movement of goods but also the flow of ideas, cultures, and technologies.

Silk: The Fabric of Royalty: Silk, a luxurious and highly sought-after fabric, was the pride of China. The secret of silk production, tightly guarded by the Chinese for centuries, eventually spread along the Silk Road. This fine textile was a symbol of royalty and affluence, and it quickly became a valuable commodity in markets from Rome to Constantinople.

Spices: The Flavor of Trade: Spices, including pepper, cinnamon, cloves, and nutmeg, were another coveted category of goods exchanged along these trade routes. These aromatic treasures added flavor, aroma, and preservation qualities to food and were highly prized by both the culinary and medicinal worlds.

China's Silk Production: China was the epicenter of silk production, with its sericulture (the cultivation of silkworms) and weaving techniques remaining unparalleled. The production of silk involved a labor-intensive process, from raising silkworms to spinning silk threads and weaving fabric.

The Chinese mastery of these techniques gave them a near-monopoly on silk production for centuries.

The West's Thirst for Silk: The demand for silk in the West was insatiable. Roman elites, in particular, developed a taste for this luxurious fabric, which became a symbol of status and wealth. As a result, the Roman Empire heavily relied on trade with the East to satisfy this demand, creating a trade deficit that spanned centuries.

The Spice Trade: Spices, on the other hand, were primarily sourced from regions such as the Spice Islands (modern-day Indonesia), India, and Southeast Asia. These spices were not only used for culinary purposes but also for medicinal and preservative qualities. Spices were highly valued and were often worth their weight in gold.

Trade Routes and Cultural Exchange: The trade in silk and spices along the Silk Road was not limited to goods. It also facilitated the exchange of cultures, ideas, and technologies. The transmission of knowledge, such as papermaking and the concept of zero, was a significant byproduct of these exchanges.

Challenges of the Silk Road: While the Silk Road was a testament to human ingenuity and the desire for trade and exchange, it was not without challenges. The vast distances, harsh terrains, and political complexities of the regions it traversed presented obstacles to traders and merchants. Bandits and marauders also posed significant threats to caravans.

The Maritime Silk Road: In addition to overland routes, the maritime Silk Road emerged as another vital conduit for trade. It connected the East with regions in Southeast Asia, the Indian subcontinent, the Middle East, and East Africa. This maritime trade route was instrumental in the exchange of spices, textiles, ceramics, and more.

Shifts in Trade Patterns: Over time, trade patterns along the Silk Road evolved. The rise of the Mongol Empire facilitated safe passage for traders, leading to increased trade and cultural exchanges between the East and West. Later, the emergence of maritime trade routes during the Age of Exploration further transformed global trade dynamics.

European Voyages of Discovery: European explorers such as Vasco da Gama and Christopher Columbus embarked on voyages of discovery in search of direct sea routes to Asia. These explorations eventually led to the discovery of new trade routes, including the sea route to India, which circumvented the overland Silk Road.

Impact on World History: The trade in silk and spices has had a profound impact on world history. It contributed to the rise and fall of empires, shaped cultural interactions, and influenced culinary traditions. The desire for access to these valuable commodities drove exploration, colonization, and the forging of new global connections.

Cultural Exchange: Along with silk and spices, the Silk Road facilitated the exchange of religions, philosophies, art, and technology. Buddhism, Islam, Christianity, and other belief systems found their way along these routes, leading to the spread of faiths and cultural cross-pollination.

Modern Significance: The legacy of the Silk Road endures in the modern world. It serves as a symbol of the interconnectedness of human societies and the enduring value of trade and exchange. Today, the "Belt and Road Initiative," a modern infrastructure and economic development project initiated by China, seeks to revive and expand the ancient Silk Road routes, fostering greater connectivity and cooperation among nations.

In summary, the trade in silk and spices along the Silk Road and maritime routes is a testament to the enduring human desire for exchange and the pursuit of valuable goods.

Beyond commerce, it forged cultural connections, expanded knowledge, and shaped the course of history. The legacies of silk and spices are woven into the fabric of civilizations, leaving an indelible mark on the global tapestry of culture, trade, and human interaction.

The Silk Road, often described as the world's first international trade route, occupies a pivotal place in world history due to its profound impact on cultures, economies, and the exchange of knowledge. This ancient network of interconnected trade routes, stretching from East Asia to the Mediterranean, acted as a bridge between the East and the West, facilitating the movement of goods, ideas, and people. Its role in world history can be examined from various perspectives.

Ancient Origins and Significance: The origins of the Silk Road can be traced back to ancient China, where silk production was a closely guarded secret. The demand for this luxurious fabric, with its shimmering beauty and exceptional texture, was insatiable in the West, particularly in the Roman Empire. The Silk Road became the primary avenue for the West to obtain this prized commodity.

Cultural Exchange and Syncretism: One of the most profound impacts of the Silk Road was the exchange of cultures, religions, and ideas. Along its extensive routes, traders, pilgrims, and explorers interacted, leading to a rich cross-pollination of cultures. Buddhism, for example, spread from India to China and beyond, while Islamic civilization and art absorbed elements from Persia, India, and Central Asia. This cultural syncretism gave rise to unique artistic expressions, architectural styles, and belief systems.

Spread of Knowledge: The Silk Road also acted as a conduit for the transmission of knowledge. Chinese inventions like papermaking, printing, and gunpowder made their way to the West, significantly impacting the course of history.

Conversely, innovations from the West, such as the compass and advanced mathematical concepts, found their way to the East. This exchange of scientific and technological knowledge helped advance human civilization.

Economic Engine: The Silk Road was a vibrant economic engine that fueled trade between regions that were previously isolated. Besides silk, it facilitated the exchange of precious metals, spices, textiles, gems, and exotic goods like peacocks and rhinoceros horns. The Silk Road played a critical role in stimulating economic growth and development in the civilizations along its routes.

Exploration and Expeditions: The Silk Road sparked a spirit of exploration and adventure. Marco Polo's famous journey along the Silk Road in the 13th century is a testament to the allure of these trade routes. His accounts, along with those of other travelers, helped Europeans gain a broader understanding of the East and encouraged further exploration, ultimately leading to the Age of Exploration and the discovery of new trade routes.

Crossroads of Empires: The Silk Road became a meeting point for various empires and cultures, including the Roman, Persian, Indian, Chinese, and Islamic empires. It was at the crossroads of these great powers that trade, diplomacy, and conflict intersected. These interactions often shaped the political landscapes of regions and led to the rise and fall of empires.

Challenges and Perils: While the Silk Road facilitated exchanges and prosperity, it also posed challenges and perils. Traversing vast and diverse terrains, merchants faced harsh climates, bandits, and political instability. Despite these obstacles, the allure of the trade routes and the potential rewards spurred travelers and merchants to undertake perilous journeys.

Decline and Revival: The Silk Road's prominence gradually waned during the later centuries due to the rise of maritime routes and geopolitical shifts. However, in contemporary times, China's "Belt and Road Initiative" seeks to revive and expand the Silk Road's legacy by investing in infrastructure, trade, and cultural exchange along its historical routes. This modern initiative aims to rejuvenate ancient connections and foster cooperation among nations.

Cultural Heritage and Tourism: Today, many regions along the Silk Road have preserved their cultural heritage, including ancient cities, trading posts, and historical landmarks. These sites draw tourists and researchers interested in exploring the remnants of this remarkable period in history. UNESCO has recognized several sections of the Silk Road as World Heritage Sites, further emphasizing their cultural significance.

Global Interconnectedness: The Silk Road's legacy of interconnectedness continues to be relevant in the modern world. It underscores the importance of global trade, cooperation, and cultural exchange. As societies become increasingly interconnected through trade, travel, and communication, the Silk Road serves as a symbol of the enduring human quest for connection and exchange.

In summary, the Silk Road's role in world history is multifaceted and profound. It acted as a conduit for the exchange of goods, cultures, knowledge, and ideas, fostering connections between East and West. Its legacy endures in contemporary times, serving as a reminder of the enduring human desire for exploration, trade, and cultural exchange, and the remarkable impact such exchanges can have on the course of human history.

BOOK 2
CONFUCIANISM
THE MORAL COMPASS OF ANCIENT CHINA (551 BCE - 479 BCE)
BY A.J. KINGSTON

Chapter 1: The World of Ancient China (551 BCE)

In 551 BCE, the world was a vastly different place compared to today, marked by a rich tapestry of geographic and cultural diversity. This period in history was characterized by distinct civilizations, each with its own unique geography, culture, and societal norms.
China: Birth of Confucius: In the eastern part of Asia, the Chinese civilization was flourishing. It was during this time that Confucius, one of the most influential philosophers in history, was born. Confucius's teachings would later form the basis of Confucianism, a philosophical and ethical system that profoundly shaped Chinese culture and governance.
China's Geography: Geographically, China was diverse, encompassing vast plains, fertile river valleys, and rugged mountain ranges. The Yellow River (Huang He) and the Yangtze River played pivotal roles in the agricultural development and economic prosperity of ancient China. These rivers supported a burgeoning population engaged in farming, trade, and various cultural activities.
India: Birth of Mahavira: To the south of China, the Indian subcontinent was experiencing its own cultural and philosophical developments. Around the same time as Confucius, Mahavira, the founder of Jainism, was born in ancient India. Jainism would become one of the major religious and philosophical traditions in India, emphasizing non-violence (ahimsa) and asceticism.
Indian Geography: India's geography was incredibly diverse, with its vast expanse covering everything from the fertile Gangetic plains to the rugged terrain of the Himalayas. The Indian subcontinent was home to multiple distinct kingdoms, each with its own language, culture, and traditions. This

diversity was reflected in the wide range of religious beliefs and practices found across the region.

Greece: Birth of Pericles: In the western part of the world, ancient Greece was witnessing significant cultural and political developments. In 551 BCE, Pericles, a prominent Athenian statesman, was born. Pericles would go on to lead Athens during its "Golden Age," a period of great cultural achievements and democratic reforms.

Greek Geography: Greece's geography was characterized by a rugged and mountainous landscape, with numerous islands dotting the Mediterranean Sea. These geographical features influenced the development of city-states, each with its own government and culture. The interconnectedness of these city-states, facilitated by the Mediterranean Sea, played a crucial role in the exchange of ideas and goods.

Persia: Achaemenid Empire: In the Middle East, the Achaemenid Empire, led by Cyrus the Great, was expanding its territory. By 551 BCE, this empire had already achieved remarkable feats, including the conquest of Babylon. The Achaemenid Empire's governance and administrative innovations laid the groundwork for future Persian empires.

Persian Geography: The Achaemenid Empire spanned a vast geographical area, including modern-day Iran, Iraq, and parts of Turkey and Egypt. Its diverse geography encompassed arid deserts, fertile river valleys, and mountainous regions. The empire's central location made it a hub for trade and cultural exchange between East and West.

The year 551 BCE marked a significant point in history when diverse civilizations were thriving across different regions of the world. Each of these civilizations had its own unique geography, culture, and societal norms. The interactions and exchanges between these civilizations would continue to shape the course of history, influencing everything from philosophy and religion to governance and trade. This period of geographic and cultural diversity laid the foundation for the rich tapestry of human history that would unfold in the millennia to come.

During ancient times, philosophical and religious traditions began to emerge, laying the foundations for belief systems and ethical philosophies that continue to influence human thought and culture today. These early traditions reflected the profound questions and moral inquiries of their respective societies and have left a lasting legacy in the world's intellectual and spiritual history.

Confucianism: In ancient China during the 6th century BCE, Confucius (551-479 BCE) developed Confucianism, a moral and ethical philosophy. Confucianism emphasized the importance of filial piety, respect for authority, and ethical conduct in personal and social life. It played a significant role in shaping Chinese culture, governance, and social values. Confucianism also advocated for the cultivation of virtues and the pursuit of a harmonious society through moral self-improvement.

Daoism (Taoism): Daoism, or Taoism, is another ancient Chinese philosophy that emerged around the same time as Confucianism. Laozi is traditionally considered the founder of Daoism, and his text, the "Tao Te Ching," is a central Daoist scripture. Daoism emphasizes living in harmony with the Dao (Tao), often translated as "the Way." It advocates for simplicity, spontaneity, and a non-interfering attitude toward natural processes. Daoism has had a profound influence on Chinese culture, particularly in the realms of art, poetry, and traditional medicine.

Jainism: In ancient India, Mahavira (599-527 BCE) founded Jainism, a religious and philosophical tradition that emphasizes non-violence (ahimsa), truthfulness, and asceticism. Jainism holds that all living beings have a divine spark within them and should be treated with utmost compassion. It played a significant role in shaping ethical and spiritual thought in India and contributed to the development of the doctrine of karma and reincarnation.

Greek Philosophy: Ancient Greece was a crucible for philosophical thought during the 6th century BCE. Prominent Greek philosophers like Thales, Pythagoras, and Heraclitus engaged in critical inquiry about the nature of reality, the cosmos, and the human condition. Socrates (469-399 BCE) is perhaps the most famous of these philosophers. His method of questioning, known as the Socratic method, aimed to stimulate critical thinking and self-examination. Socrates' student, Plato, and Plato's student, Aristotle, made substantial contributions to Greek philosophy and laid the groundwork for Western philosophical traditions.

Zoroastrianism: Zoroastrianism, founded by the prophet Zoroaster (Zarathustra) in ancient Persia, is one of the world's oldest monotheistic religions. It introduced the concept of a single, supreme god (Ahura Mazda) and the dualistic struggle between good and evil. Zoroastrianism influenced subsequent monotheistic religions, including Judaism, Christianity, and Islam, with concepts such as judgment, heaven, and hell.

Ancient Egyptian Religion: In ancient Egypt, religious beliefs and practices centered around a pantheon of gods and the worship of pharaohs as divine rulers. The Egyptian Book of the Dead, a collection of funerary texts, provided guidance on the afterlife and influenced religious thought and practices in the region.

These early philosophical and religious traditions reflect humanity's quest for meaning, morality, and understanding of the cosmos. They addressed fundamental questions about existence, ethics, and the nature of reality, providing guidance and spiritual solace to individuals and communities. These traditions have had a lasting impact on culture, ethics, and spirituality, shaping the diverse array of belief systems and philosophies that continue to shape our world today.

Social structure and governance are fundamental aspects of human societies that have evolved over millennia, reflecting the values, needs, and complexities of different cultures and civilizations. These systems have played a crucial role in organizing communities, distributing power, and ensuring order within societies. Examining the dynamics of social structure and governance across various historical periods and regions provides insights into the diversity of human societies and their approaches to organization and leadership.

Ancient Mesopotamia and the Emergence of Kingship: In ancient Mesopotamia, one of the world's earliest civilizations, the Sumerians established city-states around 3500 BCE. These city-states had complex social hierarchies, with priests, rulers, and laborers occupying distinct roles. The emergence of kingship marked a significant development in governance, as rulers gained both political and religious authority. The Code of Hammurabi, one of the earliest known legal codes (circa 1754 BCE), provided a framework for justice and governance, highlighting the role of laws in early statecraft.

Egyptian Pharaohs and Divine Rule: Ancient Egypt's social structure and governance were deeply influenced by religious beliefs. Pharaohs, considered divine rulers, held absolute power over the land and its people. The construction of monumental structures such as the pyramids and temples exemplified the close relationship between governance and religious authority. The pharaoh's role as both a political and spiritual leader underscored the fusion of religion and state in Egyptian society.

Greek Democracy and Citizen Participation: In ancient Greece, the city-state of Athens pioneered the concept of democracy around the 5th century BCE. Athenian democracy was characterized by citizen participation in decision-making through assemblies and juries. While it was not a true universal democracy, as it excluded women, slaves, and non-citizens, it marked a significant step towards inclusive governance. Greek philosophers like Plato and Aristotle also contributed to political thought by examining the merits and drawbacks of different forms of governance.

Roman Republic and the Rule of Law: The Roman Republic, established in the 6th century BCE, featured a unique system of governance. It was characterized by a separation of powers among various branches of government, including the Senate and the popular assemblies. The concept of the rule of law, embodied in the Twelve Tables, emphasized legal principles and the protection of individual rights. The Roman Republic's governance system laid the foundation for later republican forms of government.

Feudalism in Medieval Europe: Medieval Europe saw the emergence of feudalism, a hierarchical social structure and governance system. At the top of the feudal hierarchy was the monarch, followed by nobles, knights, clergy, and peasants. Feudal lords granted land (fiefs) in exchange for military service and loyalty. This decentralized system of governance was marked by local authority and a lack of centralized state control. The Catholic Church played a significant role in legitimizing authority and moral governance during this period.

Chinese Imperial Dynasties and Bureaucracy: China's long history is marked by the rule of various imperial dynasties. Chinese governance was characterized by a centralized bureaucracy, with officials selected through a rigorous examination system based on Confucian principles. The emperor, considered the "Son of Heaven," held supreme authority, but governance was carried out through a complex administrative structure. The Great Wall of China, a monumental feat of engineering, served both defensive and symbolic purposes, highlighting the relationship between governance and state security.

Islamic Caliphates and Religious Leadership: The Islamic world witnessed the rise of various caliphates, beginning with the Rashidun Caliphate after the death of the Prophet Muhammad in the 7th century CE. Islamic governance combined religious leadership with political authority. Caliphs were not just political rulers but also spiritual leaders, guiding the Muslim community (Ummah). The caliphate system evolved over time, leading to the establishment of the Umayyad, Abbasid, and other dynastic caliphates.

Medieval Japan and the Shogunate: Medieval Japan featured a unique governance structure marked by feudal lords known as daimyos and a centralized military government led by the shogun. The emperor held a symbolic position, while the shogun wielded de facto power. This system, known as shogunate, emphasized hierarchical authority and military rule. Japanese feudalism also encompassed a code of conduct called Bushido, governing the behavior of samurai warriors.

Early Modern Europe and the Nation-State: The Renaissance and the Enlightenment in early modern Europe led to significant changes in governance and social structure. The rise of nation-states, such as England, France, and Spain, marked a shift from feudalism to centralized authority under monarchs. Enlightenment philosophers like John Locke and Montesquieu articulated ideas about individual rights, separation of powers, and the social contract, influencing the development of modern political thought and governance.

Modern Governance Systems: The modern era has witnessed diverse forms of governance, including constitutional monarchies, republics, democracies, and authoritarian regimes. Concepts of human rights, representation, and the rule of law have gained prominence. The role of governance extends to addressing complex global challenges, such as climate change, economic inequality, and human rights violations.

In summary, the history of social structure and governance reflects the dynamic evolution of human societies, from early civilizations to the complex governance systems of the modern world. These systems have been shaped by cultural, religious, and philosophical influences, as well as by the quest for justice, order, and individual rights. Understanding the historical development of social structure and governance provides valuable insights into the complexities of human organization and the enduring quest for effective governance and social cohesion.

Chapter 2: Confucius: Life and Early Influences (551 - 539 BCE)

Confucius, also known as Kong Fuzi or Kong Qiu, was a Chinese philosopher and educator who lived during the Spring and Autumn Period of ancient China, specifically from 551 BCE to 479 BCE. His early years were marked by a deep curiosity, a quest for knowledge, and a desire to bring about positive social change through education and ethical principles.

Birth and Family Background: Confucius was born on September 28, 551 BCE, in the state of Lu, which is located in modern-day Shandong Province, China. He was born into a modest family known as the Kong family. His father, Kong He, and his mother, Yan Zhengzai, were not from aristocratic backgrounds, but they valued education and scholarship.

Early Education and Love for Learning: Confucius demonstrated an early love for learning and a keen interest in ancient Chinese literature and history. He is said to have started his education at a young age, studying the Chinese classics, poetry, and music. His passion for learning was evident, and he quickly developed a reputation for being an avid student.

Teaching Career and Ethical Values: At the age of 22, Confucius began his teaching career. He opened a school where he imparted his knowledge and wisdom to a small group of disciples. His teaching philosophy emphasized ethical values, social harmony, and moral rectitude. Confucius believed that individuals could cultivate themselves morally and contribute to a just and harmonious society through education and the practice of virtuous conduct.

Travels and Seeking Knowledge: Confucius was not content with merely teaching in his local community. He embarked on a journey throughout ancient China, visiting various states and seeking knowledge from different scholars and teachers. His travels allowed him to gain a broader perspective on governance, ethics, and the social issues of his time.

Government Service and Political Aspirations: Confucius had a strong desire to serve in a government role and bring about positive reforms. He held various government positions in the state of Lu, including roles as a magistrate and an adviser to the Duke of Lu. However, his attempts at implementing his ideas of good governance and ethical leadership often met with resistance and political intrigue.

Exile and Period of Reflection: After facing political setbacks and opposition from influential factions in Lu, Confucius was forced into exile. During this period, which lasted for about 12 years, he continued to study, write, and reflect on his philosophical ideas. It was during his exile that Confucius further refined his thoughts on ethics, morality, and governance.

Return to Lu and Continuing Influence: Confucius eventually returned to Lu, where he spent his final years teaching and compiling his teachings into a collection of texts known as the "Analects." These texts contain the recorded sayings and ideas of Confucius and his disciples. His teachings emphasized the importance of benevolence (ren), righteousness (yi), and filial piety (xiao) as essential virtues for individuals and society.

Legacy: Confucius' influence on Chinese culture, ethics, and governance has been profound and enduring. His ideas laid the foundation for Confucianism, a philosophical and ethical system that continues to shape Chinese society and culture to this day. Confucianism has also had a significant impact on the broader East Asian region and has been a source of guidance in areas such as education, family values, and government administration.

In summary, Confucius' early years were marked by a thirst for knowledge, a commitment to ethical principles, and a passion for teaching. His life's work, including his teachings and writings, has left an indelible mark on the intellectual and ethical landscape of China and beyond, making him one of the most influential philosophers and educators in human history.

Confucius, one of history's most influential philosophers, drew inspiration from a diverse range of teachers and philosophical traditions that were prevalent in ancient China during his lifetime. These influences played a significant role in shaping his philosophical outlook and the development of Confucianism.

Influential Teachers:

Master Kong Fu (Kong Fu Zi): Confucius, known as Kong Qiu, or Master Kong, in his early years, learned from his father, Kong He, and his mother, Yan Zhengzai. While his parents were not scholars or philosophers, they instilled in him a love for learning and a strong work ethic.

Master You (You Ruo): Confucius is believed to have studied under Master You, a teacher known for his expertise in ancient Chinese rituals and music. This early exposure to ritual and music influenced Confucius' emphasis on the importance of proper conduct and social harmony.

Laozi: According to some accounts, Confucius met Laozi, the legendary founder of Daoism (Taoism), during his travels. While there is limited historical evidence of this encounter, it is said that Confucius was struck by Laozi's wisdom and philosophy, which emphasized the Dao (Tao) as an underlying principle of harmony and spontaneity.

Philosophical Roots:
Ruism (Confucianism): Confucius is often associated with the Ruist (Confucian) school of thought. Ruism places a strong emphasis on ethical conduct, virtue, and the cultivation of moral character. Confucius believed that individuals could become exemplary leaders and contribute to a harmonious society by adhering to ethical principles such as ren (benevolence), yi (righteousness), and li (ritual propriety). His teachings focused on the importance of family, respect for tradition, and the development of an ideal moral society.

Daoism (Taoism): While Confucianism and Daoism are distinct philosophical traditions, Confucius' exposure to Daoist ideas, particularly the concept of the Dao (Tao), influenced his thinking. The Daoist emphasis on naturalness, simplicity, and harmony resonated with Confucius' vision of a just and harmonious society. However, Confucius' approach to achieving harmony differed from that of Daoism, as he stressed the importance of moral cultivation and social ethics.

Yijing (I Ching): The Yijing, or Book of Changes, is an ancient Chinese divination text that played a role in shaping Confucian thought. Confucius was a proponent of using the Yijing as a tool for ethical guidance and decision-making. He believed that by understanding the patterns and changes in the natural world reflected in the Yijing, individuals could gain insights into moral conduct and governance.

Classical Chinese Literature: Confucius was deeply influenced by classical Chinese literature and historical texts, including the Shijing (Book of Songs), Shujing (Book of Documents), and Chunqiu (Spring and Autumn Annals). These texts provided him with a rich source of wisdom, historical narratives, and examples of virtuous rulers and leaders. Confucius often referred to these texts in his teachings to illustrate moral principles and the importance of tradition.

Confucius' intellectual journey was marked by a quest for moral wisdom and a desire to establish a framework for ethical behavior and harmonious governance. His synthesis of these diverse influences laid the foundation for Confucianism, a philosophical tradition that continues to shape Chinese culture, ethics, and governance, as well as the broader East Asian region, to this day.

Confucius was not only a philosopher and teacher but also a well-traveled scholar who embarked on a journey across ancient China during a time when travel was a challenging and arduous undertaking. His travels, which spanned several decades, were instrumental in shaping his philosophical outlook and the development of Confucianism. These journeys were marked by encounters with diverse people, exposure to various regional cultures, and a deep commitment to learning and self-improvement.

Early Wanderings and Pursuit of Knowledge: Confucius began his travels as a young man, driven by a burning desire for knowledge and a sense of duty to study and understand the world around him. His wanderings took him to different states and regions within China, where he sought out renowned scholars and teachers to expand his intellectual horizons.

Seeking Wisdom from Sages and Scholars: Confucius had a deep respect for learning and sought wisdom from both ancient texts and living scholars. He visited the states of Wei, Song, and Chen, among others, to engage in intellectual exchanges with renowned thinkers and teachers of his time. His encounters with these sages and scholars broadened his perspective and deepened his understanding of ethics, governance, and social order.

Reflection and Contemplation in Exile: At one point in his life, Confucius faced political setbacks and was forced into exile for about 12 years. During this period, he continued his travels within the state of Lu and its neighboring regions. Exile provided him with ample time for reflection and contemplation, allowing him to refine his philosophical ideas and teachings.

Embracing Cultural Diversity: Confucius' travels exposed him to the rich tapestry of cultural diversity within ancient China. He encountered people from various backgrounds and regions, each with their own customs, traditions, and dialects. This exposure to cultural diversity likely contributed to his emphasis on the importance of harmony and social cohesion in society.

Collecting Ancient Texts and Wisdom: Confucius had a deep reverence for classical Chinese literature and ancient texts. During his travels, he collected and studied numerous historical documents, including the Shijing (Book of Songs), Shujing (Book of Documents), and Chunqiu (Spring and Autumn Annals). These texts served as valuable sources of wisdom and historical insights that he incorporated into his teachings.

Encounters with Leaders and Rulers: Confucius sought audiences with rulers and leaders of various states during his travels. He believed that his teachings on ethical governance and the cultivation of moral character could help guide rulers in the just administration of their states. While some rulers were receptive to his ideas, others were less receptive, and Confucius faced challenges in convincing them of the merits of his philosophical principles.

Educational Endeavors and Teaching: Throughout his travels, Confucius remained committed to his role as a teacher. He attracted a group of disciples who accompanied him on his journeys, and he continued to impart his wisdom and ethical teachings to them. Confucius' teaching style emphasized dialogue, critical thinking, and the importance of moral self-improvement.

Legacy of Confucius' Travels: Confucius' travels were instrumental in shaping not only his own philosophical outlook but also the legacy of Confucianism. His commitment to lifelong learning, intellectual curiosity, and engagement with diverse cultures and ideas became core values within the Confucian tradition. Confucianism's emphasis on the importance of education, ethical conduct, and social harmony can be traced back to the experiences and encounters of Confucius during his extensive travels.

In summary, Confucius' travels were a testament to his unwavering commitment to the pursuit of knowledge and his dedication to the betterment of society through ethical principles. His encounters with scholars, leaders, and diverse cultures enriched his understanding of human nature, governance, and the moral responsibilities of individuals in society. Confucius' journeys continue to inspire those who seek wisdom and strive for ethical living, and they remain a foundational aspect of his enduring legacy in the world of philosophy and education.

Chapter 3: Formation of Confucian Philosophy (532 - 517 BCE)

Confucius' philosophical developments represent a journey of intellectual growth and refinement that profoundly influenced not only his own thinking but also the course of Chinese philosophy and culture. His ideas evolved over time, shaped by his experiences, reflections, and interactions with scholars and thinkers of his era. These philosophical developments laid the foundation for Confucianism, one of the most enduring philosophical and ethical systems in history.

Early Ethical Foundations: Confucius' early philosophical foundations were rooted in a deep concern for ethics, virtue, and social harmony. He believed that ethical conduct and moral character were essential for individual well-being and societal order. Confucius' teachings emphasized the cultivation of virtues such as benevolence (ren), righteousness (yi), and filial piety (xiao) as the key to living a meaningful and harmonious life.

The Importance of Ritual and Propriety (Li): As Confucius traveled and engaged in philosophical discourse, he increasingly emphasized the importance of ritual and propriety (li) as essential components of a just and orderly society. Li referred to the observance of social norms, customs, and ceremonies that governed various aspects of life, from personal behavior to state governance. Confucius believed that observing li was crucial for maintaining social harmony and moral order.

Education and Self-Cultivation: Confucius placed a strong emphasis on education and the role of teachers in guiding students toward moral self-improvement. He believed that individuals could develop virtuous character through the study of classical texts, the observation of ethical role models, and rigorous self-examination. Confucius' approach to education emphasized the importance of character development alongside intellectual learning.

Social and Political Philosophy: Confucius' philosophical developments extended to the realms of politics and governance. He articulated his vision of a just and virtuous ruler who governs with benevolence and righteousness, known as the "gentleman" (junzi). Confucius believed that a virtuous ruler could set an example for the entire society, leading to a harmonious and well-ordered state. His teachings emphasized the moral responsibilities of rulers and officials in ensuring the welfare of the people.

Emphasis on Family and Relationships: Confucius' philosophy underscored the significance of familial relationships and their role in shaping an individual's moral character and social behavior. Filial piety, the respect and devotion shown to parents and ancestors, was considered a foundational virtue in Confucianism. Confucius believed that the practice of filial piety extended to broader social relationships, fostering harmony within families and communities.

The Golden Mean and Moderation: As Confucius' ideas matured, he articulated the concept of the "Doctrine of the Mean" (Zhongyong), which emphasized the importance of moderation and balance in all aspects of life. Confucius believed that individuals should avoid extremes and strive for a balanced and harmonious approach to ethics, conduct, and governance. The Doctrine of the Mean became a central concept in Confucian philosophy.

Reflections on the Past and Present: Throughout his life, Confucius engaged in a critical examination of ancient texts, historical records, and the actions of past rulers. He believed that studying the mistakes and successes of the past could provide valuable lessons for the present and the future. His reflections on history and governance contributed to his vision of a just and stable society.

The Compilation of the "Analects": Confucius' philosophical developments were captured in the "Analects" (Lunyu), a collection of sayings and ideas attributed to him and recorded by his disciples. These teachings provided a systematic framework for Confucian thought and became a foundational text of Confucianism. The "Analects" continue to be studied and revered as a source of moral and ethical guidance.

In summary, Confucius' philosophical developments evolved from an initial emphasis on ethics and virtue to a broader framework encompassing education, governance, family, and social harmony. His ideas on ritual, propriety, moderation, and the role of the junzi have left an indelible mark on Chinese culture and have continued to influence ethical thinking and social values for over two millennia. Confucius' enduring legacy lies in his vision of a just and harmonious society built upon the moral cultivation of individuals and the observance of ethical principles.

The importance of ethics and virtue in human life is a fundamental aspect of moral philosophy that has been explored by thinkers, philosophers, and scholars across cultures and throughout history. Ethics and virtue encompass the principles and qualities that guide our actions, interactions, and character, contributing to the well-being of individuals and the harmony of societies.

Ethics as the Foundation of Morality: Ethics, at its core, is the study of moral principles that govern human behavior. It provides a framework for individuals to distinguish right from wrong, good from bad, and just from unjust actions. Ethics serves as the foundation upon which moral decisions are made, and it guides our conduct in various aspects of life.

Virtue as Moral Excellence: Virtue, on the other hand, refers to the moral excellence or positive character traits that individuals cultivate in themselves. Virtuous qualities include benevolence, honesty, integrity, compassion, courage, and humility, among others. Virtues are considered to be inherent elements of ethical living and are essential for the development of a morally upright and virtuous person.

The Pursuit of Virtue: Ethics and virtue are intimately connected, as ethics provides the principles that guide the cultivation of virtuous character. The pursuit of virtue is a lifelong endeavor that involves conscious efforts to develop and embody these positive qualities. It requires self-reflection, self-discipline, and a commitment to ethical principles.

The Role of Ethics in Decision-Making: Ethics plays a pivotal role in decision-making, influencing the choices individuals make in various contexts, from personal relationships to professional settings. When faced with moral dilemmas or complex decisions, ethical principles serve as a moral compass, helping individuals navigate through ethical challenges and make choices aligned with their values.

Ethics in Professional Life: In the professional realm, ethics is particularly significant. Ethical conduct in business, healthcare, law, and other fields is vital for building trust, maintaining integrity, and fostering responsible practices. Ethical guidelines and codes of conduct exist to ensure that professionals uphold moral standards and act in the best interests of their clients, customers, and the public.

Virtue Ethics: Virtue ethics is a philosophical approach that places a central focus on the cultivation of virtuous character as the primary aim of moral living. This ethical perspective, which has roots in the works of Aristotle and Confucius, emphasizes the development of virtues as a means to lead a good and fulfilling life. Virtue ethics encourages individuals to strive for moral excellence and to embody virtues in their daily interactions and choices.

Ethical Theories and Perspectives: Various ethical theories and perspectives have emerged throughout history to explore the nature of ethics and virtue. These include utilitarianism, deontology, virtue ethics, relativism, and care ethics, among others. Each theory offers a distinct framework for evaluating moral actions and ethical principles, providing valuable insights into the complexities of ethical thought.

Virtue and Moral Education: Moral education and character development are integral components of nurturing virtuous individuals within society. Schools, religious institutions, and families play a crucial role in instilling ethical values and virtues in the younger generation. Through education and guidance, individuals can learn to discern right from wrong and develop the moral character necessary for ethical living.

The Connection Between Ethics and Society: Ethical behavior is not solely an individual concern; it has profound implications for the well-being and cohesion of society. A society that values and upholds ethical principles tends to be more just, stable, and harmonious. Ethical societies promote fairness, equity, and the common good, fostering a sense of trust and community among their members.

Ethical Challenges in a Complex World: In today's complex and interconnected world, ethical challenges abound. Issues such as environmental sustainability, social justice, technological advancements, and global conflicts pose intricate moral dilemmas. Ethical discourse and ethical decision-making are crucial in addressing these challenges and finding solutions that align with moral values.

The Role of Cultural and Religious Values: Cultural and religious values often shape an individual's ethical framework and the virtues they prioritize. Different cultures and religions offer unique perspectives on ethics and virtue, influencing the moral values and principles that guide individuals within these cultural contexts. The diversity of ethical perspectives enriches the global discourse on ethics and virtue.

Ethical Leaders and Role Models: Ethical leaders and role models play a vital role in shaping societal norms and values. Their actions and behavior set an example for others to follow, inspiring individuals to cultivate virtues and uphold ethical standards. Ethical leadership fosters a culture of integrity and accountability within organizations, communities, and nations.

In summary, the importance of ethics and virtue cannot be overstated in human life. Ethics provides the moral framework that guides our choices and actions, while virtue represents the moral qualities that individuals aspire to embody. Together, they contribute to personal well-being, social harmony, and the development of virtuous individuals and communities. As individuals and societies grapple with the complexities of the modern world, the timeless principles of ethics and virtue continue to serve as beacons of moral guidance and ethical living.

Moral principles are the cornerstone of an ideal society, guiding individuals and communities toward values that promote justice, fairness, and the common good. An ideal society is characterized by a shared commitment to these principles, which shape the social fabric, governance, and interactions among its members. These principles serve as a moral compass, helping society navigate complex issues and challenges while striving for a harmonious and equitable existence.

Justice as a Foundational Principle: Justice is often considered the bedrock of moral principles in an ideal society. It involves the fair and equitable distribution of resources, opportunities, and rights among all members of society. In an ideal society, justice ensures that no one is marginalized or oppressed based on factors such as race, gender, socioeconomic status, or any other characteristic.

Equality and Equity: Equality and equity are integral components of justice in an ideal society. While equality aims to treat all individuals the same, equity recognizes that different individuals may require different resources and support to achieve equal opportunities and outcomes. An ideal society strives for both equality and equity, addressing systemic inequalities and promoting social inclusion.

Human Rights and Dignity: Respecting and upholding human rights is a fundamental moral principle in an ideal society. Every individual is entitled to basic rights and freedoms, including the right to life, liberty, security, and dignity. An ideal society protects these rights, ensuring that all its members are treated with respect and compassion.

Rule of Law and Accountability: An ideal society operates under the rule of law, where laws are just, transparent, and applied consistently. The rule of law ensures that individuals are held accountable for their actions, regardless of their position or status. This principle promotes a sense of trust and fairness in society.

Ethical Governance and Leadership: Ethical governance and leadership are essential for an ideal society. Leaders are expected to uphold ethical standards, act in the best interests of the people, and ensure that policies and decisions are grounded in moral principles. Ethical governance fosters trust, cooperation, and the pursuit of the common good.

Social Responsibility and Solidarity: Members of an ideal society recognize their social responsibility toward one another and practice solidarity. This means that individuals support and assist those in need, fostering a sense of community and mutual care. Social responsibility extends to environmental stewardship, as an ideal society takes measures to protect the planet for future generations.

Compassion and Empathy: Compassion and empathy are vital moral principles that promote understanding and kindness among individuals in an ideal society. These qualities enable people to connect with the experiences and suffering of others, motivating them to take actions that alleviate suffering and promote well-being.

Non-Violence and Conflict Resolution: An ideal society values non-violence and seeks peaceful means of resolving conflicts. Conflict resolution methods emphasize dialogue, negotiation, and compromise, avoiding harm to individuals and communities. The pursuit of peace and reconciliation is paramount.

Ethical Economy and Sustainability: Economic activities in an ideal society adhere to ethical principles. Economic systems prioritize the well-being of all citizens, minimize inequality, and promote sustainable practices that protect the environment. Economic decisions consider the long-term consequences on society and the planet.

Educational Excellence and Moral Development: Education in an ideal society places a strong emphasis on moral development and ethical education. Schools and educational institutions aim not only to impart knowledge but also to cultivate virtuous character in students. Education instills values such as integrity, empathy, and responsibility, preparing individuals to contribute positively to society.

Cultural Diversity and Inclusivity: An ideal society celebrates cultural diversity and inclusivity, recognizing the richness that different cultures bring. It promotes the exchange of ideas, art, and traditions while fostering a sense of unity amid diversity. Inclusivity ensures that all voices are heard and valued.

Sustainable Development and Environmental Stewardship: Environmental ethics are integral to an ideal society's moral principles. Sustainability and environmental stewardship guide decisions about resource management and ecological conservation. Society takes responsibility for its ecological footprint and seeks to minimize harm to the natural world.

Continuous Self-Improvement: Individuals in an ideal society are committed to continuous self-improvement. They reflect on their actions, seek personal growth, and cultivate virtues that align with moral principles. This commitment extends to a lifelong journey of ethical development.

Responsibility for Future Generations: Members of an ideal society recognize their responsibility toward future generations. They strive to leave a legacy of ethical values, a just society, and a sustainable world that will benefit those who come after them.

Social Institutions that Uphold Moral Principles: In an ideal society, social institutions such as the legal system, educational institutions, government, and religious organizations play a role in upholding and promoting moral principles. These institutions are aligned with the values of justice, equality, and ethical governance.

The Collective Pursuit of the Common Good: An ideal society places the collective pursuit of the common good at its core. It recognizes that the well-being of each individual is interconnected with the well-being of the entire community. Members of society work together to address challenges, reduce inequalities, and create conditions that promote the flourishing of all.

In summary, moral principles are the guiding light of an ideal society, shaping its values, actions, and aspirations. Justice, equality, human rights, ethical governance, and compassion are among the foundational principles that underpin an ideal society's quest for a just, harmonious, and morally upright existence. These principles not only provide a vision for an ideal society but also serve as a moral compass that continues to inspire individuals and communities in their pursuit of a better world.

Chapter 4: The Analects: Core Teachings of Confucius (512 - 479 BCE)

The "Analects" (Lunyu), also known as the "Analects of Confucius," is a collection of sayings, ideas, and teachings attributed to the Chinese philosopher Confucius and his disciples. Compiled over several centuries, the "Analects" holds immense significance in the realms of philosophy, ethics, education, and Chinese culture. Its compilation, preservation, and impact on society are central to understanding its enduring importance.

Compilation of the Analects: The "Analects" was not written by Confucius himself but rather compiled by his disciples and later generations of scholars. The compilation process occurred over several centuries, with various individuals contributing to the collection. Key figures in the compilation include Confucius' disciples such as Zengzi, Zisi, and others, who documented his teachings and conversations. It is believed that Confucius' ideas were transmitted orally before being recorded in written form.

Preservation and Transmission: The preservation of the "Analects" throughout history is a testament to its enduring significance. Despite the challenges posed by time, political changes, and cultural shifts, the text has been meticulously copied, annotated, and studied by generations of scholars. The commitment to preserving Confucian teachings ensured that the "Analects" remained a foundational text in Chinese culture.

Structure and Contents: The "Analects" consists of a series of short passages, dialogues, and aphorisms attributed to Confucius and his disciples. It is organized into twenty chapters, each addressing different aspects of life, ethics, governance, and personal conduct. The content covers a wide range of topics, including filial piety, virtue, morality, leadership, education, and the pursuit of the junzi (gentleman).

Significance of the Analects:

Philosophical Foundation: The "Analects" serves as a foundational text of Confucianism, one of the most influential philosophical and ethical systems in Chinese history. It provides insights into Confucius' moral philosophy, emphasizing the importance of virtue, benevolence, and ethical conduct.

Moral and Ethical Guidance: The "Analects" offers moral and ethical guidance for individuals and society. It provides practical wisdom on how to lead a virtuous life, navigate complex social relationships, and contribute to the well-being of society.

Educational Text: The "Analects" has been a cornerstone of traditional Chinese education. It has been used to teach students about ethics, morality, and the ideals of Confucianism. The text's emphasis on character development and learning has influenced educational systems in China for centuries.

Political and Governance Philosophy: The "Analects" addresses principles of governance and leadership, advocating for rulers to be virtuous and just. Confucius' ideas on ethical governance have had a profound impact on Chinese political thought and leadership ideals.

Cultural and Social Influence: The "Analects" has deeply influenced Chinese culture and societal norms. Concepts such as filial piety, respect for elders, and the pursuit of moral excellence have been central to Chinese cultural values for centuries.

Global Influence: Beyond China, the "Analects" has had a global impact on ethics, philosophy, and the study of Chinese culture. It has been translated into numerous languages and continues to be studied and admired by scholars worldwide.

Interpretation and Adaptation: The "Analects" has been interpreted and adapted by scholars and thinkers throughout history. Commentaries, annotations, and adaptations of the text have enriched its understanding and application in various cultural and historical contexts.

Ethical Reflection: The "Analects" encourages readers to engage in ethical reflection and self-improvement. It challenges individuals to assess their own actions and behaviors in light of Confucian principles.

In summary, the "Analects" is not just a compilation of Confucian teachings but a foundational text that has shaped the moral, ethical, and cultural landscape of China and beyond. Its enduring significance lies in its ability to provide timeless wisdom and ethical guidance to individuals and societies, fostering a commitment to virtuous living and the pursuit of a harmonious and just society. The "Analects" continues to be a source of inspiration and reflection for those seeking moral and ethical guidance in the modern world.

Confucianism, one of the most influential philosophical and ethical systems in Chinese history, is characterized by several key philosophical concepts that shape its worldview and guide the behavior and values of individuals. These concepts provide a foundation for understanding the principles and teachings of Confucianism:

1. Ren (仁) - Benevolence or Humaneness:

Ren is considered the central virtue in Confucianism. It represents the quality of compassion, kindness, and empathy toward others. It is the essence of being a virtuous and humane person.

Confucius emphasized that individuals should cultivate ren in their character, treating others with respect and benevolence.

2. Li (礼) - Rituals and Propriety:

Li refers to the observance of social norms, customs, and rituals that govern various aspects of life, from personal behavior to social interactions.

It emphasizes the importance of maintaining proper conduct, showing respect for tradition, and promoting social harmony through proper etiquette and decorum.

3. Xiao (孝) - Filial Piety:

Filial piety is the virtue of showing respect, obedience, and care to one's parents and ancestors. It is considered a fundamental virtue in Confucianism.

Confucius believed that practicing filial piety within the family would extend to broader society, fostering harmony and moral values.

4. Yi (义) - Righteousness or Justice:

Yi represents the moral quality of doing what is right and just, even in the face of personal sacrifice or hardship.

Confucian ethics stress the importance of acting with righteousness and standing up for moral principles.

5. Zhi (智) - Wisdom:

Wisdom involves the ability to make sound judgments, understand the world, and apply moral principles in decision-making.

Confucianism encourages the cultivation of wisdom to navigate complex moral dilemmas.

6. Xin (信) - Honesty and Trustworthiness:

Xin emphasizes the importance of honesty, sincerity, and trustworthiness in one's words and actions.

Building and maintaining trust in relationships and society is a core Confucian value.

7. Junzi (君子) - The Gentleman or Noble Person:
The junzi is an idealized ethical and moral exemplar in Confucianism. This person embodies virtues such as ren, li, yi, and xiao.
The junzi strives to be a morally upright individual who serves as a role model for others.

8. Tian (天) - Heaven or the Way:
Tian represents the natural order, the moral and cosmic framework that governs the universe.
Confucius believed that aligning with Tian's moral principles would lead to a harmonious and righteous life.

9. Rectification of Names (正名, zhèngmíng):
This concept emphasizes the importance of using proper names and titles to accurately reflect social roles and relationships.
Confucianism argues that a well-ordered society depends on individuals fulfilling their roles and responsibilities correctly.

10. Family as the Foundation: - Confucianism places a strong emphasis on the family as the foundational unit of society. Family values, including filial piety and respect for elders, are central to Confucian ethics. - The family serves as a model for ethical behavior and social harmony.

11. Continuity with the Past: - Confucianism values the study of classical texts and the wisdom of previous generations. Learning from history and tradition is seen as essential for moral and cultural continuity.

12. Education and Self-Cultivation: - Confucianism places a strong emphasis on education as a means of moral development. Self-cultivation, through the study of classical texts and reflection, is central to becoming a virtuous person.

These key concepts form the ethical framework of Confucianism, guiding individuals in their pursuit of moral excellence, social harmony, and a just society. They continue to influence Chinese culture, ethics, governance, and personal values to this day, and have also had a significant impact on the broader East Asian cultural sphere.

The "Analects of Confucius" has been a source of profound interpretation and influence since its compilation in ancient China. This collection of sayings and teachings attributed to Confucius and his disciples has sparked a rich tradition of philosophical analysis, commentary, and adaptation, resulting in a multifaceted impact on Chinese culture, philosophy, ethics, and beyond.

Interpretations:

Interpreting the "Analects" has been a longstanding endeavor, as scholars and thinkers have sought to glean deeper insights from its verses. Several major interpretations and schools of thought have emerged over time:

Confucian Tradition:

Confucian scholars have traditionally been at the forefront of interpreting the "Analects." They view it as a guide to ethical living and governance, emphasizing the importance of virtues like ren (benevolence), li (ritual propriety), and filial piety.

Confucian interpretations often focus on practical applications of Confucian principles in personal conduct, family relationships, and governance.

Neo-Confucianism:

Neo-Confucianism, which emerged during the Song Dynasty (960–1279), built upon Confucian teachings, including those found in the "Analects." Neo-Confucian scholars, such as Zhu Xi, incorporated elements of Daoism and Buddhism into their interpretations.

They explored metaphysical and cosmological aspects of Confucianism, integrating them into a comprehensive worldview.

Legalism:
Legalist interpretations of the "Analects" take a different perspective. Legalists were often critical of Confucian ideas, particularly those that emphasized benevolence and virtue. They focused on the practical application of strict laws and harsh punishments for social control.

New Confucianism:
In the modern era, New Confucianism, led by figures like Xiong Shili and Mou Zongsan, offered new interpretations of the "Analects." They aimed to revitalize Confucianism in response to challenges from Western thought and modernization.

New Confucian interpretations explored the compatibility of Confucian values with democracy, human rights, and global ethics.

Influence:
The "Analects" has had a profound and enduring influence, not only in China but also throughout East Asia and beyond:

Chinese Culture:
The "Analects" has played a central role in shaping Chinese culture. It has influenced social norms, ethical values, and cultural practices.

Concepts like filial piety, respect for elders, and the pursuit of virtue are deeply embedded in Chinese society, thanks in part to the "Analects."

Education:
The "Analects" has been a fundamental text in Chinese education for centuries. It has been used to teach students about ethics, moral values, and the ideals of Confucianism.

Its emphasis on character development and self-cultivation continues to be relevant in educational settings.

Ethical Governance:
Confucian principles from the "Analects" have influenced governance and leadership in China. Rulers have often

drawn upon Confucian values, emphasizing benevolence, righteousness, and ethical governance.

Throughout Chinese history, emperors and officials have sought guidance from Confucian texts, including the "Analects."

East Asian Philosophy and Culture:

The "Analects" has not only shaped China but also influenced the ethical and philosophical thought of neighboring East Asian countries, including Japan, Korea, and Vietnam.

It has contributed to the development of East Asian cultural norms, values, and social systems.

Global Influence:

The "Analects" has gained recognition and respect on a global scale. It has been translated into numerous languages and studied by scholars worldwide.

Its teachings on ethics, virtue, and social harmony have resonated with individuals and cultures beyond East Asia.

Modern Applications:

In contemporary China, the "Analects" continues to be a source of ethical guidance, informing debates on topics such as business ethics, social responsibility, and personal conduct.

Its adaptability and timeless wisdom make it relevant in the modern world.

Cross-Cultural Dialogues:

The "Analects" has been a focal point for cross-cultural dialogues and exchanges. It has facilitated discussions between Western and Chinese scholars on topics related to ethics, philosophy, and governance.

It has contributed to a deeper understanding of Chinese culture and values in the global context.

In summary, the "Analects of Confucius" remains a foundational text that has influenced Chinese culture, philosophy, and ethics for over two millennia. Its interpretations have evolved over time, reflecting the changing intellectual and cultural landscape. Its enduring influence extends far beyond China, making it a vital part of the global dialogue on ethics, morality, and the human condition. The "Analects" continues to inspire individuals and societies in their pursuit of moral excellence and social harmony.

Chapter 5: The Five Relationships and Moral Conduct (505 - 484 BCE)

The concept of the Five Fundamental Relationships (Wu Lun) is a central tenet of Confucian thought, emphasizing the importance of social harmony, ethical conduct, and hierarchical relationships within society. These five relationships define various interpersonal dynamics and responsibilities, providing a framework for ethical behavior and social order in Confucian philosophy.

Ruler and Subject (君臣关系, Jūn Chén Guānxì):

This relationship pertains to governance and leadership within a society. The ruler is responsible for governing justly and benevolently, while subjects have a duty to be loyal, obedient, and law-abiding.

Confucianism stresses that rulers should prioritize the well-being of their subjects and govern with virtue and wisdom. Subjects, in turn, owe their allegiance and obedience to the ruler.

Father and Son (父子关系, Fù Zǐ Guānxì):

The father-son relationship is a familial one, emphasizing the duties and responsibilities between parents and children. Confucianism places great importance on filial piety, the virtue of respecting and caring for one's parents.

Children are expected to be obedient, respectful, and caring toward their parents, while parents are responsible for providing for and guiding their children with love and wisdom.

Husband and Wife (夫妻关系, Fūqī Guānxì):

This relationship centers on marriage and family life. Confucianism emphasizes the complementary roles of husbands and wives in a harmonious family.

Husbands are expected to provide for and protect their wives, while wives are encouraged to support and nurture their husbands. Mutual respect and cooperation are essential for a successful marriage.

Elder Sibling and Younger Sibling (兄弟关系, Xiōngdì Guānxì):

The sibling relationship extends to the broader family and social context. It emphasizes the importance of respect, care, and cooperation among siblings.

Elder siblings are expected to serve as role models and offer guidance to their younger siblings, while younger siblings should show deference and seek the advice of their elder siblings.

Friend and Friend (朋友关系, Péngyǒu Guānxì):

The friend-to-friend relationship is not bound by hierarchy or familial ties but is equally important in Confucianism. Friends are regarded as companions on the path of virtue and personal growth.

True friends are expected to uphold moral values, provide support, and offer sincere counsel to each other. Friendship is characterized by trust, loyalty, and mutual respect.

These Five Fundamental Relationships are central to Confucian ethics and social philosophy, as they establish a moral framework for individuals to navigate their roles and responsibilities in society. Confucius believed that by upholding these relationships with virtue and sincerity, individuals could contribute to social harmony, stability, and the overall well-being of the community.

It is important to note that while Confucianism places great emphasis on these relationships, the interpretation and application of these principles have evolved over time. In modern societies, there is often a more egalitarian view of these relationships, with a focus on mutual respect, shared responsibilities, and gender equality. Nonetheless, the Five

Fundamental Relationships continue to serve as a foundation for ethical conduct and social cohesion in many cultures influenced by Confucian values.

Ethics and conduct hold a central place in Confucian thought, shaping the moral framework and guiding principles of individuals and society. Rooted in the teachings of Confucius (Kong Fuzi or Kongzi) and further developed by subsequent Confucian philosophers, this ethical system emphasizes the cultivation of virtuous character, social harmony, and the practice of ethical principles in everyday life.

Ren (仁) - The Virtue of Benevolence and Humaneness:

At the core of Confucian ethics is the concept of ren, often translated as benevolence or humaneness. Ren represents the highest moral virtue and is considered the foundation of a virtuous life.

Confucius taught that individuals should cultivate ren in their character, which involves showing compassion, kindness, and empathy toward others. Ren is the key to harmonious social relationships and ethical conduct.

Li (礼) - Rituals and Propriety:

Li, or rituals and propriety, is another fundamental concept in Confucian ethics. It refers to the observance of social norms, customs, and rituals that govern various aspects of life, from personal behavior to social interactions.

Li emphasizes the importance of maintaining proper conduct, showing respect for tradition, and promoting social harmony through appropriate etiquette and decorum.

Xiao (孝) - Filial Piety:

Filial piety is a cornerstone of Confucian ethics and involves the virtue of showing respect, obedience, and care to one's parents and ancestors. It is considered a fundamental virtue in Confucianism.

Confucius believed that practicing filial piety within the family would extend to broader society, fostering harmony and moral values.

Yi (义) - Righteousness or Justice:
Yi represents the moral quality of doing what is right and just, even in the face of personal sacrifice or hardship. It is closely linked to the concept of moral integrity.

Confucian ethics stress the importance of acting with righteousness and standing up for moral principles.

Zhi (智) - Wisdom:
Wisdom in Confucian ethics involves the ability to make sound judgments, understand the world, and apply moral principles in decision-making.

Cultivating wisdom is essential for navigating complex moral dilemmas and making choices that align with ethical values.

Xin (信) - Honesty and Trustworthiness:
Xin emphasizes the importance of honesty, sincerity, and trustworthiness in one's words and actions. It involves keeping one's promises and maintaining integrity in all dealings.

Building and maintaining trust in relationships and society is a core Confucian value.

Junzi (君子) - The Gentleman or Noble Person:
The junzi is an idealized ethical and moral exemplar in Confucianism. This person embodies virtues such as ren, li, yi, and xiao.

The junzi strives to be a morally upright individual who serves as a role model for others, upholding ethical principles in all aspects of life.

Tian (天) - Heaven or the Way:
Tian represents the natural order, the moral and cosmic framework that governs the universe in Confucian thought.

Confucius believed that aligning with Tian's moral principles would lead to a harmonious and righteous life.

Rectification of Names (正名, zhèngmíng):

This concept emphasizes the importance of using proper names and titles to accurately reflect social roles and relationships. It contributes to the clarity of social interactions and responsibilities.

Confucianism argues that a well-ordered society depends on individuals fulfilling their roles and responsibilities correctly.

Family as the Foundation:

Confucianism places a strong emphasis on the family as the foundational unit of society. Family values, including filial piety and respect for elders, are central to Confucian ethics.

The family serves as a model for ethical behavior and social harmony.

Continuity with the Past:

Confucianism values the study of classical texts and the wisdom of previous generations. Learning from history and tradition is seen as essential for moral and cultural continuity.

Education and Self-Cultivation:

Confucianism places a strong emphasis on education as a means of moral development. Self-cultivation, through the study of classical texts and reflection, is central to becoming a virtuous person.

Confucian ethics emphasize the importance of applying these principles in daily life, cultivating virtuous character, and contributing to the well-being of society. Ethical conduct, guided by ren, li, and other virtues, is seen as the path to personal fulfillment and social harmony in Confucian thought. While interpretations and applications of Confucian ethics may vary, the enduring influence of these principles continues to shape ethical values, behavior, and relationships in East Asian societies and beyond.

Confucian values, deeply rooted in Chinese philosophy and ethics, have had a profound impact on daily life in East Asian societies. These values, which emphasize virtues such as benevolence, respect for tradition, filial piety, and social harmony, guide the behavior, interactions, and choices of individuals in various aspects of their lives.

Family and Filial Piety:

One of the most prominent applications of Confucian values can be observed within the family unit. Filial piety, or the virtue of showing respect, obedience, and care to one's parents and ancestors, is a fundamental aspect of Confucianism. In daily life, this manifests as:

Respect for Elders: Younger family members show respect to their elders through gestures like bowing, using honorifics, and providing assistance to older family members.

Care for Aging Parents: Adult children are often expected to care for their aging parents, both financially and emotionally, ensuring their well-being.

Ancestral Worship: Families conduct rituals to honor deceased ancestors, maintaining a strong connection to their cultural heritage.

Education and Self-Cultivation:

Confucianism places a strong emphasis on education and self-cultivation as a means of moral development. In practice:

Focus on Academic Excellence: Students are encouraged to excel academically, with the belief that education leads to personal growth and contributes to society.

Study of Classical Texts: Confucian classics, including the "Analects," are studied to cultivate ethical values, wisdom, and a sense of tradition.

Lifelong Learning: The pursuit of knowledge and self-improvement is considered a lifelong endeavor, even beyond formal education.

Social Relationships and Harmony:

Confucian values also guide social interactions and the promotion of social harmony:

Respect for Authority: People often show respect for authority figures, including teachers, employers, and government officials.

Courtesy and Etiquette: Politeness, courtesy, and adherence to social etiquette are valued in daily interactions.

Conflict Resolution: Efforts are made to resolve conflicts harmoniously, avoiding confrontations that disrupt social equilibrium.

Work and Professional Ethics:

In the professional realm, Confucian values influence work ethics and business practices:

Ethical Business Conduct: Business leaders are expected to prioritize ethical conduct in their dealings, demonstrating honesty and integrity.

Respect for Employees: Employers are encouraged to treat employees with fairness, respect, and consideration, fostering a harmonious work environment.

Long-Term Perspective: There is an emphasis on long-term business relationships and reputation rather than short-term gains.

Community and Civic Engagement:

Confucian values extend to community and civic life:

Community Service: Volunteering and community service are viewed as opportunities to contribute to the greater good and strengthen social bonds.

Participation in Governance: Civic engagement is encouraged, with an emphasis on responsible citizenship and participation in local governance.

Gender Roles and Family Dynamics:

While traditional gender roles have been influenced by Confucian values, modern interpretations are evolving:

Respect for Gender Roles: Traditional gender roles emphasize men as providers and women as caregivers, with an expectation that women will prioritize family responsibilities.

Changing Gender Norms: Modern society is challenging traditional gender roles, with greater emphasis on gender equality and women's empowerment.

Global Influence:

Confucian values have transcended national borders and are influential in many East Asian societies, including China, Japan, South Korea, and Vietnam. They have also been a point of interest for scholars, policymakers, and individuals worldwide who seek to understand and incorporate these values into their own lives.

Adaptation to Modern Life:

As societies modernize, the application of Confucian values continues to evolve:

Balancing Tradition and Modernity: People strive to strike a balance between honoring tradition and adapting to the demands of modern life.

Critical Examination: Confucian values are critically examined, and discussions take place about their relevance in contemporary society.

Interplay with Other Values: Confucian values often coexist with other value systems, such as democracy, human rights, and individualism, leading to complex ethical and cultural landscapes.

In summary, Confucian values play a multifaceted and dynamic role in the daily lives of individuals in East Asian societies and beyond. These values shape family dynamics, educational pursuits, social interactions, work ethics, and civic engagement. While they provide a moral compass and a sense of tradition, they also adapt to the changing realities of the modern world, reflecting the ongoing interplay between tradition and modernity. As societies continue to evolve, Confucian values remain a source of inspiration for personal and collective ethical growth, fostering harmony and virtuous living.

Chapter 6: Confucianism's Impact on Education and Governance (490 - 475 BCE)

Confucian educational principles have played a significant role in shaping the educational systems and values of East Asian societies, particularly China, for over two millennia. Rooted in the teachings of Confucius (Kong Fuzi or Kongzi), these principles emphasize the moral and ethical development of individuals as a foundation for a harmonious and just society. Within the framework of Confucian education, several key principles and concepts are central to understanding its philosophy and application.

1. Moral Education (德育, Dé Yù):
Confucian education places a strong emphasis on moral development. The cultivation of virtuous character, particularly the Confucian virtues of benevolence (ren), righteousness (yi), propriety (li), wisdom (zhi), and trustworthiness (xin), is considered the primary goal of education. Students are not only taught academic subjects but also guided in the development of ethical principles and values that will shape their behavior and interactions throughout life.

2. Filial Piety (孝, Xiào):
Filial piety, the virtue of showing respect and devotion to one's parents and ancestors, is a core Confucian value. Confucian education instills the importance of filial piety from a young age, emphasizing the roles and responsibilities of children in caring for and honoring their parents. This principle reinforces the idea that family values and social harmony begin within the family unit.

3. The Analects (论语, Lúnyǔ):

Confucian education relies heavily on the study of classical texts, with the "Analects of Confucius" being a foundational text. Students engage in the study and interpretation of Confucian classics, including the "Analects," to gain insight into the teachings and wisdom of Confucius. This textual approach is central to the moral and intellectual development of individuals.

4. Rectification of Names (正名, Zhèngmíng):

The concept of the rectification of names emphasizes the importance of using proper names and titles to accurately reflect social roles and relationships. In education, this principle underscores the need for clarity in communication and the acknowledgment of one's social responsibilities and duties. By adhering to correct names and titles, individuals ensure clarity in their interactions and avoid confusion or misunderstandings.

5. The Role of the Teacher (师道, Shī Dào):

Confucian education places the teacher in a position of great responsibility and respect. Teachers are not only instructors but also moral exemplars and guides for their students. They are expected to embody Confucian virtues and serve as role models for ethical behavior. The teacher-student relationship is characterized by trust, respect, and a commitment to mutual growth.

6. Emphasis on Self-Cultivation (修身养性, Xiū Shēn Yǎng Xìng):

Confucian education emphasizes the importance of self-cultivation and lifelong learning. Students are encouraged to engage in continuous self-improvement, reflection, and personal growth. This process of self-cultivation is seen as essential for becoming a virtuous and morally upright individual.

7. The Importance of Rituals and Propriety (礼, Lǐ):

Rituals and propriety (li) are fundamental to Confucian education. They encompass the observance of social norms, customs, and rituals that govern various aspects of life, from personal behavior to social interactions. Students are taught to uphold proper conduct and etiquette in their daily lives, contributing to social harmony and order.

8. Family as the Foundation (家庭教育, Jiātíng Jiàoyù):
Confucian education recognizes the family as the foundational unit of society. Family values, including filial piety and respect for elders, are central to the educational process. Students are taught that the principles of ethical behavior and social harmony begin within the family, and these values are carried forward into the broader society.

9. The Role of Ritual Music (礼乐, Lǐ Yuè):
Ritual music, along with rituals (li), holds a significant place in Confucian education. It is believed that music has the power to shape individuals' emotions and character. Music and rituals are used to instill a sense of harmony, order, and moral sensibility in students. Through the appreciation of music and participation in rituals, students are exposed to the cultural and ethical heritage of their society.

10. Lifelong Learning and Social Responsibility:
Confucian education instills a sense of social responsibility in students. Beyond acquiring knowledge and moral principles, individuals are encouraged to use their education for the betterment of society. Lifelong learning and the application of ethical values in various roles, including as citizens and community members, are emphasized.

In summary, Confucian educational principles encompass a holistic approach to education that focuses on moral development, intellectual growth, and the cultivation of ethical values. These principles have left an enduring legacy in East Asian societies, influencing educational systems, family dynamics, and social interactions. While modern education systems have evolved and adapted, the foundational principles of Confucian education continue to shape the moral and ethical fabric of these societies, emphasizing the importance of virtue, social harmony, and lifelong self-improvement.

Confucianism, with its profound ethical and philosophical underpinnings, has exerted a significant influence on governance throughout the history of East Asian societies. This influence has shaped the principles, practices, and expectations of rulers and governments, guiding their approach to leadership, administration, and the relationship between the state and its citizens. The impact of Confucianism on governance can be observed through several key aspects.

1. Moral Authority and Righteous Governance:

One of the central tenets of Confucianism is the concept of moral authority. Confucian philosophy asserts that leaders should govern with benevolence (ren), righteousness (yi), and propriety (li). This ethical approach to governance emphasizes the importance of just and virtuous leadership.

Confucian rulers were expected to lead by example, embodying the moral principles they wished to instill in their subjects. This approach to governance aimed to create a virtuous and harmonious society, where leaders set the moral tone for their administration.

2. Social Hierarchy and Harmony:

Confucianism promotes the idea of a well-ordered society with clear social hierarchies and roles. This hierarchical structure, based on the Five Fundamental Relationships, includes the ruler-subject, father-son, husband-wife, elder sibling-younger sibling, and friend-friend relationships. Each relationship is defined by specific duties and responsibilities.

In governance, this hierarchical model was extended to the relationship between the ruler and subjects. The ruler was seen as a paternal figure, and subjects were expected to show loyalty, obedience, and filial piety, mirroring the filial piety expected within families. This structure aimed to create social harmony and stability.

3. Education and the Cultivation of Virtue:
Confucianism places great emphasis on education and the cultivation of moral virtue. Rulers were encouraged to invest in education, creating a well-educated and morally upright bureaucracy. Education was not only about acquiring knowledge but also about instilling ethical values.

The civil service examination system, which became a hallmark of Confucian governance, was designed to select government officials based on their knowledge of Confucian classics and their ability to apply Confucian principles in their roles. This system ensured that government officials were well-versed in Confucian ethics and philosophy.

4. Filial Piety and the Role of Family:
Filial piety, a fundamental Confucian virtue, extends beyond the family to governance. Rulers were expected to treat their subjects with the same care and benevolence that children were expected to show their parents. This concept of "ruling as a parent" emphasized the ruler's responsibility to protect and provide for the well-being of the people.

Confucianism's emphasis on the family as the foundational unit of society also influenced governance. The family served as a model for proper social relationships, with the hierarchical structure of the family mirroring that of the state.

5. Ethical Administration and Justice:
Confucian rulers were expected to govern with fairness and justice, upholding the principles of righteousness (yi) and propriety (li). Ethical administration aimed to ensure that laws were just, punishments were proportionate, and the interests of the people were protected.

Rulers were encouraged to consult with their advisors and ministers, seeking wise counsel and making decisions in the best interest of the state and its people. The ethical dimension of governance extended to the conduct of government officials, who were expected to act with integrity and uphold moral standards.

6. Governance as Service:

Confucianism promotes the idea that governance is a service to the people. Rulers were seen as serving the welfare of their subjects and the state, rather than pursuing personal interests or power. This perspective aligned with the concept of ren (benevolence) and emphasized the ethical duty of leaders.

The idea of selfless service and the pursuit of the common good guided rulers in their decision-making processes and policies. It encouraged them to prioritize the well-being and prosperity of the state and its citizens.

7. Continuity and Adaptation:

Over centuries, Confucianism has demonstrated its adaptability. While it provided a foundational framework for governance, it also allowed for flexibility and adaptation to changing circumstances. Rulers could incorporate Confucian principles into their governance while adapting to the specific needs and challenges of their time.

Confucian governance principles remained influential even as societies underwent significant transformations, adapting to new political systems and modernization.

In summary, Confucianism has had a profound and enduring influence on governance in East Asian societies. Its ethical and moral principles have shaped the conduct of rulers, the structure of governments, and the relationship between the state and its citizens. While Confucianism's influence has evolved over time, its emphasis on moral leadership, social hierarchy, and ethical governance has left a lasting legacy in the region's political and social fabric.

The role of scholar-officials, also known as literati or mandarins, in ancient China was a pivotal and influential one that spanned over many centuries and dynasties. These individuals were highly educated and held positions of authority in the government bureaucracy. Their role was multifaceted, encompassing not only administrative and governance responsibilities but also a deep commitment to Confucian values, scholarship, and ethical conduct.

1. Education and the Civil Service Examination System:
Central to the role of scholar-officials was their rigorous education and selection through the civil service examination system. These individuals were typically well-versed in Confucian classics, including the "Analects" and the "Book of Rites," and other literary and philosophical works.

To become scholar-officials, aspiring candidates had to pass a series of examinations at the local, provincial, and imperial levels. These examinations tested their knowledge of Confucianism, history, law, and administrative skills. Successful candidates were awarded prestigious positions in the government bureaucracy.

2. Government Administration and Leadership:
Scholar-officials occupied key administrative positions within the government. They were responsible for a wide range of tasks, including taxation, law enforcement, local governance, and infrastructure development. Some of the most senior officials held positions like governors, judges, or advisors to the emperor.

Scholar-officials played a crucial role in shaping government policies, advising rulers on matters of state, and implementing reforms. Their expertise in Confucian ethics and governance principles influenced the moral and ethical dimensions of government decisions.

3. Ethical Governance and Confucian Values:
An essential aspect of the role of scholar-officials was the application of Confucian values in governance. Confucianism emphasizes virtues such as benevolence (ren), righteousness (yi), propriety (li), wisdom (zhi), and trustworthiness (xin). Scholar-officials were expected to embody and promote these virtues in their official duties.

Their commitment to ethical governance involved ensuring fair and just treatment of the population, upholding moral standards, and seeking the well-being of the state and its citizens. They were often viewed as moral exemplars and role models for the society.

4. Social Harmony and Hierarchy:
Scholar-officials were instrumental in maintaining social harmony and reinforcing the hierarchical structure of Chinese society. They played a key role in upholding the Confucian principle of the "Five Fundamental Relationships," which included the ruler-subject relationship. They were expected to model proper behavior in their interactions with the common people.

By adhering to these social norms and hierarchies, scholar-officials contributed to the stability of the state and the preservation of traditional values. They facilitated the smooth functioning of the Confucian-inspired social order.

5. Cultural Preservation and Scholarship:
Scholar-officials were also patrons of the arts and played a significant role in the preservation and promotion of Chinese culture and traditions. They supported the creation of poetry, calligraphy, literature, and the arts. Many of them were accomplished writers and scholars in their own right.

Their scholarly pursuits extended beyond the realm of government administration, contributing to the richness of Chinese intellectual and cultural heritage. Their writings often focused on Confucian philosophy, history, ethics, and social commentary.

6. Challenges and Reforms:

Throughout Chinese history, scholar-officials faced various challenges and periods of reform. Some periods saw them advocating for political and social reforms, such as during the Song Dynasty's Neo-Confucian revival. Others faced difficulties in dealing with external threats, such as invasions by nomadic tribes.

Scholar-officials played pivotal roles in advocating for changes in government policies, and their influence varied depending on the dynasty and the specific historical context.

7. Enduring Legacy:

The legacy of scholar-officials in ancient China is enduring. Their commitment to Confucian values, ethical governance, and scholarship left a lasting impact on Chinese culture, government, and society. Their role as moral and intellectual leaders continues to be celebrated in Chinese history and literature.

The influence of scholar-officials extended beyond their lifetimes, shaping the trajectory of Chinese civilization and contributing to the Confucianization of East Asian societies. Their commitment to education, ethics, and governance laid the foundation for the Confucian traditions that continue to resonate in contemporary East Asia.

In summary, the role of scholar-officials in ancient China was a vital and complex one that blended governance, scholarship, and ethics. These individuals were not only administrators but also guardians of Confucian values and cultural heritage. They played a pivotal role in shaping Chinese society, governance, and intellectual life, leaving an enduring legacy that continues to be celebrated and studied today.

Chapter 7: Challenges and Critiques of Confucianism (475 - 479 BCE)

Confucianism, with its emphasis on tradition, hierarchy, and ethical values, has not been without its critics and opponents throughout history. While it has been a dominant and enduring philosophical and ethical system in East Asia, it has also faced challenges, critiques, and opposition from various quarters. These critics and opponents have offered alternative viewpoints and philosophical frameworks, often highlighting perceived shortcomings of Confucianism or advocating for different systems of thought.

1. Mohism (墨家, Mòjiā):

Mohism was one of the earliest philosophical schools to emerge in ancient China as a rival to Confucianism. Founded by Mozi (Mo Tzu), Mohism advocated for universal love (jian'ai) and impartial caring for all people, regardless of their social status or relationships. This contrasted with Confucianism's emphasis on familial love and hierarchy.

Mohists criticized Confucianism for what they saw as its elitism and failure to address the welfare of all members of society. They advocated for utilitarian principles and the promotion of the greatest good for the greatest number.

2. Daoism (道家, Dàojiā):

Daoism, particularly in its early philosophical form, challenged many aspects of Confucianism. Daoists, such as Laozi (Lao Tzu), emphasized the Dao (Tao), a concept of the "Way" or the natural order of the universe. They advocated for a more spontaneous and intuitive way of living, in contrast to Confucianism's emphasis on ritual and social norms.

Daoists criticized Confucianism for what they viewed as rigid and artificial constructs of society. They valued simplicity, humility, and the pursuit of harmony with nature over Confucian ideals of hierarchy and social order.

3. Legalism (法家, Fǎjiā):

Legalism, associated with thinkers like Han Feizi, was another philosophical school that opposed Confucianism. Legalists advocated for strict laws, harsh punishments, and centralized state control to maintain order and obedience. They viewed Confucianism's emphasis on moral virtue as insufficient for effective governance.

Legalists criticized Confucianism for its perceived idealism and argued that a strong and authoritarian state was necessary to ensure stability and compliance with the law.

4. Buddhism (佛教, Fójiào):

Buddhism, which was introduced to China from India, presented a challenge to Confucianism's dominance in the realm of spirituality and ethics. Buddhists emphasized the path to enlightenment and the transcendence of worldly suffering, which contrasted with Confucianism's focus on ethical conduct within the social realm.

Some Confucian scholars criticized Buddhism for its perceived world-denying nature and questioned its compatibility with Confucian values and social responsibilities.

5. Neo-Confucianism (宋明理学, Sòng-Míng Lǐxué):

While not direct opponents, Neo-Confucian thinkers introduced significant modifications to traditional Confucianism. Figures like Zhu Xi sought to integrate Confucianism with elements of Daoism and Buddhism. They emphasized metaphysical and cosmological aspects, focusing on the investigation of the principle (li) that underlies all phenomena.

This philosophical shift within Confucianism led to debates and critiques from traditional Confucian scholars who felt that Neo-Confucianism was straying from the original teachings of Confucius.

6. Intellectual Critics:

Within Confucianism itself, there were scholars who offered internal critiques and challenged certain aspects of the tradition. Wang Yangming, for instance, questioned the emphasis on ritual and external conduct, advocating for the importance of inner moral intuition (liangzhi).

These intellectual critics contributed to the ongoing evolution and refinement of Confucian thought, stimulating debates about its core principles.

7. Modern and Political Critics:

In modern times, Confucianism has faced criticism from political and intellectual circles for its perceived role in reinforcing traditional hierarchies and authoritarianism. Some argue that Confucian values have been used to justify oppressive political regimes.

Critics have also pointed out gender biases within Confucianism, as it has historically emphasized male superiority and the subordination of women.

It is important to note that while Confucianism faced opposition and critique, it also underwent adaptation and evolution in response to these challenges. Throughout its long history, Confucianism has proven to be a dynamic and resilient tradition, absorbing and responding to various criticisms and influences while maintaining its core ethical principles. Additionally, many of these critiques were rooted in specific historical and cultural contexts, and Confucianism continues to play a prominent role in the moral and ethical fabric of East Asian societies today.

Confucianism, as a venerable philosophical and ethical

tradition that has endured for over two millennia, has not remained static in the face of critiques and challenges. It has demonstrated a remarkable capacity for adaptation, self-reflection, and response to various criticisms throughout its history. Confucian scholars and thinkers have engaged with critics, both from within their own tradition and from other philosophical schools, and have sought to address perceived shortcomings while preserving the core values and principles of Confucianism.

1. Engagement with Mohism:
Confucianism encountered an early challenge from Mohism, which emphasized universal love and impartial care for all people. Confucian thinkers, including Mencius (Mengzi), engaged in intellectual debates with Mohists. While Confucianism did not adopt Mohist principles wholesale, it did recognize the importance of benevolence (ren) as a central virtue. Confucianism emphasized that benevolence should begin within the family and expand outward to the broader society, addressing some of the concerns raised by Mohists about the welfare of all.

2. Integration of Daoist Ideas:
Daoism, with its emphasis on the Dao (Tao) as the natural order, simplicity, and harmony with nature, presented a contrasting worldview to Confucianism's focus on ritual and hierarchy. Neo-Confucian scholars, such as Zhu Xi, sought to integrate elements of Daoist thought into Confucianism. They emphasized the importance of understanding the metaphysical principle (li) that underlies all phenomena, bridging the gap between Confucian and Daoist ideas.

3. Response to Legalism:
Legalism's emphasis on strict laws, harsh punishments, and centralized state control challenged Confucian principles of moral governance. Confucian scholars acknowledged the need for laws and governance but argued that moral

education and ethical leadership were essential components of effective governance. They advocated for a balanced approach that combined legal measures with moral guidance to ensure social order.

4. Engagement with Buddhism:
The arrival of Buddhism in China posed questions about the compatibility of Buddhist teachings with Confucian values and ethics. Confucian scholars engaged with Buddhists in debates and discussions. While Confucianism maintained its distinct ethical and social focus, it absorbed certain elements of Buddhist thought, such as the concept of filial piety extending beyond the family to society, and incorporated them into Confucian ethics.

5. Response to Intellectual Critics:
Within Confucianism itself, there were intellectuals who offered internal critiques and sought to refine Confucian thought. Wang Yangming, for instance, challenged the emphasis on ritual and external conduct, advocating for the importance of inner moral intuition (liangzhi). His ideas contributed to the development of Neo-Confucianism and influenced subsequent generations of Confucian thinkers.

6. Addressing Gender Biases:
Critics, both historical and modern, have pointed out gender biases within Confucianism, as it traditionally emphasized male superiority and the subordination of women. In response to these critiques, contemporary Confucian scholars have engaged in discussions about gender equality and sought to reinterpret Confucian principles to promote greater gender inclusivity and respect for women's rights.

7. Adaptation to Modern Challenges:
In the modern era, Confucianism has faced challenges related to its perceived role in reinforcing authoritarianism and hierarchies in East Asian societies. Confucian scholars have engaged with these critiques by emphasizing the

ethical and humanistic aspects of Confucianism, promoting values such as social justice, human rights, and democratic governance. They have sought to demonstrate that Confucianism can be a source of inspiration for addressing contemporary societal challenges.

8. Global Engagement:
Confucianism has increasingly engaged with global philosophical and ethical dialogues. Scholars have explored the compatibility of Confucian principles with universal values and human rights, seeking to demonstrate that Confucianism can be a relevant and enriching perspective in a global context.

9. Continued Moral Reflection:
Throughout its history, Confucianism has encouraged moral reflection and self-improvement. Confucian scholars have responded to critiques by continuously examining and refining their ethical principles and values. They have sought to ensure that Confucianism remains a dynamic and relevant ethical framework for addressing the complex moral challenges of society.

In summary, Confucianism's response to critiques has been characterized by a willingness to engage with diverse perspectives, adapt to changing circumstances, and undergo intellectual and philosophical development. While it has preserved its core values and principles, Confucianism has also demonstrated a capacity for evolution and reinterpretation, ensuring its enduring relevance in the complex landscape of philosophical and ethical thought. It remains a living tradition that continues to inspire ethical reflection and dialogue in East Asia and beyond.

The "Zhuangzi," attributed to the ancient Chinese philosopher Zhuang Zhou (also known as Chuang Tzu), is a foundational text in Daoism (Taoism) that offers philosophical alternatives to the prevailing Confucian and Legalist schools of thought. This work is a collection of stories, parables, and philosophical reflections that challenge conventional wisdom, explore the nature of reality, and advocate for a Daoist worldview. Within the "Zhuangzi," several key philosophical alternatives to Confucianism and Legalism emerge:

1. Embracing Naturalness (Ziran):

The "Zhuangzi" places a strong emphasis on the concept of ziran, often translated as "naturalness" or "spontaneity." Zhuangzi argues that individuals should align themselves with the natural order of the Dao (Tao), rather than trying to conform to rigid social norms and conventions, as advocated by Confucianism.

While Confucianism emphasizes ritual, propriety, and moral cultivation, the "Zhuangzi" suggests that true virtue arises from a state of effortless and uncontrived spontaneity. It encourages individuals to live in harmony with the Dao, embracing their innate nature rather than trying to mold themselves into prescribed roles and behaviors.

2. Rejecting Social Hierarchies:

Confucianism places a strong emphasis on social hierarchies and the Five Fundamental Relationships, which prescribe specific roles and duties for individuals based on their social status. In contrast, the "Zhuangzi" challenges these hierarchies and advocates for a more egalitarian and fluid view of society.

The text contains stories and parables that illustrate the absurdity of rigid social distinctions. It suggests that distinctions between rulers and subjects, rich and poor, and wise and foolish are arbitrary and artificial. Instead, the "Zhuangzi" proposes a vision of a world where such distinctions are irrelevant, and all individuals are treated with equal respect and compassion.

**3. The Relativity of Values:
The "Zhuangzi" introduces the idea that values and judgments are relative and context-dependent. It challenges the absolute moral standards promoted by Confucianism and Legalism. Instead of rigid moral principles, the text suggests that what is considered good or bad depends on one's perspective and the circumstances.

This relativism is exemplified in stories where actions that might be seen as morally reprehensible in one context are celebrated as virtuous in another. The "Zhuangzi" encourages readers to question their preconceived notions of right and wrong and to view ethics as a more fluid and nuanced concept.

**4. Skepticism and Paradox:
The "Zhuangzi" employs a style of philosophical skepticism and paradox that challenges conventional wisdom and the certainties of Confucian and Legalist thought. It often uses humor and absurdity to provoke thought and reflection.

Zhuangzi's famous butterfly dream anecdote, in which he questions the boundary between dream and reality, illustrates this skeptical approach. The text encourages readers to question their assumptions about the nature of reality and knowledge, promoting a more open and flexible mindset.

**5. The Pursuit of Wu Wei:
Wu wei, often translated as "non-action" or "effortless action," is a central concept in Daoism that is explored in the "Zhuangzi." While Confucianism emphasizes the active cultivation of virtue and the fulfillment of social roles, the "Zhuangzi" suggests that true virtue can be found in a state of wu wei.

Wu wei involves letting go of striving and forcing outcomes, instead allowing things to unfold naturally. It is a state of flow where one acts spontaneously in accordance with the

Dao, without conscious effort. This stands in contrast to Confucian ideals of moral effort and self-cultivation.

6. Appreciation of the Relational Dao:

The "Zhuangzi" presents the Dao as a dynamic and relational concept rather than a fixed set of principles or rules. It suggests that the Dao cannot be captured through rigid definitions or categories. This view contrasts with Confucianism's emphasis on the importance of moral norms and social order.

The text encourages individuals to engage with the world in a more intuitive and flexible manner, appreciating the interconnectedness of all things and recognizing that the Dao is constantly evolving.

In summary, the "Zhuangzi" offers philosophical alternatives to Confucianism and Legalism that challenge traditional views of ethics, society, and reality. It advocates for a Daoist worldview characterized by naturalness, relativism, skepticism, and the pursuit of wu wei. These alternatives provide a counterbalance to the rigid moral and social structures of Confucianism and Legalism, inviting readers to embrace a more fluid and open-minded approach to life and philosophy.

Chapter 8: The Legacy of Confucianism in Ancient China

Confucianism's enduring influence on Chinese culture is a testament to its profound and lasting impact on the country's history, values, social structure, and worldview. For over two millennia, Confucianism has shaped the way Chinese society functions, providing a moral and philosophical framework that continues to play a central role in various aspects of Chinese life. Here, we explore how Confucianism's influence persists and thrives in contemporary Chinese culture:

1. Ethical Foundation:
Confucianism has provided a strong ethical foundation for Chinese culture. Its emphasis on virtues such as benevolence (ren), righteousness (yi), propriety (li), wisdom (zhi), and trustworthiness (xin) has influenced the moral values of individuals and communities. These virtues remain fundamental to Chinese ethical thought and are often taught to children as part of their moral education.

2. Family Values:
The Confucian emphasis on filial piety (xiao) and respect for parents and ancestors continues to be a core value in Chinese families. The family unit remains central in Chinese culture, and the practice of ancestral worship and the importance of family gatherings during festivals are manifestations of Confucian values.

3. Education and Scholarly Tradition:
Confucianism has historically placed a high value on education and scholarship. This emphasis on learning and self-improvement has persisted in Chinese culture. China has a rich tradition of scholars and intellectuals, and academic achievement is highly regarded in society. The civil service examination system, rooted in Confucian ideals, has been

replaced by modern educational institutions, but the emphasis on academic excellence endures.

4. Social Harmony and Order:

Confucianism's focus on social harmony and order has had a lasting impact on Chinese culture. Chinese society places importance on maintaining stability, respecting authority, and upholding social norms. The Confucian idea that individuals should fulfill their roles and responsibilities within society continues to influence behavior and interactions.

5. Government and Leadership:

Confucian principles have influenced the expectations placed on political leaders. The concept of the "Mandate of Heaven," which suggests that rulers must govern justly and responsibly to maintain their legitimacy, is deeply rooted in Confucian thought. The idea of virtuous leadership and moral governance continues to shape political discourse in China.

6. Cultural Practices and Rituals:

Many Chinese cultural practices and rituals are influenced by Confucianism. These include traditional wedding ceremonies, funeral rites, and festivals. Confucian ideas about propriety (li) and proper conduct in social situations continue to guide these rituals.

7. Language and Literature:

Confucian classics, such as the "Analects" and the "Book of Rites," have had a profound influence on Chinese language and literature. These texts have provided rich sources of wisdom and have been studied and referenced by generations of Chinese scholars and writers.

8. Art and Aesthetics:

Confucian values have also influenced Chinese art and aesthetics. Traditional Chinese paintings, calligraphy, and ceramics often incorporate Confucian themes and motifs.

The emphasis on balance, harmony, and simplicity in Chinese art reflects Confucian ideals.

9. Global Influence:

Confucianism has not only shaped Chinese culture but has also had a significant impact on neighboring East Asian countries, including Japan, Korea, and Vietnam. These countries have absorbed Confucian values and adapted them to their own cultures.

10. Contemporary Adaptations:

While Confucianism remains influential, it has also evolved in response to modern challenges. Contemporary Confucian scholars engage with issues such as environmental ethics, gender equality, and social justice, demonstrating the adaptability of Confucian thought in addressing contemporary societal concerns.

In summary, Confucianism's enduring influence on Chinese culture is evident in its profound impact on ethics, family values, education, social harmony, government, and various cultural practices. It continues to shape the collective consciousness of the Chinese people, providing a moral and philosophical compass that guides individuals and society as a whole. While adapting to changing times, Confucianism remains a vital and enduring aspect of Chinese cultural identity.

Confucianism's influence in later Chinese dynasties continued to evolve and adapt to the changing political, social, and intellectual landscape. While it remained a dominant philosophical and ethical system, it underwent transformations and faced challenges in different historical periods. Here's a glimpse of how Confucianism fared in some of China's later dynasties:

1. Han Dynasty (206 BCE - 220 CE):

The Han Dynasty is often considered the golden age of Confucianism. Confucian principles of government, emphasizing benevolent rule, ethical leadership, and the importance of education, played a central role in shaping Han governance. The state-sponsored civil service examination system, rooted in Confucian thought, was established during this period to select officials based on merit and knowledge of Confucian classics.

Confucianism's influence extended to education, where it became the dominant intellectual framework. Confucian classics, including the "Analects" and the "Book of Rites," were central to the curriculum. The Han Dynasty solidified Confucianism's position as the official state ideology.

2. Tang Dynasty (618 - 907):

The Tang Dynasty continued to uphold Confucian principles in governance and education. Confucian classics remained at the core of the imperial examination system, which assessed candidates for government positions based on their knowledge of Confucian texts.

During the Tang Dynasty, Confucianism coexisted with Daoism and Buddhism. Intellectual exchange between these philosophical traditions led to the development of Neo-Confucianism, a philosophical synthesis that incorporated elements of Daoist and Buddhist thought.

3. Song Dynasty (960 - 1279):

The Song Dynasty marked the flourishing of Neo-Confucianism, particularly under the influence of scholars like Zhu Xi. Neo-Confucianism sought to combine Confucian principles with metaphysical and cosmological ideas, emphasizing the study of the "Four Books" (Analects, Mencius, the Doctrine of the Mean, and the Great Learning).

Neo-Confucianism became the dominant intellectual and philosophical framework in Song Dynasty China. It shaped state policy, influenced educational institutions, and had a profound impact on the literati class.

4. Ming Dynasty (1368 - 1644):

The Ming Dynasty continued to uphold Confucian values in governance and education. The imperial examination system remained central, and knowledge of Confucian texts was a prerequisite for government officials. The Ming Dynasty is known for its restoration of Confucian rituals and the publication of the Ming edition of the "Confucian Classics."

Ming scholars, such as Wang Yangming, made significant contributions to Confucian thought by emphasizing the importance of inner moral intuition (liangzhi) and the unity of knowledge and action.

5. Qing Dynasty (1644 - 1912):

The Qing Dynasty, ruled by the Manchu ethnic group, continued to embrace Confucianism as the official ideology. However, the Qing rulers also incorporated elements of their own Manchu culture and governance, resulting in a syncretic approach.

During the late Qing Dynasty, China faced internal challenges, foreign invasions, and the impact of Western ideas. Scholars like Kang Youwei and Liang Qichao advocated for Confucian reform and modernization, reflecting the tension between traditional Confucian values and the need to adapt to changing circumstances.

6. Modern and Contemporary China:

In the 20th century, Confucianism faced significant challenges during periods of political turmoil and ideological change. The May Fourth Movement of 1919, which called for the rejection of traditional values and the adoption of Western ideas, questioned the relevance of Confucianism in modern China.

The Chinese Communist Party, under Mao Zedong, initially rejected Confucianism as part of the "Four Olds" during the Cultural Revolution (1966 - 1976). However, in more recent decades, there has been a revival of interest in Confucianism in China, both as a cultural heritage and as a source of ethical and moral guidance in society.

Today, Confucian values continue to influence Chinese culture, ethics, and social relationships. They also play a role in China's approach to governance and social harmony.

In summary, Confucianism's influence in later Chinese dynasties remained strong, shaping governance, education, and cultural practices. While it faced challenges and adaptations in response to evolving intellectual currents and historical contexts, Confucianism continues to be an enduring and influential aspect of Chinese culture and identity.

Confucianism has deeply influenced Chinese culture, giving rise to a rich tapestry of symbols and practices that reflect its moral, ethical, and social principles. These cultural symbols and practices, rooted in Confucianism, continue to shape various aspects of Chinese life today:

1. Filial Piety (Xiao):

Filial piety is one of the core values of Confucianism, emphasizing respect and devotion to one's parents and ancestors. This practice involves rituals such as ancestor worship, tomb-sweeping ceremonies, and the veneration of family elders. Ancestral tablets, family altars, and offerings of food and incense are common symbols of filial piety in Chinese households.

2. Confucian Rituals and Ceremonies:

Confucian rituals and ceremonies are an integral part of Chinese culture. These ceremonies often include coming-of-age rituals, marriage ceremonies, and funerals. Traditional wedding ceremonies, for example, often incorporate Confucian principles, such as the exchange of vows emphasizing loyalty and respect.

3. Confucian Temples and Ancestral Halls:

Confucian temples and ancestral halls (known as "xiangtang" or "zongci") are dedicated to the veneration of Confucius and one's ancestors. These structures serve as cultural symbols of Confucian values and offer spaces for ceremonies, lectures, and the display of Confucian texts and teachings.

4. Confucian Literature and Classics:
Confucian classics, including the "Analects," the "Mencius," and the "Doctrine of the Mean," are foundational texts of Confucianism. These writings have shaped Chinese literature and scholarship for centuries. Confucian principles of ethics, propriety, and governance are woven into Chinese literary works, poetry, and historical writings.

5. Scholarship and Education:
Confucianism's emphasis on education and scholarship has left an indelible mark on Chinese culture. The pursuit of knowledge and moral self-cultivation are highly valued in Chinese society. Educational institutions, books, and scholarly traditions are symbols of the Confucian commitment to self-improvement and intellectual growth.

6. Social Hierarchies and Respect for Elders:
Confucianism has influenced social hierarchies and the practice of showing respect to elders and authority figures. The practice of bowing, addressing individuals by their titles and honorifics, and adhering to proper etiquette in various social settings are expressions of Confucian respect for social order.

7. The Family as the Basic Unit of Society:
Confucianism regards the family as the fundamental unit of society. Family values, including the importance of the parent-child relationship, have profound cultural significance. The practice of arranging family gatherings during festivals and holidays reinforces the centrality of family life.

8. Moral Conduct and Virtue:
Confucian values of benevolence (ren), righteousness (yi), propriety (li), wisdom (zhi), and trustworthiness (xin) continue to inform Chinese notions of moral conduct and virtue. These values are often invoked in discussions of ethics and proper behavior.

9. Government and Governance:
Confucian principles have influenced Chinese approaches to governance and leadership. The concept of the "Mandate of Heaven," which suggests that rulers must govern justly to maintain legitimacy, reflects Confucian ideals of virtuous leadership.

10. Cultural Conservatism and Tradition:
Confucianism's emphasis on preserving cultural traditions and customs has contributed to the conservation of traditional Chinese practices, including language, art, music, and dress. Traditional clothing, such as the qipao and changshan, is symbolic of this cultural conservatism.

In summary, Confucianism's impact on Chinese culture is evident in a wide range of symbols and practices that reflect its moral and social teachings. These cultural expressions continue to resonate in contemporary Chinese society, providing a strong foundation for ethical conduct, social harmony, and the preservation of cultural traditions. Confucianism remains a living and influential force in the cultural identity of the Chinese people.

Chapter 9: Confucianism Beyond China: Global Influence

Confucianism, originally developed in ancient China, gradually spread to East Asia over centuries through cultural diffusion, trade, and interactions between Chinese scholars and neighboring societies. Its influence extended to countries such as Japan, Korea, and Vietnam, where it not only shaped the moral and ethical values of these cultures but also played a significant role in their political and social systems. Here's an overview of how Confucianism spread to East Asia:

1. Korea:

Confucianism was introduced to Korea during the Three Kingdoms period (c. 4th century CE) through contact with China. Korean scholars and officials began to study Confucian texts and embrace Confucian ideals, including the importance of virtue, social order, and ethical conduct.

The Goryeo Dynasty (918 - 1392) marked a significant period of Confucian influence in Korea. King Taejo of Goryeo adopted Confucian principles in governance, leading to the establishment of Confucian academies and the incorporation of Confucian rituals into Korean court culture.

The Joseon Dynasty (1392 - 1910) solidified Confucianism's status as the state ideology. Confucian civil service examinations were introduced, modeled after the Chinese system, and the study of Confucian classics became the foundation of education. Confucian values, such as respect for elders and the emphasis on filial piety, became integral to Korean society.

2. Japan:

Confucianism reached Japan during the early medieval period through trade with China and the Korean Peninsula. The Japanese adapted Confucian ideas to their own cultural context, blending them with existing indigenous beliefs and practices.

During the Edo period (1603 - 1868), Confucianism gained prominence in Japan, particularly among the samurai class. Confucian scholars, known as "bunjin," played a significant role in shaping Japanese intellectual and ethical thought. Neo-Confucianism, with its emphasis on moral cultivation and metaphysical principles, became influential.

Confucian values influenced Japanese social etiquette, education, and the Bushido code of the samurai. Confucian principles of loyalty, honor, and righteousness were integrated into Japanese ethical systems.

**3. Vietnam:

Confucianism was introduced to Vietnam during the Chinese domination of the region, which lasted for over a thousand years. Vietnamese scholars adopted Confucian texts and the Chinese script for writing.

The Ly and Tran Dynasties (11th to 14th centuries) saw the integration of Confucian principles into Vietnamese governance and education. The Confucian civil service examination system was implemented, modeled after the Chinese system.

Vietnamese Confucianism emphasized social harmony, ethical conduct, and the importance of education. Confucian scholars played key roles in the administration of the country.

**4. Continued Influence:

In contemporary East Asia, Confucianism's influence remains evident in various aspects of culture, education, and ethics. While these countries have undergone significant modernization and cultural change, Confucian values continue to shape social norms, family dynamics, and ethical conduct.

In South Korea, for example, Confucian ideals of education, respect for elders, and social order remain deeply ingrained in society. In Japan, Confucian ethics continue to influence business practices and the educational system. In Vietnam, Confucian values of respect for authority and education continue to be important.

In summary, Confucianism spread to East Asia through cultural exchange and historical interactions, leaving a lasting impact on the moral, ethical, and social values of countries such as Korea, Japan, and Vietnam. While these societies have adapted Confucian principles to their own cultural contexts, the enduring influence of Confucianism is still evident in their traditions and social norms today.

Confucianism has played a significant role in shaping the cultures and societies of both Korea and Japan, albeit in unique ways influenced by their distinct historical contexts. Here's an exploration of how Confucianism has manifested in these two East Asian nations:

Confucianism in Korea:

Introduction and Adoption:

Confucianism was introduced to Korea during the Three Kingdoms period (c. 4th century CE) through contact with China. Korean scholars and officials began to study Confucian texts and embrace Confucian ideals, including the importance of virtue, social order, and ethical conduct.

Influence on Governance:

The Goryeo Dynasty (918 - 1392) marked a significant period of Confucian influence in Korea. King Taejo of Goryeo adopted Confucian principles in governance, leading to the establishment of Confucian academies and the incorporation of Confucian rituals into Korean court culture. The governance system was restructured based on Confucian ideals of benevolence, justice, and moral leadership.

Joseon Dynasty:
The Joseon Dynasty (1392 - 1910) solidified Confucianism's status as the state ideology. Confucian civil service examinations were introduced, modeled after the Chinese system, and the study of Confucian classics became the foundation of education. Confucian values, such as respect for elders and the emphasis on filial piety, became integral to Korean society.

Role of Confucian Scholars:
Korean Confucian scholars, known as "sadaebu," played a central role in shaping Korean culture, politics, and education. They emphasized the importance of moral cultivation, scholarship, and public service.

Confucian Rituals and Ancestral Worship:
Confucian rituals, including ancestral worship, became a prominent part of Korean culture. Ancestral tablets, family altars, and ceremonies like Chuseok (Korean Thanksgiving) and Seollal (Lunar New Year) continue to reflect Confucian values of filial piety and respect for ancestors.

Confucianism in Japan:

Adaptation and Syncretism:
Confucianism reached Japan during the early medieval period through trade with China and Korea. The Japanese adapted Confucian ideas to their own cultural context, blending them with existing indigenous beliefs and practices.

Influence on Samurai and Bushido:
During the Edo period (1603 - 1868), Confucianism gained prominence in Japan, particularly among the samurai class. Confucian scholars, known as "bunjin," played a significant role in shaping Japanese intellectual and ethical thought. Neo-Confucianism, with its emphasis on moral cultivation and metaphysical principles, became influential.

Confucian values, such as loyalty, honor, and righteousness, were integrated into the Bushido code of the samurai.

Confucian ethics influenced the conduct and behavior of the warrior class.

Education and Scholarship:

Confucianism also had a profound impact on Japanese education. Confucian classics, including the "Analects" and the "Mencius," were studied extensively in Japan. Educational institutions, modeled after Chinese Confucian academies, emphasized the study of these texts.

Influence on Government:

Confucian principles of governance, emphasizing ethical leadership and the well-being of the people, influenced Japanese politics and administration. Confucian scholars served as advisers to Japanese rulers.

Cultural Practices:

Confucianism influenced various cultural practices in Japan, including the adoption of Chinese-style clothing and the incorporation of Confucian rituals into ceremonies such as weddings and funerals.

In summary, Confucianism has had a lasting impact on both Korean and Japanese cultures, shaping their values, ethics, education, and social systems. While the influence of Confucianism is evident in various aspects of these societies, it has also been adapted and integrated in ways that reflect the unique historical and cultural contexts of Korea and Japan. Confucianism continues to be an important part of the cultural heritage of both nations, contributing to their sense of identity and tradition.

Confucianism, with its profound ethical and philosophical teachings, has had a profound and enduring impact on Asian societies. This influence extends across a range of areas, including culture, ethics, politics, education, and social norms. From its origins in ancient China, Confucianism's influence has radiated outward, shaping the values and practices of numerous Asian nations, including China, Korea, Japan, Vietnam, and beyond.

At the heart of Confucianism are the teachings of Confucius (551-479 BCE), a philosopher and educator whose ideas emphasized the cultivation of moral virtues, ethical conduct, and the importance of harmonious relationships within society. His philosophy laid the groundwork for a societal framework that has left an indelible mark on Asian cultures.

Ethical Foundations:

One of the most enduring impacts of Confucianism is its strong ethical foundations. Confucianism places a central emphasis on moral virtues, such as benevolence (ren), righteousness (yi), propriety (li), wisdom (zhi), and trustworthiness (xin). These virtues serve as guiding principles for individuals in their interactions with others and in the conduct of their lives.

Social Harmony and Relationships:

Confucianism places a premium on the importance of harmonious relationships within society. This includes the idea of filial piety, which emphasizes respect for one's parents and ancestors, as well as the Five Relationships: ruler and subject, father and son, husband and wife, elder brother and younger brother, and friend and friend. These relationships form the basis of social order and are seen as critical to maintaining harmony.

Education and Scholarship:

Confucianism's emphasis on the importance of education has had a profound influence on Asian societies. Confucius believed that education was the key to moral development and personal improvement. This belief has resulted in a strong tradition of scholarship and the establishment of educational institutions throughout Asia dedicated to the study of Confucian classics.

Politics and Governance:

Confucianism's influence on politics and governance is particularly evident in China and other East Asian countries. The idea of the "Mandate of Heaven," which suggests that rulers must govern justly to maintain legitimacy, reflects Confucian ideals of virtuous leadership. Confucian principles have often been integrated into political systems, influencing the behavior of rulers and officials.

Cultural Practices and Traditions:

Confucianism has shaped cultural practices and traditions in Asian societies. Ancestral worship, for example, is a common practice rooted in Confucianism. Families maintain ancestral altars and engage in rituals to honor their ancestors, reflecting the importance of filial piety and maintaining connections with one's lineage.

Gender Roles and Family Structure:

Confucianism has also had a significant impact on gender roles and family structure. Traditional gender roles often emphasize the importance of women as virtuous wives and mothers, while men are expected to be the primary providers. These roles are deeply rooted in Confucian ideas of family and social order.

Adaptations and Evolutions:

While Confucianism has left an indelible mark on Asian societies, it is essential to recognize that its impact has evolved and adapted over time. Different regions and historical periods have interpreted and incorporated Confucian ideas in various ways, leading to unique cultural expressions and adaptations.

Contemporary Relevance:

In contemporary times, the influence of Confucianism remains relevant in many Asian societies. While modernization and globalization have brought changes, Confucian values of respect for authority, moral conduct, and social harmony continue to be valued and emphasized.

Challenges and Critiques:

It's also important to acknowledge that Confucianism has faced challenges and critiques. Some argue that its emphasis on hierarchy and conformity can stifle individuality and social progress. Others contend that Confucianism has been used to justify oppressive social norms, particularly with regard to gender roles.

In sum, Confucianism's impact on Asian societies is vast and multifaceted. It has influenced cultural practices, social norms, political systems, and ethical values for centuries. While it has faced critiques and adaptations, its enduring influence is a testament to the profound and lasting legacy of Confucius and his philosophy in shaping the moral and ethical fabric of Asia. Confucianism's enduring influence can still be seen in the values and traditions of Asian societies today.

Chapter 10: Confucianism in the Modern World

Confucianism, a philosophy with deep historical roots in China, continues to exert a significant influence on contemporary Chinese society and culture. While China has undergone dramatic social, economic, and political changes in recent decades, Confucian values and principles remain an integral part of the country's fabric. Here, we explore the role of Confucianism in contemporary China.

1. Moral and Ethical Framework:
Confucianism provides a moral and ethical framework that shapes the behavior of individuals and communities in China. Concepts such as benevolence (ren), righteousness (yi), and propriety (li) continue to guide Chinese people in their personal and social lives. These values emphasize ethical conduct, empathy, and respect for others.

2. Family Values and Filial Piety:
The importance of the family and filial piety, a fundamental Confucian concept, still holds great significance in contemporary China. Chinese families often prioritize the well-being and happiness of their elders, maintaining strong connections across generations. Traditional festivals like the Spring Festival (Chinese New Year) underscore the importance of family reunions.

3. Education and Scholarship:
Confucianism's emphasis on education has influenced China's education system. The rigorous study of Confucian classics remains a key aspect of Chinese education, particularly in the humanities and social sciences. Confucian values of scholarship, diligence, and moral development continue to be promoted in Chinese schools and universities.

4. Political Governance:

Confucian principles have influenced the Chinese government's approach to governance. While China is governed by a one-party system, the ruling Communist Party has integrated certain Confucian elements into its ideology. Concepts like social harmony, moral leadership, and the idea of the "mandate of heaven" have been invoked to justify the party's rule.

5. Social Harmony and Stability:

Confucianism promotes the idea of social harmony and stability as essential components of a well-functioning society. This concept aligns with the Chinese government's emphasis on maintaining social stability and controlling potential sources of unrest.

6. Influence on Business and Ethics:

Confucian values of trustworthiness, honesty, and integrity continue to play a role in Chinese business ethics. These values are seen as crucial in fostering trust in commercial transactions, both domestically and internationally.

7. Cultural Practices and Rituals:

Confucian rituals and customs, such as ancestral worship and rites, continue to be observed in China. Ancestral halls and ancestral tablets are maintained in many households, and ceremonies like Qingming Festival (Tomb-Sweeping Day) are observed to pay respects to ancestors.

8. Cultural Identity and Heritage:

Confucianism remains an essential part of China's cultural identity and heritage. It informs Chinese literature, art, philosophy, and social norms. The philosophy of Confucius is studied and respected as a foundational aspect of Chinese culture.

9. Adaptation and Modernization:

While Confucianism remains influential, it has also adapted to modernity. China's rapid economic development and globalization have brought changes to traditional values and social structures. Younger generations may reinterpret Confucian principles in ways that align with contemporary life.

10. Challenges and Critiques:
Confucianism has faced challenges and critiques within China. Some argue that it can reinforce hierarchical social structures and limit individual freedom. Others believe that it has been co-opted by the government to legitimize authoritarian rule.

In summary, Confucianism continues to play a significant role in contemporary China, providing a moral, ethical, and cultural framework that shapes various aspects of Chinese society. While it has adapted to modernity and faced critiques, its enduring influence reflects its deep-seated importance in China's cultural and historical heritage. Confucian values continue to influence the behavior and mindset of individuals, families, and communities across China.

Confucian values, rooted in the teachings of Confucius and developed over millennia in East Asia, have relevance beyond the region's borders. These values encompass moral principles, ethical conduct, and a social philosophy that emphasize harmony, benevolence, righteousness, and filial piety. When considered in the context of global ethics, Confucian values offer insights and perspectives that can contribute to a more inclusive and harmonious world. Here's an exploration of Confucian values and their potential impact on global ethics:

1. Humaneness (Ren/仁): At the core of Confucianism is the concept of ren, often translated as "humaneness" or "benevolence." It emphasizes compassion, empathy, and a genuine concern for the well-being of others. In a global context, the principle of ren encourages individuals and nations to treat one another with kindness, respect, and a sense of shared humanity. It promotes the idea of universal care and concern for all human beings, transcending cultural and national boundaries.

2. Righteousness (Yi/义): Yi is another fundamental Confucian value associated with moral integrity and doing what is right. In global ethics, the concept of yi encourages individuals and nations to uphold justice, fairness, and ethical principles in their interactions with others. It calls for a commitment to addressing global issues such as poverty, inequality, and environmental sustainability with a strong sense of moral responsibility.

3. Filial Piety (Xiao/孝): While originally focused on the respect and devotion to one's parents, the concept of filial piety can be expanded to emphasize the importance of honoring and caring for the elderly, vulnerable, and disadvantaged members of society. In a global context, this value encourages a sense of social responsibility toward those in need, irrespective of cultural or national boundaries.

4. Ritual Propriety (Li/礼): Li refers to the observance of ritual propriety and social etiquette. In global ethics, it can be interpreted as promoting respect for diverse cultures, customs, and traditions. Recognizing and respecting cultural differences while fostering a sense of shared values and mutual understanding can contribute to a more inclusive and harmonious global community.

5. Loyalty (Zhong/忠): Loyalty, as a Confucian value, emphasizes faithfulness and commitment to one's relationships and responsibilities. In a global context, this value encourages nations and individuals to fulfill their commitments and obligations in international agreements, treaties, and partnerships. It promotes trust and cooperation among nations.

6. Harmony (He/和): Harmony is a central theme in Confucianism, emphasizing the importance of balance, cooperation, and avoiding conflict. In global ethics, the value of harmony suggests that nations should seek diplomatic solutions to conflicts, prioritize dialogue and cooperation, and work together to address global challenges.

7. Continuity (Chuan/传): The Confucian emphasis on the transmission of knowledge, culture, and values from one generation to the next underscores the importance of intergenerational ethics. This value encourages a global perspective on preserving and passing on cultural heritage, ecological sustainability, and ethical principles for future generations.

8. Self-Cultivation (Xiu/Xiushen/修身): Confucianism places a strong emphasis on personal moral development and self-improvement. In global ethics, the value of self-cultivation suggests that individuals and nations should continually strive for moral growth and self-awareness, seeking to become better stewards of the planet and contributors to a more just and ethical world.

9. Humility (Qian/谦): Humility is an important Confucian virtue that encourages individuals to avoid arrogance and excessive pride. In global ethics, this value promotes a spirit of humility in international relations, fostering cooperation, compromise, and mutual respect among nations. It encourages humility in the face of complex global challenges.

10. Adaptation and Syncretism: Confucianism has demonstrated a capacity for adaptation and syncretism throughout its history, incorporating ideas from other philosophical and religious traditions. In a global context, this adaptability can encourage an openness to diverse perspectives and the integration of valuable ethical insights from different cultures and belief systems.

In summary, Confucian values offer a rich ethical framework that can contribute to global ethics by promoting compassion, justice, mutual respect, and social responsibility. While rooted in East Asian culture, these values possess universal relevance and can serve as a bridge for fostering ethical dialogue and cooperation on a global scale. Embracing the wisdom of Confucianism alongside other ethical traditions can contribute to building a more inclusive and harmonious world.

Confucianism, a philosophical and ethical tradition with deep historical roots, faces both challenges and opportunities in the 21st century. As the world undergoes rapid social, technological, and cultural changes, Confucianism is confronted with the need for adaptation while preserving its core values. Here, we explore the challenges and adaptations of Confucianism in the contemporary era:

1. Modernization and Globalization:

Challenge: The processes of modernization and globalization have brought significant changes to societies worldwide, impacting traditional value systems, including Confucianism.

Adaptation: Confucianism has adapted to modernity by emphasizing its relevance in addressing contemporary challenges. It seeks to harmonize traditional values with modern aspirations for progress, social justice, and global cooperation.

2. Changing Family Structures:

Challenge: Evolving family structures, such as smaller nuclear families and increased urbanization, can challenge Confucian ideals of strong family bonds and filial piety.

Adaptation: Confucianism promotes the importance of family values while acknowledging the diversity of family structures in the contemporary world. It emphasizes the essence of care and support for family members, regardless of family size or composition.

3. Gender Equality:
Challenge: Confucianism has been criticized for traditional gender roles that may perpetuate inequality and limit individual freedoms.
Adaptation: Contemporary Confucian scholars and practitioners are reevaluating and interpreting Confucian texts in ways that promote gender equality and inclusivity. They are working to integrate Confucian principles with modern feminist perspectives.

4. Environmental Concerns:
Challenge: Traditional Confucian thought did not explicitly address ecological issues, making it necessary to adapt to contemporary environmental challenges.
Adaptation: Some Confucian scholars are developing "eco-Confucianism" by emphasizing the value of harmony with nature. They seek to align Confucian ethics with environmental sustainability and responsible stewardship of the planet.

5. Political Systems and Governance:
Challenge: In countries where Confucianism has historical influence, there is a need to reconcile Confucian ideals with democratic principles and human rights.
Adaptation: Scholars are exploring ways to integrate Confucian values such as benevolence, justice, and moral leadership with democratic governance, emphasizing accountable and just governance.

6. Education and Technology:
Challenge: The digital age and advancements in technology have transformed the way education is delivered and accessed, challenging traditional Confucian models.

Adaptation: Confucianism continues to promote the value of education, but it adapts to include modern educational methods and technological tools. The focus remains on moral and ethical development alongside academic knowledge.

7. Cultural Revival and Identity:
Challenge: In East Asian societies, there is a tension between embracing cultural heritage and adopting Western values and lifestyles.
Adaptation: Confucianism can serve as a source of cultural identity and pride while engaging in cross-cultural dialogues. It emphasizes the importance of cultural preservation and intercultural understanding.

8. Interfaith Dialogue:
Challenge: In a pluralistic world, Confucianism encounters other religious and philosophical traditions, requiring adaptability and dialogue.
Adaptation: Confucianism can engage in interfaith dialogues to promote mutual understanding and cooperation among different belief systems, contributing to global harmony and ethical discussions.

9. Ethical Business Practices:
Challenge: Confucian values can be applied to modern business ethics, but they must adapt to address issues like corporate responsibility and globalization.
Adaptation: Confucianism promotes ethical conduct in business by emphasizing values such as trustworthiness, integrity, and social responsibility, aligning with contemporary standards of ethical business practices.

10. Globalization of Confucianism:
Challenge: As Confucianism gains global interest and recognition, it faces the challenge of retaining its core values while adapting to diverse cultural contexts.

Adaptation: Confucianism can engage in cross-cultural dialogues and intercultural exchanges to share its wisdom while respecting the uniqueness of other cultures. It emphasizes the universality of ethical values.

In summary, Confucianism faces a series of challenges in the 21st century, primarily driven by globalization, technology, and evolving social norms. However, it also offers opportunities for adaptation and relevance by emphasizing its core values of benevolence, righteousness, and ethical conduct in addressing contemporary ethical, social, and environmental concerns. As it navigates these challenges, Confucianism can contribute to a more harmonious and inclusive global society.

BOOK 3
THE GREAT WALL
ENGINEERING MARVEL OF ANCIENT CHINA (7TH CENTURY BC - 17TH CENTURY AD)
BY A.J. KINGSTON

Chapter 1: The Origins of a Defensive Vision (7th Century BC)

In the 7th century BC, ancient China was a realm of dynamic changes, both internally and externally, that would lay the foundation for future strategies and the development of defenses. During this period, several early threats and challenges emerged, compelling Chinese states to innovate and adapt to ensure their survival and sovereignty.

One of the primary threats during this time was the constant competition and conflict among various states and regions within China. This era, known as the Spring and Autumn Period (approximately 771-476 BC), was marked by power struggles, territorial disputes, and warfare between feudal states. These conflicts were often driven by ambitions for expansion, resource control, and political dominance.

The primary objective of many states during this period was to secure their territories and resources. This need for defense prompted the development of early defensive structures and strategies. City walls and fortifications became essential for safeguarding the populations and resources of these states from potential invaders. The concept of city walls, which later evolved into the iconic Great Wall of China, began as a response to these threats.

The construction of walls around cities and settlements was an early manifestation of the importance placed on defense. These walls served as physical barriers to protect against external attacks and provided a sense of security for the people within. Walls were constructed using a variety of materials, including earth, wood, and stone, depending on the region and available resources.

Furthermore, the idea of a "defensive vision" began to take shape during this period. Leaders and statesmen recognized the need for a coherent strategy to defend their territories effectively. This included fortifying key locations, maintaining well-trained armies, and devising tactics to repel potential invaders. Defensive alliances between states were also established to enhance collective security.

One of the prominent military strategists of this era was Sun Tzu, who authored "The Art of War." This seminal work provided valuable insights into military tactics, strategy, and the importance of adaptability on the battlefield. While Sun Tzu's teachings were initially focused on warfare between states within China, his principles of strategy and tactics have had enduring influence and relevance far beyond the borders of ancient China.

External threats also loomed on the northern frontier during the 7th century BC. Nomadic tribes, particularly the Xiongnu, posed a significant challenge to the settled Chinese states. These nomadic tribes were skilled horse riders and hunters, making them formidable opponents in raids and skirmishes. They sought to expand their territory into Chinese lands, posing a constant threat to border regions.

In response to these external threats, the Chinese states began to strengthen their northern defenses. Early defensive structures, such as watchtowers and outposts, were established along the northern borders. These structures served as early warning systems, allowing states to detect and respond to potential incursions by nomadic tribes.

Additionally, diplomacy played a role in managing external threats. Chinese states engaged in negotiations and alliances with neighboring tribes to maintain a degree of stability on the northern frontier. Treaties and agreements were forged to establish mutual non-aggression and trade relationships.

Trade along the Silk Road, a network of interconnected trade routes that extended from China to the Mediterranean, brought both opportunities and challenges. While trade enriched Chinese states with valuable goods, it also exposed them to foreign influences and potential security risks. States had to strike a balance between reaping the economic benefits of trade and protecting their territories from external threats.

The emergence of Confucianism, a philosophical and ethical system that emphasized the importance of moral conduct, social harmony, and the well-being of the state, also played a role in early defense strategies. Confucian principles encouraged virtuous leadership and the maintenance of a just and stable society. These values contributed to the idea that strong, ethical governance was essential for a state's defense.

In summary, the 7th century BC was a pivotal period in ancient China marked by internal conflicts, external threats, and the need for defense. It saw the development of early defensive structures, military strategies, and diplomatic efforts to secure Chinese territories. These early responses to threats and challenges laid the groundwork for the more elaborate defense systems and strategies that would evolve over the centuries, culminating in the construction of the Great Wall of China and the establishment of enduring principles of defense.

Ancient China developed a range of defensive strategies and structures over the centuries to protect its territories from external threats. These strategies and structures evolved in response to changing geopolitical conditions and technological advancements. Here, we delve into the key elements of ancient Chinese defensive systems and their historical significance:

1. City Walls and Fortifications:

City walls and fortifications were fundamental components of ancient Chinese defensive systems. These walls served as formidable barriers against invading forces, offering protection to the city's inhabitants and valuable resources. Initially constructed during the Spring and Autumn Period (8th to 5th centuries BC), these walls evolved over time, becoming more elaborate and resilient. They were often built using earth, wood, stone, or a combination of these materials, depending on the region and available resources.

The most iconic example of these defensive structures is the Great Wall of China, which was constructed, expanded, and maintained over several dynasties. It represented one of the most extensive and enduring defensive projects in human history. The Great Wall was not a single continuous wall but a series of walls, watchtowers, and fortifications spanning thousands of miles. It played a crucial role in protecting China's northern borders from nomadic invasions.

2. Watchtowers and Signal Beacons:

Watchtowers were strategically placed along city walls and defensive lines to provide a vantage point for guards and soldiers to monitor the surrounding terrain. They served as early warning systems, allowing defenders to detect approaching enemy forces and signal for reinforcements.

Signal beacons were an essential part of the communication network. They were used to transmit urgent messages over long distances. A series of signal fires or smoke signals could relay information quickly, facilitating coordinated responses to threats.

3. Defensive Alliances:

Chinese states often formed defensive alliances with neighboring states to enhance their collective security. These alliances were forged through treaties and agreements that stipulated mutual defense in the event of an attack. The idea was to deter potential invaders by presenting a united front.

One notable example is the alliance between the states of Qi, Chu, Jin, and Qin during the Warring States Period (5th to

3rd centuries BC). This alliance, known as the "Baigou Covenant," aimed to counter the expansionist ambitions of the state of Yan.

4. Natural Barriers and Terrain:

China's diverse geography provided natural defensive advantages. Mountain ranges, rivers, and rugged terrain often acted as natural barriers that hindered the movement of invading forces. These geographical features were strategically incorporated into defense plans, with fortifications and garrisons positioned to take advantage of the terrain.

For instance, the Yangtze River in southern China served as a formidable natural barrier against northern invasions. The ancient state of Chu, located south of the Yangtze, used the river's protection to its advantage.

5. Diplomacy and Treaties:

Diplomacy played a crucial role in managing external threats. Chinese states engaged in negotiations with neighboring tribes and states to maintain a degree of stability along their borders. Treaties and agreements were signed to establish non-aggression pacts and facilitate trade.

For example, the Western Han Dynasty (206 BC - 9 AD) established diplomatic relations with the Xiongnu, a powerful nomadic confederation, through a series of treaties. These treaties helped reduce hostilities and ensured peaceful coexistence for a time.

6. Defensive Warfare and Tactics:

Ancient China developed various defensive warfare strategies and tactics to repel invading forces. These tactics included guerrilla warfare, ambushes, and the use of defensive structures like trenches and moats. The goal was to weaken the enemy's advance and create favorable conditions for counterattacks.

Sun Tzu's "The Art of War" provided valuable insights into military strategy and tactics, emphasizing the importance of adaptability, intelligence gathering, and deception. These principles guided Chinese military thought for centuries and remain influential in military theory worldwide.

In summary, ancient China's defensive strategies and structures were multifaceted and adapted to the changing geopolitical landscape. City walls, fortifications, watchtowers, and the Great Wall of China stood as physical barriers against invaders. Defensive alliances, diplomacy, and natural terrain added additional layers of protection. The lessons learned from these historical defense systems continue to inform military strategy and the preservation of cultural heritage today.

The early concepts of wall building in ancient China were born out of necessity, driven by a combination of geographical, political, and military factors. These concepts laid the groundwork for the development of the iconic Great Wall of China and the enduring importance of defensive structures in Chinese history.

The concept of building walls for defense dates back to China's earliest dynastic periods, with evidence of walls and fortifications found in archaeological sites from the Shang Dynasty (c. 1600–1046 BC) and the Zhou Dynasty (c. 1046–256 BC). These early walls were relatively simple and constructed using readily available materials like earth and wood. Their purpose was to protect settlements and early urban centers from attacks by neighboring tribes and marauders.

One of the primary drivers for wall construction during this era was the frequent conflict and warfare between rival states and factions. The period known as the Spring and Autumn Period (c. 771–476 BC) and the subsequent Warring

States Period (c. 475–221 BC) were characterized by intense power struggles and territorial disputes among feudal states. As a result, city walls and fortifications became vital for safeguarding populations, resources, and territorial boundaries.

The early walls were typically built around cities, towns, and strategic locations such as passes and river crossings. These walls served as physical barriers to protect against external threats and provided a sense of security for the people living within their confines. Walls varied in size and complexity depending on the wealth and resources of the state or city constructing them. Some were relatively modest, while others were more formidable, featuring multiple layers of walls, gates, and watchtowers.

The construction techniques used in the early walls were basic but effective. Earth and wooden structures were reinforced with layers of compacted soil and rocks, making them resilient against assaults. Watchtowers were strategically placed along the walls to provide vantage points for sentries and defenders to monitor the surrounding landscape for potential threats.

One of the early principles guiding wall construction was the strategic positioning of walls to take advantage of natural terrain features. Mountains, rivers, and rugged terrain often served as natural barriers that complemented the walls' defensive capabilities. Settlements and fortifications were strategically located at key points, combining the protection of the walls with the advantages of natural defenses.

It's important to note that the early concept of wall building in ancient China was not limited to static defensive structures. Walls were part of a broader defensive strategy that included the training and organization of armies, the use of tactics to repel invaders, and diplomatic efforts to secure alliances with neighboring states.

The idea of a "defensive vision" began to take shape during this early period. Leaders and statesmen recognized the need for a coherent strategy to defend their territories effectively. This included fortifying key locations, maintaining well-trained armies, and devising tactics to repel potential invaders.

The concepts and principles of wall building evolved over time, especially as China transitioned from a collection of warring states to a unified empire under the Qin Dynasty (221–206 BC). The Qin Dynasty is renowned for constructing the initial portions of what would become the Great Wall of China. These early walls were built to consolidate and protect the newly unified empire's northern frontier from the threats posed by nomadic tribes, particularly the Xiongnu.

The Great Wall's construction was a monumental undertaking that spanned centuries and multiple dynasties. It involved connecting and extending existing walls and fortifications, creating a vast network of defensive structures. The Great Wall of China, as it is commonly known today, stands as a testament to the enduring legacy of early wall-building concepts in China.

In summary, the early concepts of wall building in ancient China were shaped by the need for defense in a tumultuous period marked by conflict and territorial disputes. These concepts evolved over time, culminating in the construction of the Great Wall of China, an iconic symbol of China's historical commitment to safeguarding its territories and people. The principles of strategic positioning, the use of natural terrain, and the integration of walls into broader defensive strategies continue to influence military and architectural thinking today.

Chapter 2: The Warring States Period and Early Defensive Structures (475 - 221 BC)

The turbulent era of the Warring States in ancient China, spanning from approximately 475 BC to 221 BC, was a period of profound political, military, and social upheaval. During this era, the once-unified Zhou Dynasty fragmented into numerous independent states, each vying for supremacy. This tumultuous period laid the groundwork for significant developments in Chinese history, including the eventual unification of China under the Qin Dynasty and the emergence of philosophical and military thought that would shape the nation for centuries to come.

The decline of the Zhou Dynasty, which had ruled China for centuries, set the stage for the Warring States Period. The Zhou kings had become nominal figureheads with little real authority, while regional rulers known as "zhuhou" or "feudal lords" gained increasing autonomy. Disputes over land, resources, and power escalated, leading to the emergence of powerful states that sought to expand their territories and influence.

One of the defining features of the Warring States Period was the intense competition and conflict between these states. Historians typically identify seven major states during this era: Qin, Qi, Chu, Yan, Han, Zhao, and Wei, although there were others as well. These states engaged in a complex web of alliances, rivalries, and shifting allegiances as they sought to gain dominance.

The pursuit of territorial expansion was a driving force behind the conflicts of this period. States engaged in military campaigns to conquer neighboring regions and absorb smaller states into their domains. Battles were fought with increasingly sophisticated tactics and weaponry, including the use of cavalry, chariots, and crossbows.

Diplomacy also played a pivotal role during the Warring States Period. States formed alliances and engaged in intricate negotiations to bolster their positions. Diplomatic marriages, political marriages where members of one state's ruling family married into another, were common strategies to secure alliances and peace agreements. The state of Qi, for example, used this tactic to form an alliance with the powerful state of Chu.

The emergence of renowned military strategists and philosophers during this era significantly impacted China's future. Among the most notable figures was Sun Tzu, the author of "The Art of War." Sun Tzu's treatise on military strategy and tactics remains influential not only in China but also globally. His teachings emphasized the importance of intelligence, deception, and adaptability on the battlefield, principles that continue to guide military thought.

In addition to military strategists, the Warring States Period saw the rise of influential philosophers who profoundly shaped Chinese thought. Confucius, the founder of Confucianism, lived during this era. He sought to address the moral and ethical dilemmas of the time, emphasizing the importance of benevolence, righteousness, and social harmony. Confucian principles would go on to play a central role in Chinese culture, ethics, and governance.

Confucius was not alone in his philosophical endeavors. Other prominent philosophers, such as Laozi, the founder of Daoism, and Mozi, the founder of Mohism, offered alternative visions of how to address the turmoil of the Warring States Period. These philosophical schools explored questions of ethics, morality, and the nature of governance, contributing to a rich tapestry of intellectual thought during the era.

One of the key developments of this period was the concept of "xingfa" or "legalism." Legalism advocated for strict laws, harsh punishments, and centralized control to maintain order and enforce the authority of the ruling state. The state of Qin, under the leadership of Shang Yang, famously implemented legalist policies, setting the stage for Qin's eventual unification of China.

The competition and conflict among the states eventually led to a state of exhaustion and depletion of resources. As the smaller states were absorbed by larger ones, the balance of power shifted. The state of Qin, under the ambitious ruler Qin Shi Huang, emerged as the dominant force.

In 221 BC, Qin Shi Huang successfully unified China, marking the end of the Warring States Period and the beginning of the Qin Dynasty. His reign brought about significant changes, including standardizing writing, currency, and weights and measures, as well as the construction of the Great Wall of China. Despite the harsh legalist policies, his centralized rule set the stage for the later Han Dynasty and the establishment of imperial China.

In summary, the turbulent era of the Warring States in ancient China was a time of intense conflict, diplomacy, and intellectual ferment. It witnessed the rise of influential philosophers and military strategists whose ideas continue to shape China and the world today. This period of chaos and transformation ultimately paved the way for the unification of China and the establishment of imperial rule, leaving a lasting legacy on the nation's history and culture.

The emergence of defensive measures in ancient China was a response to the ever-present threats and challenges faced by various states and regions. Over the centuries, Chinese leaders and military strategists developed a range of measures to protect their territories, resources, and populations. These defensive strategies evolved in tandem with changes in technology, political dynamics, and external threats.

1. City Walls and Fortifications:
City walls and fortifications were among the earliest defensive measures employed by Chinese states. These walls were constructed around cities, towns, and key settlements to serve as physical barriers against invading forces. They were typically made from materials like earth, wood, and stone, depending on the region and available resources. The walls provided protection for urban centers and acted as deterrents to potential attackers.

2. Watchtowers and Beacon Towers:
Watchtowers were strategically placed along city walls and defensive lines to provide elevated vantage points for guards and sentries to monitor the surrounding terrain. These watchtowers played a crucial role in early warning systems, allowing defenders to detect approaching enemy forces and signal for reinforcements.

Beacon towers, also known as signal towers, were used to transmit urgent messages over long distances. By lighting signal fires or sending smoke signals, messages could be relayed swiftly, facilitating coordinated responses to threats or emergencies.

3. Natural Barriers and Terrain:
China's diverse geography provided natural defensive advantages. Mountain ranges, rivers, and rugged terrain often acted as natural barriers that hindered the movement of invading forces. Chinese states strategically positioned settlements and fortifications at key points to take advantage of these natural defenses.

4. Diplomacy and Treaties:
Diplomacy played a significant role in managing external threats. Chinese states engaged in negotiations and alliances

with neighboring states and tribes to maintain a degree of stability along their borders. Treaties and agreements were forged to establish non-aggression pacts, trade relationships, and mutual defense agreements.

5. Defensive Alliances:

Chinese states often formed defensive alliances with neighboring states to enhance their collective security. These alliances were forged through treaties and agreements that stipulated mutual defense in the event of an attack. The goal was to deter potential invaders by presenting a united front against external threats.

6. Defensive Warfare and Tactics:

Ancient China developed various defensive warfare strategies and tactics to repel invading forces. These tactics included guerrilla warfare, ambushes, and the use of defensive structures like trenches and moats. The objective was to weaken the enemy's advance and create favorable conditions for counterattacks.

7. Military Training and Organization:

The training and organization of armies were crucial aspects of defensive measures. Well-trained and disciplined soldiers were essential for effectively repelling invaders. Chinese states invested in military training to ensure that their armies were prepared to defend their territories.

8. Use of Diplomatic Marriages:

Diplomatic marriages were a common strategy to secure alliances and maintain peace. Members of one state's ruling family would marry into another state's ruling family, creating familial ties and fostering goodwill between states. This practice helped prevent conflicts and promote diplomatic relations.

9. Development of Defensive Philosophy:

Philosophical and ethical systems, such as Confucianism, emphasized the importance of moral conduct, social harmony, and just governance as essential elements of defense. These philosophical principles contributed to the idea that strong, ethical leadership was necessary for a state's security and stability.

In summary, the emergence of defensive measures in ancient China was a multifaceted response to the complex and dynamic challenges faced by Chinese states. These measures encompassed physical defenses, diplomacy, alliances, and the cultivation of ethical and philosophical values. They were essential in safeguarding territories and ensuring the security and well-being of the population, ultimately contributing to the endurance and resilience of ancient Chinese states.

The construction of the Great Wall of China, one of the most iconic architectural marvels in human history, was a monumental undertaking that spanned centuries and dynasties. It began as a series of disconnected defensive walls and fortifications, which over time, evolved into the extensive and continuous structure known today as the Great Wall. This remarkable feat of engineering and human labor required careful planning, innovation, and the contributions of multiple dynasties and leaders.

The idea of constructing defensive walls in northern China dates back to the early dynastic periods, with evidence of such walls dating as far back as the Shang Dynasty (c. 1600–1046 BC) and the Zhou Dynasty (c. 1046–256 BC). These early walls served as protection for settlements and early urban centers, safeguarding them against incursions by neighboring tribes and marauders. However, it was during the Warring States Period (c. 475–221 BC) that the concept of connecting these walls and fortifications began to take shape.

The need for a more extensive and cohesive defensive structure became apparent as Chinese states engaged in intense competition and conflict during the Warring States Period. The primary threat came from nomadic tribes in the north, particularly the Xiongnu, who posed a significant challenge to China's northern states. The states of Qin, Yan, and Zhao, among others, recognized the necessity of fortifying their northern borders to deter these nomadic threats.

The state of Qin, under the leadership of Shang Yang, was one of the most proactive in fortifying its northern frontier. Shang Yang implemented legalist policies that emphasized centralized control and strict enforcement of laws. These policies included the development of infrastructure and defenses, laying the groundwork for the Great Wall's future expansion.

The first significant efforts to connect and extend these early walls occurred during the reign of Qin Shi Huang, the first emperor of the Qin Dynasty (221–206 BC). Qin Shi Huang is renowned for his ambitious and often brutal unification of China. Recognizing the strategic importance of the walls, he initiated a project to link and expand these defensive structures, creating a more comprehensive northern defense line.

The Great Wall constructed during the Qin Dynasty was a significant engineering feat. It was built using a variety of materials, including earth, wood, and stone. Laborers, including conscripted peasants and criminals, were mobilized to construct the wall and its associated fortifications. The walls featured watchtowers and fortresses at regular intervals to provide garrisons with a vantage point for monitoring the border and defending against invaders.

Despite the impressive achievements of the Qin Dynasty in wall construction, the Great Wall as it is commonly known today was far from complete. The Qin Dynasty's unification of China was short-lived, and the construction of the wall fell into disrepair and disuse during the subsequent Han Dynasty (206 BC – 220 AD).

It was during the Han Dynasty that the Great Wall experienced significant expansion and reconstruction. Emperor Wu of Han (r. 141–87 BC) initiated large-scale efforts to fortify the northern frontier. These efforts included extending the wall farther into northern territories and rebuilding sections that had deteriorated over time.

One of the most significant contributors to the construction of the Great Wall during the Han Dynasty was General Meng Tian. Meng Tian was appointed by Emperor Wu to oversee the expansion and reinforcement of the wall. He implemented innovative engineering techniques, such as using tamped earth and stone for construction, which enhanced the wall's durability.

The expansion of the Great Wall during the Han Dynasty played a crucial role in facilitating the movement of goods and people along the Silk Road. It also served as a symbol of China's power and reach, extending its influence beyond its borders.

Over the centuries, the construction and maintenance of the Great Wall continued under various dynasties, including the Jin, Northern Wei, Northern Qi, Sui, and Tang Dynasties. Each dynasty made contributions to its extension and reinforcement, adapting the wall to the evolving geopolitical landscape.

The Ming Dynasty (1368–1644) is renowned for its significant restoration and fortification efforts on the Great Wall. During this period, the wall was reinforced with bricks and stone, and extensive watchtowers and fortresses were built. This extensive renovation and fortification efforts led to the Great Wall's enduring image as we know it today.

The construction of the Great Wall was not only a testament to the military and defensive prowess of ancient China but also a reflection of its cultural and historical significance. It symbolized the determination and resilience of the Chinese people in the face of external threats. It also served as a physical embodiment of the rich history and heritage of China.

In summary, the construction of the Great Wall of China was a protracted and complex process that spanned centuries and dynasties. It began as a series of disconnected defensive walls and fortifications and evolved into the iconic structure that stands today. The wall's construction required innovative engineering, laborious effort, and the contributions of multiple dynasties and leaders. It not only served as a defensive barrier but also played a profound role in shaping China's history, culture, and identity.

Chapter 3: Qin Dynasty: The Birth of the Great Wall (221 - 206 BC)

The reign of Qin Shi Huang, the first emperor of the Qin Dynasty (221–206 BC), marked a transformative period in Chinese history, characterized by ambitious construction projects that left a lasting impact on the nation. Qin Shi Huang's rule was defined by his determination to unify China, and his ambitious construction initiatives were integral to achieving this goal.

Qin Shi Huang's most renowned construction project was the Great Wall of China. While the concept of the Great Wall existed before his reign, he initiated significant efforts to connect and extend these defensive walls, creating a more comprehensive and formidable barrier against external threats. The purpose of the Great Wall was to protect the northern border of the Qin Empire from incursions by nomadic tribes, particularly the Xiongnu.

Under the leadership of Qin Shi Huang, the Great Wall underwent extensive expansion and reinforcement. He ordered the connection of existing walls and the construction of new sections, resulting in a more continuous and fortified structure. The wall was constructed using various materials, including earth, wood, and stone, and featured watchtowers and fortresses at regular intervals. These watchtowers provided garrisons with vantage points for monitoring the border and defending against invaders.

Qin Shi Huang's ambitious efforts to fortify the Great Wall were not limited to construction alone. He also implemented strategic reforms to bolster the defenses along the wall. One of his most significant contributions was the standardization of the written script, weights and measures, and currency.

This standardization facilitated communication, logistics, and coordination among the various regions of the empire, including those responsible for defending the Great Wall.

To oversee the construction and maintenance of the Great Wall, Qin Shi Huang appointed trusted generals and officials, including Meng Tian, who played a pivotal role in its expansion. Meng Tian implemented innovative engineering techniques, such as using tamped earth and stone, to enhance the wall's durability and effectiveness.

In addition to the Great Wall, Qin Shi Huang initiated other ambitious construction projects that reshaped the Chinese landscape. He ordered the construction of an extensive network of roads and canals to facilitate transportation and communication throughout the empire. These infrastructure projects improved the mobility of troops and resources, strengthening the empire's ability to respond to external threats.

Another significant construction project during Qin Shi Huang's reign was the standardization of measurement units and road widths. This standardization enhanced trade and commerce by streamlining transactions and facilitating the movement of goods across the empire. It also contributed to a sense of unity and uniformity within the empire.

Qin Shi Huang's most enduring and controversial construction project, however, was his mausoleum complex, famously known as the "Qin Shi Huang Mausoleum." This massive undertaking involved the creation of an elaborate tomb complex for the emperor, complete with a terracotta army of thousands of life-sized soldiers, horses, and chariots. The purpose of the terracotta army was to accompany the emperor in the afterlife and protect his spirit.

The construction of the Qin Shi Huang Mausoleum showcased the emperor's desire for immortality and his quest for eternal rule. While it was a remarkable feat of craftsmanship and engineering, it required a vast workforce, including artisans and laborers who worked under strict conditions.

Qin Shi Huang's ambitious construction projects were not without controversy. The massive labor force required for these endeavors often faced harsh conditions and heavy taxation, leading to discontent among the population. Additionally, the standardization of scripts, measures, and currency faced resistance from those who saw it as an imposition on local customs.

Despite the controversies, Qin Shi Huang's ambitious construction initiatives played a pivotal role in unifying China under a centralized rule. His legacy, including the Great Wall and the standardization of measures and script, endured for centuries and contributed to the cultural and historical foundation of China.

In summary, Qin Shi Huang's reign was marked by ambitious construction projects that reshaped China's physical and cultural landscape. His determination to unify the empire through the construction of the Great Wall, infrastructure improvements, and the standardization of measures left a profound and lasting impact on Chinese history. While his rule was not without challenges and controversies, his legacy as a visionary leader and builder of China's iconic structures endures to this day. The concept of the Great Wall of China as a unified and continuous barrier emerged gradually over centuries, with various dynasties and leaders contributing to its construction and expansion. Linking existing walls into a unified barrier was a complex and ambitious endeavor that required strategic planning, engineering innovation, and a shared vision of safeguarding China's northern borders.

The notion of defensive walls in ancient China dates back to early dynastic periods, with evidence of walls built during the Shang and Zhou Dynasties (c. 1600–1046 BC and c. 1046–256

BC, respectively). These walls were constructed around settlements and urban centers to provide protection from external threats, particularly nomadic tribes and marauders.

During the Warring States Period (c. 475–221 BC), the need for more extensive and cohesive defensive measures became apparent as Chinese states engaged in intense competition and conflict. The primary threat came from nomadic tribes in the north, particularly the Xiongnu, who posed a significant challenge to China's northern states. This period laid the groundwork for the idea of connecting and extending these walls into a comprehensive defensive structure.

The state of Qin, under the leadership of Shang Yang, was one of the most proactive in fortifying its northern frontier during the Warring States Period. Shang Yang implemented legalist policies that emphasized centralized control and strict enforcement of laws. These policies included the development of infrastructure and defenses, laying the groundwork for the Great Wall's future expansion.

The first significant efforts to link existing walls into a unified barrier occurred during the reign of Qin Shi Huang, the first emperor of the Qin Dynasty (221–206 BC). Qin Shi Huang is renowned for his ambitious unification of China, and the construction of the Great Wall was an integral part of his efforts.

Qin Shi Huang recognized the strategic importance of the walls in protecting the northern border of his empire from the Xiongnu and other threats. He initiated a project to connect and extend these defensive structures, creating a more comprehensive northern defense line. This project involved the standardization of walls, roads, and infrastructure to enhance defensive capabilities.

Under Qin Shi Huang's leadership, the Great Wall underwent extensive expansion and reinforcement. Existing walls were connected, and new sections were constructed, resulting in a more continuous and fortified structure. The wall was built using various materials, including earth, wood, and stone, with watchtowers and fortresses strategically placed along its length to provide garrisons with vantage points for monitoring the border and defending against invaders.

One of the key figures in overseeing the construction of the Great Wall during the Qin Dynasty was General Meng Tian. Meng Tian implemented innovative engineering techniques, such as using tamped earth and stone, to enhance the wall's durability and effectiveness. His contributions played a crucial role in transforming the Great Wall into a formidable defensive barrier.

Despite the impressive achievements of the Qin Dynasty in wall construction, the Great Wall as it is commonly known today was far from complete during this period. The Qin Dynasty's unification of China was short-lived, and the construction of the wall fell into disrepair and disuse during the subsequent Han Dynasty (206 BC – 220 AD).

It was during the Han Dynasty that the Great Wall experienced significant expansion and reconstruction. Emperor Wu of Han (r. 141–87 BC) initiated large-scale efforts to fortify the northern frontier. These efforts included extending the wall farther into northern territories and rebuilding sections that had deteriorated over time.

In summary, the process of linking existing walls into a unified barrier to create the Great Wall of China was a gradual and complex undertaking that spanned centuries and dynasties. It began as a series of disconnected defensive walls and fortifications and evolved into the iconic structure that stands today. The efforts of leaders like Qin Shi Huang and General Meng Tian were instrumental in transforming the Great Wall into a formidable defense against external threats, and subsequent dynasties continued to contribute to its expansion and reinforcement. The Great Wall remains a symbol of China's historical and cultural heritage, as well as its determination to protect its borders.

The Great Wall of China, an iconic symbol of Chinese history and culture, originally served a multifaceted purpose that evolved over time. Its initial construction and significance were rooted in the need for defense and protection against external threats, primarily from nomadic tribes in the north. However, as centuries passed and dynasties changed, the wall's role and meaning underwent transformations that extended beyond mere military fortifications.

The Early Defensive Imperative:

The earliest origins of the Great Wall can be traced back to ancient China's early dynastic periods, including the Shang and Zhou Dynasties (c. 1600–256 BC). During these times, rudimentary walls and fortifications were constructed around settlements to provide protection from incursions by neighboring tribes and marauders. These early walls were localized defenses, intended to safeguard specific territories.

The Warring States Period and Northern Threats:

The concept of a unified and continuous defensive barrier began to take shape during the turbulent Warring States Period (c. 475–221 BC), a time of intense competition and conflict among Chinese states. The primary threat to China's northern states came from nomadic tribes, particularly the Xiongnu, who posed a significant challenge to China's security and stability. It was during this period that the need for a more extensive and cohesive defense became apparent.

Qin Shi Huang and the Unified Wall:

The unification of China under the Qin Dynasty (221–206 BC) marked a pivotal moment in the evolution of the Great Wall. Qin Shi Huang, the first emperor of the Qin Dynasty, recognized the strategic importance of the walls in protecting the northern border of his empire. He initiated an ambitious project to connect and extend these defensive structures, creating a more comprehensive northern defense line. The primary purpose was to deter and repel external threats, particularly the Xiongnu.

The Wall's Role as a Defensive Barrier:

The Great Wall constructed during the Qin Dynasty was a significant engineering feat. It featured watchtowers and fortresses at regular intervals, providing garrisons with vantage points for monitoring the border and defending against invaders. The wall was constructed using various materials, including earth, wood, and stone, depending on the region and available resources. It served as a physical barrier that hindered the movement of enemy forces and provided a line of defense against potential attacks.

Standardization and Unification:

Qin Shi Huang's contributions to the Great Wall extended beyond construction. He implemented standardization measures, including the standardization of weights and measures, currency, and even the script. These standardization efforts enhanced communication, logistics, and coordination among different regions of the empire. The wall, in this context, symbolized not only physical defense but also the unification of diverse regions under a centralized rule.

The Han Dynasty and Expansion:

While the Qin Dynasty's rule was relatively short-lived, the construction and expansion of the Great Wall continued during the subsequent Han Dynasty (206 BC – 220 AD). Emperor Wu of Han (r. 141–87 BC) initiated significant efforts to fortify the northern frontier. Under his leadership, existing walls were extended deeper into northern territories, and sections that had deteriorated were rebuilt.

This expansion reinforced the wall's role as a defensive barrier against external threats.

Beyond Defense:

As centuries passed and dynasties changed, the Great Wall's significance extended beyond its initial role as a military fortification. It became a symbol of China's historical resilience and determination to protect its borders. The wall also facilitated the movement of goods and people along the Silk Road, fostering cultural exchange and economic development.

Cultural Symbolism:

The Great Wall began to embody cultural and historical symbolism, representing the enduring spirit of the Chinese people. It became a tangible link to China's past, reminding generations of the challenges overcome and the unity forged in the face of adversity.

Modern Significance:

In the modern era, the Great Wall has transcended its historical role to become a global icon of China. It is a UNESCO World Heritage site and a testament to human ingenuity and determination. Tourists from around the world visit the wall, not only to appreciate its historical significance but also to witness the breathtaking beauty of its winding path across diverse landscapes.

In summary:

The Great Wall of China's initial purpose and significance were firmly rooted in the need for defense against external threats, particularly from northern nomadic tribes. It evolved over time to encompass cultural, historical, and symbolic meanings that extend beyond its role as a physical barrier. Today, the Great Wall stands as a testament to China's rich history and enduring spirit, captivating the imagination of people worldwide.

Chapter 4: The Han Dynasty and Expanding the Frontier (206 BC - 220 AD)

The Han Dynasty's strategy for northern expansion marked a crucial phase in Chinese history, characterized by the consolidation and extension of Chinese territory into the vast regions north of the Yellow River. This strategy, implemented during the Western Han Dynasty (206 BC – 9 AD), sought to establish stability, security, and economic prosperity in these frontier territories while addressing the constant threat posed by nomadic tribes, particularly the Xiongnu.

1. Diplomatic Alliances and Tributary Relations:

The Western Han Dynasty initially adopted a diplomatic approach to secure its northern frontier. One of the key strategies was establishing tributary relations with neighboring nomadic tribes, including the Xiongnu. These agreements allowed the Han to maintain peaceful relations and secure the support of some nomadic leaders who were willing to pay tribute to the Chinese court in exchange for recognition and gifts.

2. Military Fortifications:

In addition to diplomacy, the Han Dynasty recognized the importance of maintaining a strong military presence along the northern border. The construction and fortification of defensive walls and garrisons played a critical role in safeguarding the frontier. These fortifications served as a physical barrier to deter invasions and allowed the Han to control key strategic points along the Silk Road.

3. Colonization and Settlement:

The Han Dynasty actively encouraged the migration of Han Chinese people into the northern frontier regions.

Colonization and settlement efforts aimed to establish a Han Chinese presence in these territories, promote agricultural development, and strengthen China's claim to the land. These settlers helped increase the productivity of the region, contributing to economic growth and stability.

4. Economic Development and Trade:

To foster economic prosperity in the northern frontier, the Han Dynasty invested in infrastructure and trade networks. Roads and canals were constructed to facilitate transportation and commerce. The opening of the Silk Road allowed for trade between China and Central Asia, bringing wealth and cultural exchange to the region.

5. Military Campaigns:

While diplomacy and fortifications were crucial components of the strategy, the Han Dynasty also recognized the need for military campaigns to deal with more aggressive nomadic tribes, particularly the Xiongnu. These campaigns, led by capable generals like Wei Qing and Huo Qubing, aimed to suppress Xiongnu incursions and protect the northern border. The success of these military campaigns contributed to a period of stability along the frontier.

6. Tributary System:

The Han Dynasty further expanded its influence by establishing a tributary system with neighboring states and tribes. This system allowed for peaceful coexistence, trade, and the exchange of goods and cultural elements. Tributary states were expected to pay tribute to the Han court in exchange for protection and recognition.

7. Marriage Alliances:

To solidify diplomatic relations and ensure peace along the northern border, the Han Dynasty often used marriage alliances. Marriages between Han Chinese princesses and the leaders of nomadic tribes, including the Xiongnu, were arranged to strengthen ties and promote cooperation.

8. Balancing Act:
Maintaining control over the northern frontier was a delicate balancing act for the Han Dynasty. The Chinese government had to manage relations with various nomadic groups, some of which were hostile, while also promoting economic development and cultural exchange in the region. This strategy required a combination of diplomatic finesse, military strength, and economic investment.

9. Legacy of Stability and Expansion:
The Han Dynasty's strategy for northern expansion laid the foundation for centuries of stability and growth in China's northern frontier regions. It allowed for the expansion of Chinese influence, the flourishing of trade and culture along the Silk Road, and the consolidation of a vast empire. While the challenges posed by nomadic tribes were persistent, the Han Dynasty's approach contributed significantly to China's territorial integrity and its historical and cultural legacy.

In summary, the Han Dynasty's strategy for northern expansion was a multifaceted approach that combined diplomacy, military strength, colonization, and economic development to secure and expand China's northern frontier. This strategy allowed for the consolidation of Chinese territory and established a foundation for cultural exchange and economic growth in the region. It played a pivotal role in shaping China's history and legacy.

The extension and improvement of the Great Wall of China represent a significant chapter in the history of this iconic structure. Over the centuries, different dynasties and leaders undertook efforts to extend, reinforce, and enhance the wall's effectiveness as a defensive barrier against external threats, particularly nomadic tribes. These endeavors contributed to the continuous evolution and expansion of the Great Wall.

1. Han Dynasty (206 BC – 220 AD):

The Han Dynasty, particularly during the Western Han period, played a pivotal role in the expansion and improvement of the Great Wall. Emperor Wu of Han (r. 141–87 BC) initiated extensive efforts to fortify the northern frontier. Existing walls were extended deeper into northern territories, and sections that had deteriorated over time were rebuilt. This expansion reinforced the wall's role as a defensive barrier and symbol of Chinese power.

2. Ming Dynasty (1368 – 1644):

The Ming Dynasty is often associated with the most recognizable and extensive construction and renovation of the Great Wall. During this period, the wall was significantly expanded and fortified to protect against the threat of the Mongols and other northern tribes. The Ming rulers ordered the construction of impressive stone fortifications, watchtowers, and gates along the wall's length. They also employed advanced engineering techniques, such as using bricks and tiles, to enhance its durability.

3. Standardization and Uniformity:

One of the key improvements made to the Great Wall was the standardization and uniformity of its construction. This was particularly evident during the Ming Dynasty, where a standardized design and construction process were implemented. This standardization allowed for consistent quality and ensured that the wall's different sections were compatible with one another.

4. Watchtowers and Fortresses:

To enhance the wall's defensive capabilities, watchtowers and fortresses were strategically placed at regular intervals. These structures served as lookout points for monitoring the border and as defensive positions for garrisons. The construction of watchtowers and fortresses was a significant improvement, as it allowed for better surveillance and rapid response to potential threats.

5. Incorporation of Natural Barriers:
In certain regions where natural geographical features could supplement the wall's defensive capabilities, they were incorporated into the design. This included using cliffs, rivers, and mountains as part of the defensive strategy, making it even more challenging for invaders to breach the barrier.

6. Signal Towers and Communication:
To improve communication and coordination along the wall, signal towers were established. These towers were equipped with signal flags, drums, and other devices to convey messages quickly across long distances. This communication network enhanced the wall's ability to respond to threats promptly.

7. Economic Impact:
The extension and improvement of the Great Wall had economic implications as well. The construction and maintenance of the wall required a significant labor force, which often involved conscripted workers and local communities. This provided employment opportunities and contributed to local economies.

8. Cultural and Historical Legacy:
As the Great Wall evolved and expanded, it became a symbol of China's historical resilience and determination to protect its borders. It embodied the enduring spirit of the Chinese people and left an indelible mark on the nation's cultural and historical identity.

9. Modern Restoration and Preservation:
In contemporary times, efforts have been made to restore and preserve sections of the Great Wall that have fallen into disrepair. UNESCO recognizes the Great Wall of China as a World Heritage site, underscoring its global cultural and historical significance. Conservation and restoration projects

aim to protect this remarkable structure for future generations.

In summary, the extension and improvement of the Great Wall of China represent a dynamic and ongoing process that has evolved over centuries. Different dynasties and leaders have contributed to its expansion and enhancement, turning it into an enduring symbol of China's history, culture, and determination to protect its northern frontier. The Great Wall's legacy continues to captivate the world and remind us of the remarkable feats of engineering and fortitude achieved by the people of ancient China.

The Han Dynasty in ancient China marked a pivotal era in the history of the Great Wall, as it not only extended the wall but also facilitated significant military and cultural exchanges along its northern frontier. This period, known for its territorial expansion, diplomatic overtures, and economic growth, saw the Great Wall serve as both a defensive fortification and a conduit for interactions between China and the diverse cultures of Central Asia.

Territorial Expansion and Defense:

During the Western Han Dynasty (206 BC – 9 AD), the expansion of Chinese territory into the vast regions north of the Yellow River was a strategic imperative. The Great Wall played a central role in this endeavor, as it provided a physical barrier against the constant threat posed by nomadic tribes, most notably the Xiongnu. The construction and extension of the wall during this period aimed to secure the northern border, deter invasions, and establish control over key strategic points.

Military Garrisons and Defense Mechanisms:

To effectively defend the northern frontier, the Western Han Dynasty established military garrisons along the Great Wall. These garrisons were strategically positioned at key junctures, including passes and watchtowers, to monitor and respond to potential threats. Soldiers stationed along the wall were tasked with patrolling the border, sending signals, and protecting the region from external incursions.

Diplomacy and Tributary Relations:
While military defenses were crucial, the Western Han Dynasty also recognized the importance of diplomacy in maintaining stability along the northern border. Diplomatic overtures included establishing tributary relations with neighboring nomadic tribes. Through these agreements, some nomadic leaders agreed to pay tribute to the Chinese court in exchange for recognition and gifts. This diplomatic approach aimed to foster peaceful coexistence and trade.

Colonization and Settlement:
To strengthen China's claim to the northern territories, the Western Han Dynasty actively encouraged the migration of Han Chinese people into these regions. Colonization and settlement efforts involved the establishment of agricultural communities and infrastructure development. The settlers played a pivotal role in increasing agricultural productivity, contributing to economic growth, and reinforcing China's presence in the frontier.

Economic Prosperity and Cultural Exchange:
One of the notable outcomes of the Han Dynasty's expansion was the flourishing of trade and cultural exchange along the Silk Road, which intersected with the Great Wall in various locations. The Silk Road facilitated the movement of goods, ideas, and people between China and Central Asia, resulting in a rich tapestry of cultural exchanges. Chinese silk, ceramics, and other goods were traded for spices, precious metals, and exotic products from distant lands.

Han Dynasty Diplomatic Envoys:
The Han Dynasty dispatched diplomatic envoys, such as Zhang Qian, to explore the western regions beyond the wall.

Zhang Qian's missions were instrumental in establishing contact with Central Asian states and tribes, including the Yuezhi and the Parthians. These diplomatic efforts paved the way for further interactions and alliances, opening up new trade routes and opportunities.

Cultural Influences and Exchange:

The contact between Chinese and Central Asian cultures along the Great Wall's frontier led to a rich exchange of ideas, religions, and artistic influences. Buddhism, for example, began to spread along the Silk Road during this time, bringing new religious beliefs and practices to China. Artistic motifs, such as those seen in Buddhist sculptures and murals, reflected the fusion of diverse cultural elements.

Legacy of the Han Frontier:

The legacy of the Han Dynasty's military and cultural exchange along the Great Wall endures in China's historical and cultural identity. The Silk Road, which ran parallel to the wall, became a symbol of the interconnectedness of civilizations. The wall itself stands as a testament to China's historical resilience and determination to safeguard its borders while embracing the influences of neighboring cultures.

The Western Han Dynasty's expansion along the Great Wall's northern frontier represented a period of dynamic interactions, where defense, diplomacy, colonization, and cultural exchange converged. The wall, once primarily a defensive fortification, evolved into a conduit for economic prosperity and cultural diversity. It serves as a lasting testament to the multifaceted history of ancient China and its engagement with the world beyond its borders.

Chapter 5: The Silk Road Connection and Economic Impact (221 - 589 AD)

The emergence of the Silk Road represents a pivotal moment in human history, marking the beginning of an interconnected world where goods, ideas, cultures, and religions flowed across vast stretches of Asia, Europe, and Africa. This network of ancient trade routes, which facilitated exchanges between the East and the West, played a profound role in shaping the civilizations and societies that thrived along its paths.

Origins of the Silk Road:
The concept of the Silk Road as a transcontinental trade route began to take shape during the Han Dynasty in China (206 BC – 220 AD). This period marked the expansion of Chinese territory into Central Asia, and the need for secure trade routes to connect China with distant regions became apparent. Chinese silk, highly coveted for its quality and craftsmanship, played a central role in initiating these exchanges.

The Silk and Spice Trade:
Silk, known as the "Queen of Textiles," became the most iconic and sought-after commodity along the Silk Road. Chinese silk was exchanged for a variety of goods, including spices, precious metals, gemstones, exotic textiles, and religious artifacts. The demand for spices, particularly from India and Southeast Asia, was driven by their use in culinary and medicinal applications.

The Role of Central Asia:
Central Asia, with its vast steppes, deserts, and oases, played a critical role as the geographical heart of the Silk Road. Cities like Samarkand, Bukhara, and Kashgar served as

important trading hubs and cultural centers where merchants, scholars, and travelers from diverse backgrounds converged. The fertile oases of Central Asia facilitated agriculture and provided rest stops for caravans traveling the arduous routes.

Cultural Exchange and Syncretism:
The Silk Road was not just a conduit for goods but also for ideas and cultures. Along the trade routes, people from different regions and civilizations came into contact, leading to a rich exchange of languages, religions, philosophies, and artistic traditions. This cultural syncretism gave rise to new beliefs, such as the spread of Buddhism from India to China, and the blending of artistic styles in visual and performing arts.

Religious Transmission:
The Silk Road was instrumental in the spread of major religions, including Buddhism, Islam, Christianity, Zoroastrianism, and others. Buddhist missionaries carried their faith from India to Central Asia, China, and Southeast Asia, leaving a profound mark on these regions. Similarly, Islam found its way to Central Asia and eventually into China and India through trade and cultural interactions.

Ancient Technological and Scientific Exchange:
The Silk Road facilitated the exchange of scientific knowledge and technological innovations. For example, the Chinese invention of papermaking spread westward, leading to the proliferation of written materials and the preservation of knowledge. Likewise, the compass, gunpowder, and advanced agricultural practices from China influenced other civilizations along the Silk Road.

The Decline and Legacy:
The decline of the Silk Road as a major trade route can be attributed to various factors, including changes in political dynamics, the rise of maritime trade routes, and the shift of

economic centers. Nevertheless, the legacy of the Silk Road endures in the form of shared cultural heritage, artistic influences, and the enduring connections between the East and the West.

The emergence of the Silk Road was a transformative moment in human history, ushering in an era of global connectivity that transcended geographical and cultural boundaries. It fostered the exchange of goods, ideas, religions, and knowledge, leaving an indelible mark on the civilizations that thrived along its extensive routes. The Silk Road stands as a testament to the enduring human desire for exploration, trade, and cultural exchange.

The Great Wall of China played a significant and multifaceted role in the Silk Road trade, both as a protective barrier and as a symbol of China's commitment to safeguarding its interests along this ancient trade route. While the Great Wall was primarily constructed as a defensive fortification, its presence influenced trade and cultural exchanges in several important ways:

1. Protection of Trade Caravans:
The Great Wall served as a formidable physical barrier against external threats, particularly raids by nomadic tribes such as the Xiongnu and Mongols. This protection allowed trade caravans to traverse the Silk Road with a greater degree of safety.

2. Secure Trade Routes:
The sections of the Silk Road that passed through regions fortified by the Great Wall offered a sense of security to traders and merchants. Knowing that they were traveling through areas protected by the wall encouraged more extensive and reliable trade.

3. Military Garrisons and Surveillance:

Along the Great Wall and its associated fortifications, military garrisons were established. These garrisons not only defended against invasions but also played a role in monitoring and regulating trade activities. They could respond to threats and provide assistance to travelers when necessary.

4. Control of Key Passes and Gates:

The Great Wall often intersected with crucial passes and gates that served as entry and exit points along the Silk Road. These strategic locations allowed the Chinese authorities to exercise control over trade routes and levy taxes on goods passing through, contributing to state revenue.

5. Trade Taxes and Customs:

The Chinese government stationed officials at key points along the wall to collect taxes and customs duties on goods entering and leaving China. These revenues were essential for the state's coffers and supported various government functions.

6. Cultural Exchange and Diplomacy:

The Great Wall was not just a physical barrier but also a symbol of China's commitment to its borders and trade routes. Diplomatic missions, envoys, and traders from other regions could witness the might of the Chinese state as they encountered the wall, fostering diplomatic relations and cultural exchange.

7. Symbol of Chinese Influence:

The Great Wall became an enduring symbol of China's territorial integrity and its resolve to protect its interests. This symbolism contributed to the perception of China as a powerful and influential civilization, attracting trade partners and cultural interactions.

8. Influence on Route Selection:

Traders and caravans often selected routes that passed through regions protected by the Great Wall, as these routes offered a greater sense of security. This, in turn, influenced the development and popularity of specific Silk Road pathways.

9. Engineering and Infrastructure Development:
The construction of the Great Wall and its associated infrastructure, such as roads and watchtowers, improved the overall infrastructure of the regions it crossed. This facilitated the movement of goods and people, further enhancing trade along the Silk Road.

10. Legacy and Cultural Significance: - The Great Wall's presence along the Silk Road left a lasting cultural and historical legacy. It serves as a reminder of the dynamic interactions between different cultures and the enduring importance of trade in shaping civilizations.

In summary, the Great Wall of China played a complex and integral role in Silk Road trade. It provided security, control, and symbolism, fostering an environment conducive to trade and cultural exchange between the East and the West. Its legacy continues to be a testament to the historical significance of this ancient trade route.

The Silk Road, a network of trade routes that connected the East and West for centuries, brought about numerous economic benefits and facilitated profound cultural exchanges. This vast network of interconnected pathways, stretching from China to the Mediterranean, allowed for the flow of goods, ideas, and cultures across regions and civilizations. Here, we explore the economic and cultural aspects of the Silk Road:

Economic Benefits:

1. Trade of Valuable Commodities:
The Silk Road was named after one of its most famous commodities, silk, which was highly sought after in the West.

Besides silk, precious metals, gemstones, spices, textiles, ceramics, and other valuable goods were traded along these routes. This trade in luxury items stimulated economic growth in the regions involved.

2. Economic Prosperity:
The trade along the Silk Road contributed to the economic prosperity of participating civilizations. Cities and regions that served as major trading hubs flourished economically due to the influx of merchants, traders, and travelers.

3. Silk Production and Export:
China, the primary producer of silk, greatly benefited from Silk Road trade. The demand for Chinese silk in the West was insatiable, leading to the establishment of the Silk Route. Chinese silk production techniques were closely guarded secrets, contributing to China's monopoly on silk production.

4. Agricultural Exchanges:
The Silk Road facilitated the exchange of agricultural products, introducing new crops and farming techniques to different regions. For example, Central Asian traders introduced rice cultivation to the Middle East.

5. Banking and Financial Institutions:
The need for reliable financial systems and institutions along the Silk Road led to the development of early banking and financial practices. Moneychangers, credit systems, and banking houses emerged to facilitate trade transactions.

6. Technological Diffusion:
The Silk Road played a role in the diffusion of technologies such as papermaking, printing, and advanced agricultural techniques. These technologies enhanced economic productivity and cultural development.

Cultural Exchange:
1. Language and Writing Systems:
The Silk Road facilitated the exchange of languages and writing systems. Multilingualism was common among

traders, and scripts like the Brahmi script from India influenced the development of scripts in Central Asia.

2. Religious Diffusion:
Major religions such as Buddhism, Islam, Christianity, and Zoroastrianism spread along the Silk Road. Buddhist monks, in particular, played a significant role in carrying their faith from India to Central Asia, China, and beyond.

3. Art and Architecture:
Artistic styles and architectural influences traveled along the Silk Road. Elements of Buddhist art, such as statues and murals, bear witness to the fusion of various cultural aesthetics.

4. Cuisine and Culinary Exchange:
The exchange of spices, recipes, and cooking techniques enriched the culinary traditions of regions along the Silk Road. Ingredients like spices, noodles, and rice became staples in various cuisines.

5. Philosophical and Intellectual Exchange:
The exchange of philosophical and intellectual ideas occurred as scholars and thinkers from different regions engaged in discussions and shared their knowledge. For instance, the spread of Greek philosophy into Central Asia and China influenced local philosophical thought.

6. Textiles and Fashion:
The exchange of textiles and fashion trends led to the blending of styles and the incorporation of foreign designs into local clothing traditions.

7. Cultural Tolerance and Syncretism:
The Silk Road fostered cultural tolerance and syncretism, as diverse cultures coexisted and influenced one another. This led to the development of hybrid cultural traditions and practices.

In summary, the Silk Road was more than just a trade route; it was a conduit for the exchange of goods, ideas, and cultures. This vibrant exchange not only enriched economies but also led to the cross-fertilization of civilizations, leaving an enduring legacy in the form of shared cultural, artistic, and intellectual heritage. The Silk Road's economic benefits and cultural exchanges continue to shape our understanding of the interconnectedness of human history and the power of trade to foster cooperation and understanding across diverse societies.

Chapter 6: Turmoil and Unification during the Sui and Tang Dynasties (589 - 907 AD)

The Sui Dynasty, which ruled China from 581 to 618 AD, is often credited with reunifying China after several centuries of division and fragmentation. This period marked a critical phase in Chinese history as it laid the foundation for the subsequent Tang Dynasty's golden era. The Sui Dynasty's reunification efforts can be understood through several key initiatives and policies:

1. The End of the Southern and Northern Dynasties:
Prior to the Sui Dynasty, China was divided into the Southern and Northern Dynasties, with various regional powers vying for control. The Sui Dynasty, founded by Emperor Wen (Yang Jian), embarked on a mission to reunify the north and south under one central authority.

2. Infrastructure Development:
One of the Sui Dynasty's most significant accomplishments was the construction of the Grand Canal, a massive waterway that connected the Yellow River in the north with the Yangtze River in the south. This project facilitated the efficient transport of goods and troops, fostering economic integration and military mobility.

3. Military Campaigns:
The Sui Dynasty conducted military campaigns to reunify northern China. Emperor Wen initiated campaigns against the Chen Dynasty in the south and the Northern Zhou Dynasty in the north, eventually defeating both and bringing their territories under Sui control.

4. Administrative Reforms:
The Sui Dynasty introduced administrative reforms to centralize and strengthen the imperial government. These

reforms included a revised legal code and the establishment of a more efficient bureaucracy.

5. Cultural Consolidation:

The Sui Dynasty worked to consolidate Chinese culture and traditions. Emperor Wen promoted Confucianism and Buddhism, fostering a sense of cultural unity among the people.

6. Standardization of Measurements:

The Sui Dynasty standardized measurements, weights, and currency, which contributed to economic stability and facilitated trade across the empire.

7. Legacy of the Sui Dynasty:

While the Sui Dynasty's reign was relatively short-lived, its achievements laid the groundwork for the prosperous Tang Dynasty that followed. The Grand Canal, in particular, continued to be a vital economic artery, enabling the efficient movement of goods and people across China.

8. Challenges and Decline:

Despite its accomplishments, the Sui Dynasty faced numerous challenges, including the heavy burden of construction projects, military expeditions, and high taxes. These pressures, combined with internal strife and external threats, contributed to the dynasty's decline.

In summary, the Sui Dynasty's reunification efforts were instrumental in bringing together the fractured regions of China during a critical period in its history. Through infrastructure development, military campaigns, administrative reforms, and cultural consolidation, the Sui Dynasty set the stage for a more unified and prosperous China in the subsequent Tang Dynasty. While the Sui Dynasty's rule was relatively brief, its impact on China's reunification and development cannot be overstated.

The Tang Dynasty, which ruled China from 618 to 907 AD, is often regarded as one of the high points of Chinese power, culture, and civilization. During this period, China experienced a golden age characterized by remarkable achievements in various fields. Here are some key aspects that illustrate the height of Chinese power during the Tang Dynasty:

1. Expansion of Territory:
The Tang Dynasty extended its territorial reach, bringing vast regions under its control, including parts of Central Asia, the Korean Peninsula, and the Tarim Basin. This territorial expansion helped China assert its dominance in East and Central Asia.

2. Economic Prosperity:
The Tang Dynasty witnessed unprecedented economic prosperity. The Grand Canal, constructed during the Sui Dynasty, continued to play a crucial role in facilitating trade and transportation, stimulating economic growth. The period saw significant advances in agriculture, including the adoption of new crops and advanced farming techniques.

3. Cultural Flourishing:
The Tang Dynasty was a cultural powerhouse. It is often celebrated for its contributions to literature, poetry, and art. Notably, the Tang era saw the flourishing of classical Chinese poetry, with poets like Li Bai and Du Fu leaving a lasting legacy. The era also witnessed remarkable advances in Chinese painting, calligraphy, and ceramics.

4. Cosmopolitan Society:
The Tang Dynasty was a cosmopolitan society characterized by cultural diversity. China's capital, Chang'an (modern-day Xi'an), was one of the world's largest and most cosmopolitan cities, with a diverse population of Chinese, foreigners, and merchants from various parts of the world. This cultural diversity contributed to a rich exchange of ideas and traditions.

5. The Silk Road:

The Tang Dynasty played a pivotal role in the Silk Road trade network. It actively promoted trade and cultural exchange along the Silk Road, allowing for the flow of goods, ideas, and cultures between East and West. This trade contributed to the economic prosperity of China.

6. Political Stability and Governance:
The Tang Dynasty established a strong centralized government with a merit-based bureaucracy. This system of governance helped maintain political stability and efficient administration, allowing the dynasty to manage its vast territories effectively.

7. Religious Tolerance:
The Tang Dynasty was characterized by religious tolerance. It welcomed the spread of Buddhism, which had a significant influence on Chinese culture and society. The dynasty also accommodated other faiths, including Daoism, Christianity, and Islam, fostering a spirit of religious pluralism.

8. Military Strength:
The Tang Dynasty maintained a formidable military force that safeguarded its borders and interests. The dynasty successfully repelled external threats and invasions, reinforcing its position as a regional power.

9. Technological Advancements:
The Tang Dynasty saw advancements in various fields, including printing technology, papermaking, and astronomical instruments. These innovations not only contributed to Chinese scientific knowledge but also had a profound impact on the wider world.

10. Decline and Fragmentation: - Despite its many achievements, the Tang Dynasty eventually faced internal strife, rebellion, and fragmentation, leading to its decline and eventual collapse. However, its cultural, economic, and political legacy continued to influence China for centuries to come.

In summary, the Tang Dynasty marked a zenith of Chinese power and influence, characterized by territorial expansion, economic prosperity, cultural flourishing, and political stability. Its contributions to art, literature, technology, and trade left an indelible mark on Chinese civilization and continue to be celebrated as a testament to the heights that a unified and dynamic China could achieve.

Chapter 7: The Ming Dynasty: The Great Wall's Golden Age (1368 - 1644 AD)

The founding of the Ming Dynasty in 1368 marked a significant period in Chinese history, and one of its key initiatives was the restoration and reconstruction of the Great Wall of China. This effort to repair and fortify the wall had important historical and strategic implications. Here is an overview of the founding of the Ming Dynasty and its actions related to the Great Wall:

1. Rise of the Ming Dynasty:

The Ming Dynasty was founded by Zhu Yuanzhang, a former peasant and Buddhist monk who rose to power during the late Yuan Dynasty, which was ruled by the Mongols. Zhu Yuanzhang led a successful rebellion against the Mongols, and in 1368, he declared himself Emperor Hongwu and established the Ming Dynasty, with its capital in Nanjing.

2. Defensive Concerns:

Upon ascending to power, the Ming Dynasty was acutely aware of the need to secure China's northern borders against potential threats from Mongol and other nomadic tribes. One of the key strategies to protect China's heartland was to restore and strengthen the Great Wall.

3. Restoration and Expansion of the Great Wall:

The Ming Dynasty initiated a massive restoration and expansion project for the Great Wall. The primary objectives were to repair existing sections of the wall that had fallen into disrepair, construct new fortifications, and extend the wall's reach in certain areas.

4. Ming Walls:

During the Ming Dynasty, the Great Wall underwent significant renovations. The walls were reinforced with bricks and stone, replacing some of the earlier sections made of tamped earth. Watchtowers, beacon towers, and military garrisons were constructed along the wall to enhance its defensive capabilities.

5. Incorporating Earlier Walls:

The Ming Dynasty incorporated sections of earlier walls into its grand design. This approach allowed them to preserve and build upon the defensive infrastructure established by previous dynasties.

6. Military Garrison Towns:

The Ming Dynasty established military garrison towns along the Great Wall, where troops were stationed to defend against potential invasions. These garrison towns served as both defensive outposts and centers for trade and communication.

7. Symbol of Chinese Unity:

The restoration and expansion of the Great Wall during the Ming Dynasty served not only as a defensive measure but also as a symbol of Chinese unity and national strength. The wall became an enduring emblem of China's commitment to protecting its borders.

8. Legacy and Cultural Significance:

The Ming Dynasty's efforts to restore and fortify the Great Wall had a lasting impact. Many sections of the wall that exist today bear the architectural hallmarks of the Ming Dynasty, including the use of bricks and stone. The Ming-era Great Wall remains a testament to China's historical commitment to defending its territory.

In summary, the founding of the Ming Dynasty in 1368 brought with it a renewed commitment to safeguarding China's northern borders through the restoration and expansion of the Great Wall. This ambitious construction project not only enhanced China's defenses but also left a significant cultural and historical legacy that continues to be celebrated and studied today.

The Ming Wall, a significant architectural achievement in Chinese history, underwent extensive fortifications and improvements during the Ming Dynasty (1368-1644). This period marked a critical phase in the development of the Great Wall of China, as it focused on strengthening its defensive capabilities and enhancing its infrastructure.

Fortifications and Improvements:

The Ming Dynasty, acutely aware of the need to defend against external threats, undertook several key measures to reinforce the Great Wall:

Brick and Stone Construction:

One of the most notable improvements during the Ming Dynasty was the extensive use of brick and stone in the construction of the wall. This transition from tamped earth to more durable materials significantly increased the wall's resilience.

Watchtowers and Beacon Towers:

The Ming Dynasty constructed numerous watchtowers and beacon towers along the Great Wall. These towers served multiple functions, including providing vantage points for monitoring the border, housing troops, and relaying signals using beacon fires to warn of impending invasions.

Fortress Cities:

Along the Great Wall, fortress cities were established as strongholds for defense. These cities were equipped with extensive fortifications, barracks for soldiers, and storage facilities for supplies, ensuring that garrisons stationed along the wall had the necessary resources to defend against attacks.

Improved Passes:

Mountain passes and strategic points along the wall were fortified to resist enemy incursions. Renowned passes like

Jiayuguan and Shanhaiguan were heavily fortified, becoming iconic symbols of the Great Wall's strength.

Gateways and Gates:

The Ming Wall featured gateways and gates at key entry and exit points. These structures served both practical and symbolic purposes, controlling access and egress while emphasizing the importance of the wall's defense.

Moats and Ditches:

In addition to the wall itself, moats and ditches were constructed in some areas to create additional obstacles for potential invaders. These defensive measures were strategically placed to impede enemy movements.

Strategic Positioning:

The Ming Dynasty carefully selected the wall's route, placing it in locations that offered natural defensive advantages. It often followed rugged terrain, such as mountains and cliffs, making it difficult for invaders to traverse.

Military Garrisons:

Along the Ming Wall, numerous military garrisons were established. These garrisons housed soldiers who were responsible for patrolling and guarding the wall, ensuring its constant vigilance.

Cultural Significance:

The fortifications and improvements made during the Ming Dynasty underscored the cultural significance of the Great Wall. It became a symbol of China's commitment to its territorial integrity and the determination to protect its heartland.

Legacy and Historical Impact:

The Ming Wall's fortifications and improvements had a profound and lasting impact:

Enhanced Defense: The Ming Dynasty's efforts significantly strengthened the wall's defensive capabilities, making it a formidable barrier against external threats.

Cultural Icon: The Ming Wall became an enduring cultural icon, representing China's historical commitment to safeguarding its borders and preserving its cultural heritage.

Tourist Attraction: Today, the Ming Wall's well-preserved sections, such as the Badaling and Mutianyu sections, attract millions of tourists from around the world. These sections offer visitors a glimpse into the Ming Dynasty's legacy and its architectural achievements.

In summary, the fortifications and improvements made to the Ming Wall during the Ming Dynasty were pivotal in enhancing its defensive capabilities and cultural significance. This period marked a critical phase in the wall's development, leaving behind a legacy that continues to captivate and inspire people to this day. The Ming Wall stands not only as a physical testament to China's history but also as a symbol of its enduring commitment to protection and preservation.

The Ming Dynasty, which ruled China from 1368 to 1644 AD, was a period of remarkable cultural and economic flourishing. This era witnessed significant developments in various fields, contributing to China's rich heritage and leaving a lasting impact on its history. Here, we explore the cultural and economic aspects of the Ming era:

Cultural Flourishing:

Literature and Poetry:

The Ming Dynasty was renowned for its literary achievements. Ming scholars produced an abundance of classical Chinese literature, including poetry, prose, and historical works. Notable poets such as Li Bai and Du Fu left their mark on Chinese poetry during this period.

The Novel:

The Ming era saw the emergence of the Chinese novel as a literary form. One of the most famous novels of all time,

"Journey to the West" by Wu Cheng'en, was written during this period. It is a classic of Chinese literature and folklore.

Ming Porcelain and Ceramics:
The Ming Dynasty was celebrated for its porcelain and ceramics production. The famous Ming blue-and-white porcelain, characterized by intricate designs in blue on white backgrounds, became highly sought after and remains iconic to this day.

Painting and Calligraphy:
The Ming Dynasty was a golden age for Chinese painting and calligraphy. Artists like Shen Zhou and Tang Yin were known for their masterful brushwork and creative expression. Ming painters developed various styles and techniques that continue to influence Chinese art.

Buddhism and Religious Art:
Buddhism thrived during the Ming Dynasty, leading to the creation of numerous Buddhist temples and religious art. Monasteries like the Shaolin Temple, famous for martial arts, played a significant role in Ming culture.

Economic Prosperity:
Agricultural Advancements:
Innovations in agriculture, including new crop varieties and advanced farming techniques, boosted food production. This, in turn, contributed to population growth and economic stability.

Trade and Commerce:
The Ming Dynasty actively promoted trade and commerce, both domestically and internationally. The establishment of the Silk Road during this period facilitated cultural exchange and economic cooperation with neighboring regions.

The Grand Canal:
The Grand Canal, constructed during earlier dynasties and expanded during the Ming Dynasty, facilitated the transportation of goods, connecting the Yellow River in the

north to the Yangtze River in the south. This massive engineering project enhanced economic integration.

Urbanization:

Ming-era China saw the growth of major cities, including the capital, Nanjing, and later, Beijing. These urban centers became hubs of economic activity, trade, and culture.

Innovation in Printing:

The Ming Dynasty witnessed innovations in printing technology. The world's first known book printed using movable type, the "Jingshi Dadian" encyclopedia, was published during this period, contributing to the spread of knowledge.

Cultural Exchanges:

Trade along the Silk Road and maritime routes fostered cultural exchanges with neighboring countries. Chinese silk, ceramics, and other goods were highly sought after, and Ming-era trade routes played a vital role in connecting China to the world.

Fiscal Reforms:

The Ming Dynasty implemented fiscal reforms to manage the empire's finances more efficiently. These reforms helped stabilize the economy and maintain a strong central government.

The cultural and economic flourishing of the Ming Dynasty played a pivotal role in shaping China's history and legacy. It left behind a rich cultural heritage, artistic achievements, and economic advancements that continue to influence China and the world today. The Ming era stands as a testament to the vibrant and dynamic nature of Chinese civilization during this period of history.

Chapter 8: Life on the Frontier: Soldiers and Communities

Garrisoning the Great Wall during various dynastic periods of Chinese history was a critical aspect of defending the northern borders and safeguarding the heartland of the empire. This practice involved stationing troops, building fortifications, and establishing a military presence along the vast stretches of the Great Wall. The concept of garrisoning the Great Wall evolved over time, reflecting the changing needs and challenges faced by different dynasties.

Early Dynasties and the Beginning of Garrisoning:

The practice of garrisoning the Great Wall can be traced back to ancient China's earliest dynasties, including the Qin Dynasty (221-206 BC) and the Han Dynasty (206 BC-220 AD). During these periods, the Great Wall was primarily constructed to deter invasions from northern nomadic tribes like the Xiongnu. Garrisons were strategically placed at key points along the wall to provide early warning of potential threats and to respond quickly to any incursions.

Ming Dynasty: A Period of Vigorous Garrisoning:

The Ming Dynasty (1368-1644) was a significant period for the Great Wall's garrisons. The Ming Dynasty recognized the wall's critical role in defense and undertook extensive efforts to fortify and maintain it. They established a comprehensive system of garrisons, military towns, and outposts along the wall to ensure constant vigilance.

These garrisons were strategically located at crucial passes, vulnerable points, and areas where threats were most likely to arise. Soldiers stationed in these garrisons were well-trained and equipped to withstand potential attacks from nomadic tribes in the north.

The Ming Dynasty also created fortress cities, such as Jiayuguan and Shanhaiguan, that served as major garrison hubs. These cities were fortified with massive walls, watchtowers, and other defensive structures to protect against enemy incursions.

Challenges Faced by Garrisoned Troops:
Garrisoning the Great Wall was no easy task. Troops stationed along the wall faced harsh living conditions, extreme weather, and the constant threat of invasion. Soldiers had to be self-sufficient and capable of withstanding long periods of isolation. Supplies, including food, water, and weaponry, had to be stockpiled in these remote garrisons to ensure their readiness for any contingencies.

Garrison Life and Cultural Exchange:
Despite the challenges, garrisons along the Great Wall played a significant role in facilitating cultural exchange. Garrisons were often melting pots of different ethnic groups and cultures. Soldiers from various regions of China, as well as foreign allies and captives, mingled in these remote outposts. This cultural diversity contributed to the exchange of ideas, languages, and traditions.

The Decline of Garrisoning:
As China's borders expanded and the nature of threats changed over time, the need for extensive garrisoning of the Great Wall gradually declined. During the Qing Dynasty (1644-1912), for example, the Manchu rulers extended the empire's territory into Inner Asia, reducing the immediate threats from the northern nomadic tribes.

Moreover, the introduction of more advanced military technologies and tactics made it less practical to rely solely on the Great Wall for defense. As a result, the focus shifted to maintaining a strong standing army capable of responding to threats on multiple fronts.

Legacy and Cultural Significance:
Garrisoning the Great Wall left a profound cultural legacy. Stories of bravery and heroism in defending the wall against

invaders became part of Chinese folklore and historical narratives. The Great Wall, with its garrisons and fortifications, remains an enduring symbol of China's commitment to protecting its territory and preserving its cultural heritage.

In summary, garrisoning the Great Wall was a vital strategy employed by various Chinese dynasties to protect their northern borders. It involved the establishment of military outposts, fortifications, and cities along the wall to defend against external threats. While the practice evolved over time and eventually declined, it left a lasting cultural legacy and contributed to the rich tapestry of China's historical narrative.

The daily life of soldiers and frontier communities along the Great Wall of China was characterized by a unique blend of challenges, resilience, and cultural exchange. These individuals, who lived and worked in the remote and often harsh environments of China's northern borderlands, played a crucial role in defending the empire and contributing to the exchange of ideas and traditions. This narrative explores the daily life of soldiers and frontier communities along the Great Wall.

Soldiers on the Frontier:
Soldiers stationed along the Great Wall had a demanding and arduous routine. Their daily life revolved around maintaining a state of readiness to defend against potential threats from northern nomadic tribes. Here are some key aspects of their daily life:

1. Training and Drills:
Soldiers engaged in regular training and drills to hone their combat skills. This included archery practice, cavalry maneuvers, and simulated battle exercises to prepare for various scenarios.

2. Guard Duty:
Guard duty was a fundamental aspect of a soldier's daily routine. Soldiers were posted in watchtowers and along the wall to keep a vigilant eye on the northern frontier. They took shifts to ensure 24/7 surveillance.

3. Patrolling the Wall:
Patrolling the wall was another critical task. Soldiers often embarked on long patrols along the wall, inspecting its integrity and checking for any signs of enemy activity.

4. Maintenance and Repairs:
Soldiers were responsible for maintaining and repairing sections of the Great Wall. This included fixing breaches, reinforcing walls, and ensuring that the fortifications remained in good condition.

5. Communication and Signaling:
Soldiers used a system of beacon fires, smoke signals, and flags to communicate with neighboring garrisons and convey important information.

Frontier Communities:
Life in frontier communities, which often included both military and civilian populations, was shaped by the need for self-sufficiency and cooperation. These communities developed their own unique way of life:

1. Agricultural Activities:
Agriculture was a vital source of sustenance for frontier communities. Residents cultivated crops like wheat, millet, and barley, as well as raised livestock such as sheep and goats.

2. Water Management:
Managing water resources was crucial in these arid regions. Communities constructed irrigation systems and dug wells to ensure a steady supply of water for both agriculture and daily needs.

3. Trade and Barter:

Frontier communities engaged in trade and barter with neighboring regions, exchanging goods like grain, silk, and ceramics for items such as furs and livestock from nomadic tribes.

4. Cultural Exchange:

Frontier communities served as meeting points for people from diverse backgrounds. Soldiers, traders, and travelers brought with them their languages, traditions, and beliefs, contributing to cultural exchange and the blending of cultures.

5. Defensive Structures:

The communities themselves often had defensive structures, including walls and watchtowers, to protect against raids or incursions. These structures mirrored the larger defensive concept of the Great Wall.

6. Family Life:

Families lived in these communities, and life revolved around family structures and traditions. Children were educated, and daily chores were divided among family members.

7. Festivals and Celebrations:

Despite the challenges of frontier life, communities celebrated festivals and cultural events. These occasions provided opportunities for socializing and preserving cultural heritage.

Cultural Exchange and Frontier Life:

One of the intriguing aspects of life on the frontier was the exchange of ideas and traditions. Soldiers, traders, and travelers often interacted with the diverse ethnic groups and cultures found in these regions. This cross-cultural exchange influenced art, cuisine, language, and even religious practices. It contributed to the rich tapestry of Chinese civilization and fostered a sense of resilience and adaptability among frontier communities.

In summary, the daily life of soldiers and frontier communities along the Great Wall of China was marked by a commitment to defense, self-sufficiency, and cultural exchange. These individuals played a crucial role in safeguarding the northern borders of the empire and contributed to the blending of cultures and traditions along the frontier. Their resilience and dedication remain an integral part of China's historical narrative.

Chapter 9: Challenges and Invasions: The Wall in Conflict

The Mongol invasions and their interactions with the Great Wall of China represent a significant chapter in the history of both the Mongol Empire and China. These invasions, led by the Mongol conqueror Genghis Khan and later by his successors, brought immense challenges to the existing political and military structures of China, including the Great Wall. This narrative explores the Mongol invasions and their impact on the Great Wall.

Genghis Khan and the Rise of the Mongol Empire:

In the early 13th century, Genghis Khan, born as Temüjin, united various Mongol tribes and embarked on a campaign of conquest that would eventually result in the creation of the vast Mongol Empire. Genghis Khan was a military genius who excelled in tactics, strategy, and organization.

The Initial Mongol Incursions:

The Mongol Empire first came into contact with the Great Wall during its early expansion efforts. In the early 1200s, Genghis Khan's armies conducted raids on northern China, including the territories protected by the Great Wall. These incursions served as a precursor to more significant invasions.

The Siege of Zhongdu (Beijing):

One of the key moments in the Mongol invasion of northern China was the siege of Zhongdu, the capital of the Jin Dynasty, in 1215. The city was protected by a section of the Great Wall, and Genghis Khan's forces laid siege to it for months. Eventually, the city fell, and this marked a significant conquest in the Mongol advance.

Integration of Northern China:

As the Mongol Empire expanded further into China, they eventually conquered the Jin Dynasty in 1234. This conquest led to the integration of northern China into the Mongol Empire, bringing vast territories that had been defended by the Great Wall under Mongol control.

Kublai Khan and the Yuan Dynasty:
After the death of Genghis Khan, his grandson Kublai Khan established the Yuan Dynasty (1271-1368), with its capital in Beijing. During this period, the Great Wall underwent significant changes. While the wall remained a symbol of defense, it was no longer a direct barrier against the Mongols, who now ruled China.

The Great Wall's Role During the Yuan Dynasty:
During the Yuan Dynasty, the Great Wall served different functions. It continued to function as a means of regulating trade and migration between northern China and the vast Mongol-controlled territories to the north and west. The wall's gateways became important trade hubs, facilitating the exchange of goods and cultures between the Mongols and the Chinese.

The Decline of the Yuan Dynasty:
The Yuan Dynasty eventually faced internal strife and external pressures, leading to its decline. The rise of the Ming Dynasty and the expulsion of the Mongols from China marked a turning point in Chinese history.

The Ming Restoration and Rebuilding the Wall:
The Ming Dynasty (1368-1644) sought to restore Chinese rule and revive traditional defenses. The Ming rulers recognized the ongoing threats from the Mongols and other northern nomadic tribes. They invested significant resources in rebuilding and reinforcing the Great Wall, transforming it into the iconic structure that is widely recognized today.

Ming Dynasty's Great Wall:
The Ming Dynasty's Great Wall was characterized by its massive scale, imposing watchtowers, and strategic placement. It extended over a vast stretch of northern China,

including both existing walls and newly constructed sections. This Ming-era Great Wall was a formidable defensive structure.

Ming-Mongol Relations:
Despite the Ming Dynasty's efforts to rebuild the Great Wall, relations with the Mongols remained complex. The Ming rulers established diplomatic ties with some Mongol groups, seeking alliances to counter other Mongol threats. This diplomatic approach reflected the evolving dynamics between China and the Mongols during this period.

Legacy and Impact:
The Mongol invasions and their interactions with the Great Wall left a lasting impact on China's history. They led to the integration of northern China into the Mongol Empire, influencing cultural exchange and trade. The Ming Dynasty's restoration of the Great Wall, in response to the ongoing Mongol threat, contributed to the wall's enduring cultural significance and its recognition as one of the world's most iconic historical landmarks.

In summary, the Mongol invasions represented a pivotal moment in the history of China and the Great Wall. These invasions, led by Genghis Khan and later Mongol leaders, reshaped the geopolitical landscape of northern China. The Great Wall evolved from being a barrier against Mongol incursions to a symbol of China's resilience and determination to protect its territory. The complex interactions between the Mongols and the Great Wall continue to be a fascinating chapter in the annals of world history.

The Great Wall of China has stood as a symbol of China's determination to protect its territory and people throughout its long history. During times of crisis, this iconic structure took on even greater significance, as it was put to the test in defending against various threats. This narrative explores how the Great Wall responded to and played a crucial role in times of crisis.

1. Early Crisis: The Xiongnu Threat:
During the Warring States Period and the early days of imperial China, the Xiongnu, a confederation of nomadic tribes in the north, posed a significant threat to the Chinese states. The construction of the earliest walls and defensive structures marked an initial response to this crisis. These walls were aimed at deterring Xiongnu incursions, and they laid the foundation for the development of the Great Wall.

2. The Mongol Invasions:
The Mongol Empire, under the leadership of Genghis Khan, launched invasions of northern China in the early 13th century. The Great Wall, which had previously served as a defense against northern threats, was put to the test during these invasions. While the Mongols breached sections of the wall, they also encountered fierce resistance from Chinese defenders.

3. The Ming Dynasty and the Mongol Threat:
The rise of the Ming Dynasty saw a resurgence of efforts to strengthen and expand the Great Wall. The Ming rulers recognized the ongoing Mongol threat and undertook extensive restoration and rebuilding projects. The result was a formidable defensive barrier that stood as a testament to China's preparedness during this period.

4. The Manchu Threat and the Qing Dynasty:
During the 17th century, the Manchu people, who would later establish the Qing Dynasty, posed a significant threat to Ming China. The Great Wall played a role in both defending against and facilitating interactions with the Manchu. Ultimately, the Manchu succeeded in conquering China, leading to the establishment of the Qing Dynasty.

5. The Opium Wars and Foreign Invasions:

In the 19th century, China faced a series of crises brought about by foreign invasions, including the Opium Wars with Britain and the Taiping Rebellion. While the Great Wall was not the primary defense against these incursions, its historical significance and symbolism as a national treasure were reaffirmed during these turbulent times.

6. The Second Sino-Japanese War:

The Great Wall played a limited role in the defense against the Japanese invasion during the Second Sino-Japanese War (1937-1945). The conflict saw the Chinese people's resilience and determination to defend their homeland, symbolized by the Great Wall, which had become a source of inspiration. During the Cultural Revolution (1966-1976), the Great Wall suffered from neglect and damage due to political upheaval and lack of maintenance. This period was a crisis of cultural heritage, and efforts to preserve and protect the Great Wall became essential in the subsequent years. In recent decades, China has undertaken significant efforts to conserve, restore, and protect the Great Wall. It has become a symbol of China's commitment to preserving its historical and cultural heritage, as well as its resolve to address modern environmental challenges. The Great Wall, beyond its historical and defensive roles, has become a global symbol of resilience and determination. It stands as a testament to human ingenuity and the enduring spirit of a nation in times of crisis. In summary, the Great Wall of China has played a multifaceted role in times of crisis throughout history. From deterring invasions to symbolizing national identity and resilience, the Great Wall has been at the heart of China's response to various challenges. Its enduring presence continues to remind us of the importance of preserving cultural heritage and standing strong in the face of adversity.

Chapter 10: The Great Wall's Enduring Legacy

Preservation and restoration efforts aimed at safeguarding the Great Wall of China constitute a vital aspect of its ongoing legacy and cultural significance. This narrative delves into the extensive initiatives, both past and present, undertaken to ensure the survival of this iconic monument.

Historical Significance and Cultural Heritage:
The Great Wall of China is not merely a physical structure; it is a symbol of China's rich history, resilience, and cultural identity. Recognizing its immense historical and cultural value, preservation efforts have been an integral part of China's commitment to safeguarding its heritage.

Early Preservation Efforts:
Efforts to preserve the Great Wall can be traced back to various dynasties throughout China's history. The Ming Dynasty, in particular, undertook extensive reconstruction and fortification projects, leaving behind a legacy of well-maintained sections of the wall.

Cultural Revolution and Neglect:
However, during the tumultuous years of the Cultural Revolution (1966-1976), the Great Wall suffered from neglect and damage due to political upheaval. Some sections were dismantled, and others fell into disrepair. This period marked a crisis in the preservation of China's cultural heritage.

Modern Conservation and Restoration:
In the latter half of the 20th century and into the 21st century, China has redoubled its efforts to preserve and restore the Great Wall. These initiatives include:

1. Conservation and Stabilization:

Conservationists and archaeologists have worked to stabilize sections of the wall that were at risk of collapse due to erosion, weathering, and human activity. This involves repairing damaged bricks and stones, reinforcing walls, and addressing structural issues.

2. Public Awareness and Education:
Promoting public awareness and education about the historical and cultural significance of the Great Wall is a crucial aspect of preservation. Museums, visitor centers, and educational programs have been established to inform visitors about the wall's history and the importance of conservation.

3. Controlled Tourism:
Managing the impact of tourism on the Great Wall is a delicate balancing act. China has implemented measures to control visitor numbers and behavior at popular sections of the wall to minimize wear and tear.

4. International Cooperation:
China has collaborated with international organizations, such as UNESCO, to seek expertise, funding, and support for preservation projects. The Great Wall was designated a UNESCO World Heritage Site in 1987.

5. Technological Advancements:
Preservation efforts benefit from advancements in technology. Modern techniques, such as remote sensing and digital mapping, are used to monitor and assess the condition of the wall. These tools aid in planning restoration projects.

6. Rebuilding and Reconstruction:
In some cases, sections of the wall that were severely damaged or dismantled have been rebuilt or reconstructed using traditional methods and materials to match the original design.

7. Local Engagement:

Engaging local communities in preservation efforts is crucial. These communities often have a deep connection to the Great Wall and play a role in its protection and maintenance.

Challenges and Ongoing Work:

Despite these concerted efforts, challenges remain. Natural erosion, climate change, and urban development in proximity to the wall continue to pose threats. Additionally, maintaining a balance between conservation and public access can be challenging.

The Enduring Legacy:

The ongoing preservation and restoration of the Great Wall underscore its enduring legacy as a symbol of China's rich history and cultural heritage. Beyond its historical significance, the Great Wall serves as a testament to humanity's commitment to safeguarding and celebrating its past.

In summary, the preservation and restoration efforts surrounding the Great Wall of China are not only a testament to China's cultural stewardship but also a reflection of the global importance of preserving our shared heritage. By safeguarding this iconic monument, China continues to honor its past and inspire future generations to appreciate the significance of cultural preservation and historical legacy.

The Great Wall of China, an iconic symbol of China's history and cultural heritage, transcends its historical context and continues to hold immense significance in the modern world. This narrative explores the multifaceted roles and impacts of the Great Wall in contemporary times.

1. Cultural and National Symbol:

The Great Wall remains a potent cultural symbol and source of national pride for the people of China. It serves as a reminder of the country's rich history, resilience, and the enduring spirit of its people. Chinese citizens, as well as people around the world, view the Great Wall as a symbol of China's past and present.

2. UNESCO World Heritage Site:

In recognition of its cultural and historical importance, the Great Wall was designated as a UNESCO World Heritage Site in 1987. This international recognition underscores its significance not only to China but also to the global community. The Great Wall's inclusion on this prestigious list ensures its protection and preservation for future generations.

3. Tourism and Economic Impact:

The Great Wall attracts millions of tourists from around the world each year. This influx of visitors contributes significantly to China's tourism industry and local economies near the wall. The tourism infrastructure around the Great Wall has expanded to accommodate the needs of travelers, including hotels, restaurants, and souvenir shops.

4. Conservation and Restoration:

China has made substantial efforts to preserve and restore the Great Wall. Conservationists and archaeologists work tirelessly to maintain the wall's structural integrity and protect it from natural erosion and human impact. Modern technologies and techniques are employed in these efforts, ensuring that the wall endures for future generations to enjoy.

5. Education and Public Awareness:

The Great Wall is not merely a physical structure but also a source of historical and cultural education. Museums, visitor centers, and educational programs have been established to inform visitors about the wall's history, significance, and the importance of its preservation. These efforts contribute to a broader understanding of Chinese culture and heritage.

6. Diplomacy and International Relations:

The Great Wall has played a role in China's diplomacy and international relations. It is often featured in official state visits and serves as a backdrop for diplomatic meetings and events. The wall's symbolism extends to China's place in the modern world and its role in global affairs.

7. Film and Popular Culture:

The Great Wall has been a recurring theme in film and popular culture worldwide. It has served as the setting for numerous films, documentaries, and literature, further cementing its status as a globally recognized icon. These portrayals contribute to the wall's enduring mystique and appeal.

8. Athletic Challenges:

In recent years, the Great Wall has been the backdrop for athletic challenges and events, including marathons and ultramarathons. These events draw participants from around the world who seek to test their physical and mental endurance against the backdrop of this historic monument.

9. Scientific Research and Exploration:

The Great Wall has also been the subject of scientific research and exploration. Archaeologists and historians continue to study its construction techniques, historical significance, and the lives of the people who built and defended it. This research adds to our understanding of ancient China and the challenges faced by its inhabitants.

10. Environmental Considerations:

As the Great Wall intersects with modern landscapes and ecosystems, there is a growing awareness of the need to balance conservation with environmental concerns. Ensuring the wall's protection while minimizing its impact on the surrounding natural environment is an ongoing challenge.

In summary, the Great Wall of China's significance in the modern world extends far beyond its historical context. It serves as a symbol of China's cultural heritage, a UNESCO

World Heritage Site, a driver of tourism and economic activity, and a source of education and diplomacy. As it continues to inspire awe and fascination, the Great Wall underscores the enduring importance of preserving our shared human heritage in the face of the challenges and opportunities of the modern era.

BOOK 4
MING DYNASTY TREASURES
ART AND CULTURE IN ANCIENT
CHINA (1368 - 1644)
BY A.J. KINGSTON

Chapter 1: The Rise of the Ming Dynasty (1368)

The founding of the Ming Dynasty in China marked a pivotal moment in the country's history, ushering in an era of stability, cultural flourishing, and enduring achievements that would leave a profound impact on the nation and its people. This narrative explores the circumstances and key figures that led to the establishment of the Ming Dynasty and its early years.

Background of Turmoil:
Before the Ming Dynasty, China had endured decades of instability, including the collapse of the preceding Yuan Dynasty, which was founded by the Mongols. The Mongol rule had led to economic hardship, social unrest, and a sense of foreign occupation among the Han Chinese.

The Rise of Zhu Yuanzhang:
Amid this backdrop of turmoil, a peasant rebellion began to take shape in the early 14th century. Zhu Yuanzhang, born into a poor family in the Anhui province, emerged as a charismatic and determined leader. He joined the Red Turban Rebellion, a popular uprising against the Mongol rule. Zhu's strategic acumen, military prowess, and ability to inspire the masses soon made him a prominent figure in the rebellion.

The Fall of the Yuan Dynasty:
Over the years, Zhu Yuanzhang's forces, which included other rebel groups, gained ground and weakened the Yuan Dynasty. The turning point came in 1368 when the Yuan Dynasty's capital, Dadu (modern-day Beijing), fell to Zhu's forces. This marked the end of Mongol rule in China and the start of a new era.

The Proclamation of the Ming Dynasty:

With the fall of the Yuan Dynasty, Zhu Yuanzhang proclaimed himself the Hongwu Emperor, the founding monarch of the Ming Dynasty. The name "Ming" means "bright" or "brilliant," reflecting the hope for a new era of clarity and prosperity. Hongwu would go on to establish his capital in Nanjing, which served as the primary seat of the Ming Dynasty for several decades.

Key Policies of the Hongwu Emperor:

The early years of the Ming Dynasty under Hongwu's rule were marked by several important policies and reforms:

Land Redistribution: To address the issue of land concentration and to reward those who had supported the rebellion, the Hongwu Emperor implemented land redistribution, granting land to peasants and reducing the power of large landowners.

Military Reforms: Recognizing the importance of a strong military, the Hongwu Emperor implemented significant military reforms, including the establishment of a hereditary military system and a standing army.

Civil Service Examinations: The Hongwu Emperor continued the Confucian tradition of civil service examinations, ensuring that officials were selected based on merit rather than birth.

The Haijin Policy: The Haijin policy, implemented in 1371, was an attempt to limit maritime trade and interactions with foreigners, focusing on self-sufficiency and reducing external influences.

Cultural Flourishing:

Under the early Ming emperors, particularly the Yongle Emperor (r. 1402-1424), China experienced a period of cultural flourishing. The Yongle Emperor moved the capital to Beijing and oversaw the construction of the Forbidden City, a magnificent palace complex that would become a symbol of Chinese imperial grandeur.

Zheng He's Voyages:
One of the most remarkable undertakings of the early Ming Dynasty was the series of voyages led by the eunuch admiral Zheng He. These expeditions, spanning from 1405 to 1433, were diplomatic, exploratory, and trade missions that reached as far as Africa and the Middle East. Zheng He's voyages showcased China's naval power and promoted Chinese culture and diplomacy on an international scale.

The End of Early Ming Expansion:
Despite the initial period of expansion and prosperity, the Ming Dynasty faced challenges in the later years of the Hongwu Emperor's rule and beyond. Economic issues, social unrest, and external threats began to strain the empire's resources and stability.

Legacy of the Ming Dynasty:
The Ming Dynasty's legacy is multifaceted and enduring. It left an indelible mark on Chinese culture, art, and governance. The Ming era witnessed remarkable achievements in fields such as porcelain production, literature, and the construction of architectural marvels like the Great Wall and the Forbidden City.

The Decline and Fall of the Ming Dynasty:
While the early Ming Dynasty was marked by stability and cultural achievement, it would eventually succumb to a series of challenges, including internal corruption, fiscal difficulties, and external threats, notably the raids by the Manchu-led Later Jin Dynasty. The Ming Dynasty's decline culminated in the Ming-Qing transition, when the Manchus overran the Ming capital and established the Qing Dynasty in 1644.

In summary, the founding of the Ming Dynasty was a pivotal moment in Chinese history, marked by the rise of Zhu Yuanzhang, the end of Mongol rule, and the establishment of an era of cultural achievement and political stability.

Despite its ultimate decline, the Ming Dynasty's legacy continues to shape China's identity and heritage, making it a critical chapter in the nation's rich history.

The overthrow of the Yuan Dynasty in China was a complex and transformative event that paved the way for the subsequent establishment of the Ming Dynasty. This historical narrative delves into the circumstances, key figures, and pivotal events that led to the downfall of the Yuan Dynasty.

1. Yuan Dynasty Rule:

The Yuan Dynasty, founded by Kublai Khan in 1271, was a foreign dynasty ruled by the Mongols, who had conquered China under the leadership of Genghis Khan. Although the Yuan Dynasty ruled for nearly a century, it faced significant challenges, including resistance from the Chinese population.

2. Social Unrest and Economic Hardship:

The Yuan Dynasty was characterized by heavy taxation, forced labor, and exploitation of the Chinese population. These oppressive policies, along with the burden of supporting Mongol rule, led to widespread social unrest and economic hardship.

3. Emergence of Rebellion Movements:

Amidst this discontent, several rebellion movements began to take shape in different regions of China. These movements were led by local leaders, bandits, and disaffected individuals who sought to resist Yuan rule.

4. The Red Turban Rebellion:

One of the most significant and influential rebellion movements was the Red Turban Rebellion, which emerged in the early 14th century. Zhu Yuanzhang, a charismatic leader from a peasant background, became a prominent figure in this rebellion. Zhu's forces, along with other rebel groups, would later play a pivotal role in the overthrow of the Yuan Dynasty.

5. Zhu Yuanzhang's Leadership:

Zhu Yuanzhang, later known as the Hongwu Emperor, emerged as a capable and determined leader. He was a master strategist and military tactician. Under his leadership, the Red Turban Rebellion grew in strength and began to challenge the Yuan Dynasty's authority.

6. The Capture of Dadu:

A significant turning point occurred in 1368 when Zhu Yuanzhang's forces captured the Yuan Dynasty's capital, Dadu (modern-day Beijing). This marked the end of Mongol rule in China and the beginning of the Ming Dynasty. Zhu proclaimed himself the Hongwu Emperor, the founding monarch of the Ming Dynasty.

7. Yuan Dynasty's Last Stand:

Despite the loss of their capital, remnants of the Yuan Dynasty continued to resist the Ming forces in various parts of China. Some regions remained under Yuan control for several years, and pockets of resistance persisted.

8. Ming Dynasty's Early Reforms:

The early years of the Ming Dynasty were marked by efforts to consolidate power, stabilize the country, and implement reforms. Hongwu Emperor Zhu Yuanzhang initiated policies such as land redistribution, military reforms, and the establishment of a merit-based civil service examination system.

9. Yuan Dynasty's Legacy:

The overthrow of the Yuan Dynasty marked the end of foreign rule in China and the restoration of Chinese governance. It also reflected the enduring aspiration of the Chinese people for self-rule and the preservation of their cultural identity.

10. The Transition to the Ming Dynasty:

The establishment of the Ming Dynasty was a pivotal moment in Chinese history, setting the stage for several centuries of cultural flourishing and stability under Ming rule.

In summary, the overthrow of the Yuan Dynasty was a complex historical process driven by widespread discontent, rebellion movements, and the leadership of figures like Zhu Yuanzhang. It represented a significant shift in China's governance, marking the end of Mongol rule and the beginning of the Ming Dynasty, an era characterized by cultural achievements and the restoration of Chinese authority. The overthrow of the Yuan Dynasty remains a testament to the resilience and determination of the Chinese people to reclaim their homeland and shape their destiny.

Chapter 2: Imperial Patronage of the Arts (1368 - 1398)

The Ming Dynasty, which ruled China from 1368 to 1644, is renowned for its robust support of the arts and culture. Under the patronage of the Ming emperors, the arts flourished, leading to remarkable achievements in literature, painting, ceramics, architecture, and more. This narrative explores the Ming court's support for the arts and its profound impact on Chinese culture.

1. Literary Renaissance:

The Ming Dynasty witnessed a literary renaissance characterized by the revival of classical Chinese literature. Emperors like the Yongle Emperor were enthusiastic patrons of literary endeavors. The court sponsored the compilation of important literary works, including the Yongle Encyclopedia, a vast compilation of knowledge, and the Siku Quanshu, a comprehensive imperial library.

2. Scholarly Pursuits:

The Ming Dynasty continued the Confucian tradition of valuing scholarship and education. The civil service examination system, based on Confucian principles, was refined during this period, promoting meritocracy. Scholars who excelled in these examinations were awarded prestigious positions in the government, encouraging intellectual achievements.

3. Painting and Calligraphy:

Ming Dynasty painters and calligraphers made significant contributions to the world of art. The court sponsored renowned artists, and imperial academies were established to nurture talent. Shen Zhou, Wen Zhengming, and Tang Yin were among the celebrated Ming painters known for their distinctive styles.

4. Porcelain Production:

The Ming Dynasty is famous for its exquisite porcelain production, particularly the Ming blue and white porcelain. The imperial kilns at Jingdezhen produced fine ceramics that were highly prized not only in China but also internationally. The court actively promoted and regulated porcelain production, resulting in beautiful and sought-after pieces.

5. Architectural Marvels:

The construction of architectural marvels reached its zenith during the Ming Dynasty. The most iconic example is the Forbidden City in Beijing, which served as the imperial palace. The Yongle Emperor ordered its construction, showcasing the grandeur of Chinese architecture and design.

6. Garden Artistry:

Ming emperors were passionate about creating exquisite gardens. These imperial gardens were designed as tranquil retreats and exemplified the Ming's appreciation for natural beauty. The classical Chinese garden style, characterized by carefully planned landscapes, intricate pavilions, and serene water features, became an enduring legacy.

7. Drama and Theater:

The Ming Dynasty also nurtured the development of Chinese drama and theater. The Kunqu opera, a refined form of traditional Chinese opera, emerged during this period. The court sponsored theatrical productions, and famous playwrights like Tang Xianzu created timeless works like "The Peony Pavilion."

8. Encouragement of Innovation:

Ming emperors encouraged artistic innovation. They appreciated the preservation of traditional arts while also supporting new forms of expression. This approach allowed artists and craftsmen to experiment with new techniques and styles.

9. Cultural Exchange:

The Ming Dynasty's cultural influence extended beyond its borders. Through trade and diplomatic missions, Ming China engaged in cultural exchanges with neighboring countries, such as Japan. These interactions facilitated the spread of Chinese art and culture throughout East Asia.

10. Enduring Legacy:

The Ming Dynasty's patronage of the arts left an indelible mark on Chinese culture. Its artistic achievements continue to inspire contemporary artists, and the Ming's cultural legacy remains a source of pride for China and a testament to the enduring power of artistic expression.

In summary, the Ming court's support for the arts played a pivotal role in shaping Chinese culture during the dynasty's reign. Through its patronage, the Ming Dynasty fostered a creative environment that led to enduring achievements in literature, painting, ceramics, architecture, and more. This cultural flourishing left an indelible legacy that continues to influence and inspire artists and enthusiasts around the world.

The early Ming Dynasty, particularly the period under the Yongle Emperor (r. 1402-1424), was marked by a remarkable artistic renaissance that left a profound impact on Chinese culture and the world. This era witnessed the flourishing of various art forms, including painting, ceramics, literature, and architecture. Below, we delve into the artistic renaissance during the early Ming Dynasty and its key characteristics:

1. The Yongle Emperor's Patronage:

The Yongle Emperor, Zhu Di, was a fervent patron of the arts and played a pivotal role in the artistic renaissance of the early Ming Dynasty. His reign saw an immense investment in cultural endeavors, making him one of the most significant artistic patrons in Chinese history.

2. The Forbidden City:
One of the most iconic architectural achievements of the Ming Dynasty was the construction of the Forbidden City in Beijing. The Yongle Emperor initiated this grand project, which would serve as the imperial palace for centuries. The architectural design of the Forbidden City showcased the Ming Dynasty's emphasis on symmetry, precision, and intricate details.

3. Porcelain Production:
Ming blue and white porcelain, with its distinctive blue motifs on a white background, became highly sought after both domestically and internationally. The imperial kilns at Jingdezhen, supported by the court, produced exquisite porcelain that reflected the Ming Dynasty's artistic prowess. These ceramics were prized for their craftsmanship and aesthetics.

4. Literature and Encyclopedias:
Under the Yongle Emperor's sponsorship, the Ming Dynasty compiled the Yongle Encyclopedia, an extensive collection of knowledge and texts. This monumental work represented a significant achievement in Chinese literature and scholarship. It covered a wide range of subjects, from history and philosophy to technology and culture.

5. Literature and Drama:
The early Ming Dynasty was a golden age for Chinese literature and drama. Playwrights like Guan Hanqing and Tang Xianzu created timeless works, and the Kunqu opera emerged as a refined form of traditional Chinese opera. The court actively supported theatrical productions and encouraged literary innovation.

6. Painting and Calligraphy:
Painting and calligraphy reached new heights during the early Ming Dynasty. The court-sponsored renowned artists, and academies were established to nurture talent. Artists

like Shen Zhou and Wen Zhengming became known for their distinctive styles, and their works are celebrated for their beauty and expressiveness.

7. Classical Gardens:

The Ming emperors were passionate about creating classical Chinese gardens. These meticulously planned landscapes featured intricate pavilions, serene ponds, and carefully arranged flora. Gardens like the Humble Administrator's Garden in Suzhou exemplified the Ming's appreciation for natural beauty and tranquility.

8. Cultural Exchange:

The early Ming Dynasty actively engaged in cultural exchange with neighboring countries, particularly through maritime trade expeditions led by figures like Zheng He. These missions promoted Chinese culture and facilitated the exchange of art, technology, and ideas with regions as far as Africa and the Middle East.

9. Legacy:

The artistic renaissance of the early Ming Dynasty left an enduring legacy. Many of the artistic achievements of this period continued to influence subsequent dynasties and artistic traditions in China. The construction of the Forbidden City, the production of Ming porcelain, and the flourishing of Ming literature and drama remain emblematic of this rich cultural era. In summary, the early Ming Dynasty, under the patronage of the Yongle Emperor, experienced a vibrant artistic renaissance that encompassed various art forms. This period's legacy continues to be celebrated for its contributions to Chinese culture and its enduring influence on art and scholarship. The early Ming Dynasty stands as a testament to the profound impact of artistic patronage on a society's cultural and creative achievements.

Chapter 3: Porcelain and Ceramics: The Ming Blue and White (1400s)

Ming blue and white porcelain is celebrated for its exquisite beauty and is considered one of the most iconic forms of Chinese ceramics. Its origins and techniques represent a significant chapter in the history of Chinese porcelain production. Here, we explore the origins and techniques behind Ming blue and white porcelain:

1. Origins:
The production of blue and white porcelain in China can be traced back to the Tang Dynasty (618-907 AD). However, it was during the Yuan Dynasty (1271-1368) that the practice gained prominence. The Mongol rulers were enthusiastic patrons of ceramic art, and their influence helped pave the way for the Ming Dynasty's mastery of blue and white porcelain.

2. Underglaze Blue:
The distinctive feature of Ming blue and white porcelain is its use of underglaze blue decoration. Underglaze blue refers to the technique of applying cobalt blue pigments directly onto the unfired porcelain. This blue pigment, derived from cobalt oxide, turns a rich blue color when fired in a kiln. The cobalt blue contrasts beautifully with the white porcelain body.

3. Painting Techniques:
The artisans who created Ming blue and white porcelain were skilled painters. They used various brushwork techniques to create intricate and detailed designs. These designs often featured traditional Chinese motifs, such as landscapes, flora, fauna, mythical creatures, and intricate geometric patterns. The painters' precision and artistic flair contributed to the porcelain's visual appeal.

4. Double Firing:

Ming blue and white porcelain typically underwent a double firing process. After the initial firing of the porcelain body and blue pigment, a clear glaze was applied to protect the decoration. The piece was then fired again at a high temperature, allowing the glaze to melt and form a glossy, translucent surface. This double firing process ensured the durability and lustrous finish of the porcelain.

5. Jingdezhen:

Jingdezhen, a city in Jiangxi province, was the epicenter of Ming blue and white porcelain production. It became renowned as the "Porcelain Capital" of China during the Ming Dynasty. The region was rich in porcelain clay and had abundant wood resources for firing kilns, making it an ideal location for ceramic production.

6. Imperial Kilns:

The Ming emperors took a keen interest in blue and white porcelain, and several imperial kilns were established to produce ceramics exclusively for the imperial court. These kilns adhered to the highest standards of craftsmanship and produced some of the most exquisite pieces of Ming blue and white porcelain.

7. Export to the World:

Ming blue and white porcelain gained international fame and was highly sought after by traders and collectors from around the world. It was exported to various regions, including Southeast Asia, the Middle East, and Europe, through the ancient maritime Silk Road and maritime routes.

8. Enduring Legacy:

The legacy of Ming blue and white porcelain endures to this day. Its timeless beauty and artistic craftsmanship continue to captivate art enthusiasts and collectors worldwide. Many collectors prize Ming blue and white porcelain as valuable historical artifacts and examples of China's rich ceramic heritage.

In summary, Ming blue and white porcelain is a testament to the artistry and technical prowess of Chinese ceramicists during the Ming Dynasty. Its origins in earlier dynasties, painting techniques, double firing process, and association with Jingdezhen make it a cherished symbol of China's ceramic heritage. Ming blue and white porcelain remains an iconic and enduring art form celebrated for its beauty and historical significance.

The Ming Dynasty (1368-1644) was a period of remarkable innovation and artistic development in Chinese ceramic production. During this time, Ming potters experimented with various techniques, designs, and styles, leading to the creation of some of the most iconic and prized ceramics in Chinese history. Here, we explore the innovations and styles that characterized Ming ceramic production:

1. Blue and White Porcelain:

Ming blue and white porcelain, as mentioned earlier, is one of the most celebrated innovations of the era. The use of cobalt blue underglaze, combined with intricate painting techniques, allowed for the creation of beautifully decorated ceramics. The distinct blue-and-white color scheme, often featuring intricate landscapes, floral motifs, and geometric patterns, became synonymous with Ming porcelain.

2. Xuande and Chenghua Styles:

Two significant periods within the Ming Dynasty, the Xuande (1426-1435) and Chenghua (1465-1487) reigns, produced ceramics with distinctive styles. Xuande ceramics are known for their elegant simplicity, often featuring sparse, freehand designs. Chenghua porcelain, on the other hand, is characterized by its refinement and delicacy, with meticulously painted motifs and a focus on intricate details.

3. Doucai Porcelain:

Doucai, meaning "contrasting colors," is a technique that gained popularity during the Ming Dynasty. It involves the use of underglaze blue in combination with overglaze enamel colors, allowing for a wider range of hues and intricate designs. Doucai porcelain pieces often feature vibrant, multicolored motifs and were highly prized during the reign of the Chenghua Emperor.

4. Wucai Porcelain:

Wucai, or "five-color" porcelain, was another innovative technique that emerged during the Ming Dynasty. This style incorporated a palette of five colors: red, green, yellow, blue, and black. Wucai ceramics are known for their bright, bold colors and often depict a wide range of subjects, from mythological creatures to floral arrangements.

5. Monochrome Glazes:

While many Ming ceramics are famous for their intricate designs, monochrome glazes also gained popularity. These ceramics featured single-colored glazes of various hues, including celadon, turquoise, and lavender. These monochromatic pieces showcased the Ming potters' mastery of glaze techniques and the subtlety of color variation.

6. Jiajing and Wanli Styles:

The Jiajing (1521-1567) and Wanli (1573-1620) reigns of the Ming Dynasty saw the continued evolution of ceramic styles. Jiajing porcelain is known for its experimentation with glaze effects, such as "chicken-bone" glaze. Wanli porcelain, on the other hand, featured a wide range of motifs, including dragons, phoenixes, and Buddhist symbols.

7. Scholar's Objects:

Ming ceramic production included a category known as "scholar's objects." These were items designed for use in scholarly pursuits, such as brush pots, incense burners, and water droppers. These objects often featured artistic and literary themes, making them highly prized by scholars and collectors.

8. Imperial Kilns and Patronage:

The Ming emperors were enthusiastic patrons of ceramic arts, and they established imperial kilns to produce ceramics exclusively for the imperial court. The standards of craftsmanship and artistic innovation reached new heights in these kilns, producing some of the finest examples of Ming ceramics.

9. Influence on Later Periods:
Ming ceramic styles and innovations had a profound influence on subsequent dynasties and regional ceramic traditions in China and beyond. Ming ceramics continue to inspire contemporary artists and collectors, and they remain highly valued in the world of art and antiques.

In summary, the Ming Dynasty was a period of remarkable innovation and artistic achievement in Chinese ceramic production. From blue and white porcelain to Doucai, Wucai, and various monochrome glazes, the Ming potters' creativity and technical expertise left a lasting legacy in the world of ceramics. The distinct styles and innovations of Ming ceramics continue to be celebrated and admired for their beauty and cultural significance.

Chapter 4: Literature and Poetry: The Ming's Scholarly Pursuits (1400s)

The Ming Dynasty (1368-1644) was a period of great literary achievement in Chinese history. It witnessed the production of significant literary works, poetry, novels, encyclopedias, and essays that left a lasting impact on Chinese culture and literature. Here are some of the literary achievements of the Ming Dynasty:

1. Ming Novels:
The Ming Dynasty is often regarded as the golden age of Chinese fiction. During this period, classical novels were written that continue to be celebrated today. Some notable examples include:

"Journey to the West" (西游记, Xiyouji): Written by Wu Cheng'en, this epic novel tells the story of the Monkey King Sun Wukong and his journey to obtain Buddhist scriptures. It is one of the Four Great Classical Novels of Chinese literature.

"Romance of the Three Kingdoms" (三国演义, Sānguó Yǎnyì): Attributed to Luo Guanzhong, this historical novel portrays the turbulent era of the Three Kingdoms and the heroic deeds of its characters, such as Liu Bei, Cao Cao, and Zhuge Liang.

"Water Margin" (水浒传, Shuǐhǔ Zhuàn): Also known as "Outlaws of the Marsh" or "All Men Are Brothers," this novel, attributed to Shi Nai'an and Luo Guanzhong, tells the story of a band of rebels who become folk heroes during the Song Dynasty.

"The Plum in the Golden Vase" (金瓶梅, Jīnpíng Méi): Written by an anonymous author, this novel is a classic of

Chinese erotic literature. It explores the life and escapades of Ximen Qing, a corrupt merchant.

2. Ming Poetry:

Ming poetry continued the classical traditions of earlier dynasties while also exploring new themes and styles. Some prominent Ming poets include:

Wang Yangming (王阳明): A philosopher and poet, Wang Yangming's poetry reflects his Confucian philosophy and his exploration of the mind's inner workings.

Tang Xianzu (汤显祖): Known for his Kunqu opera plays, Tang Xianzu was also a poet. His poetry often explores themes of love and nature.

Gong Dingzi (龚鼎孳): Gong Dingzi was a renowned poet during the late Ming period. His poetry is known for its elegance and sensitivity.

3. Encyclopedias and Reference Works:

The Ming Dynasty produced several encyclopedic works and reference books that served as valuable sources of knowledge and scholarship. The most notable among them is:

"Yongle Encyclopedia" (永乐大典, Yǒnglè Dàdiǎn): Commissioned by the Yongle Emperor, this massive encyclopedia was a comprehensive compilation of Chinese knowledge, covering topics such as literature, history, medicine, and technology. It contained over 22,000 volumes.

4. Historical Writings:

Ming historians, such as Fan Zhongyan and Ma Duanlin, made significant contributions to the recording and analysis of Chinese history. Their works, like "Jingyi Daifang Lu" and "Wenxian Tongkao," provided valuable insights into the historical events and culture of their times.

5. Essays and Prose:

Ming scholars excelled in essay writing and prose literature. They explored a wide range of topics, from philosophy to art and culture. Some notable essayists of the Ming Dynasty include Yang Shen, Yuan Hongdao, and Xu Wei.

6. Vernacular Literature:

The Ming Dynasty witnessed the popularization of vernacular literature, which made literary works more accessible to a broader audience. Novels and plays began to be written in the vernacular, allowing common people to enjoy and relate to literature.

In summary, the Ming Dynasty was a period of great literary flourishing in China. Its novels, poetry, encyclopedias, and essays continue to be celebrated for their artistic and intellectual contributions. These literary achievements not only enriched Chinese culture but also had a profound and lasting impact on world literature.

Ming literature had a profound and enduring influence on Chinese culture, shaping the way people think, express themselves, and understand their history and society. Here are some key ways in which Ming literature influenced Chinese culture:

1. Literary Canon:

The novels of the Ming Dynasty, particularly "Journey to the West," "Romance of the Three Kingdoms," and "Water Margin," have become part of the Chinese literary canon. They are taught in schools, adapted into various forms of media, and continue to be referenced in contemporary literature and popular culture.

2. Language and Writing Style:

Ming literature played a significant role in shaping the Chinese language and writing style. The classical Chinese used in these texts set a standard for elegant, expressive, and refined writing. Elements of Ming-era language and syntax continue to influence modern Chinese literature.

3. Cultural Identity:
Ming literature explored themes related to Chinese identity, culture, and values. Works like "Romance of the Three Kingdoms" and "Water Margin" delved into historical events and legendary heroes, fostering a sense of cultural continuity and pride among the Chinese people.

4. Morality and Virtue:
Many Ming literary works, including Confucian-inspired writings, emphasized moral values and virtues. These texts contributed to the propagation of Confucian ethics and moral principles throughout Chinese society, reinforcing the importance of virtuous behavior.

5. Folklore and Mythology:
Ming literature incorporated elements of Chinese folklore, mythology, and religious beliefs. Stories of gods, immortals, and legendary creatures found in these texts continue to be part of Chinese cultural and religious practices.

6. Popularization of Vernacular Literature:
Ming literature played a pivotal role in the popularization of vernacular literature, making literary works accessible to a broader audience. This shift toward the vernacular allowed for greater cultural dissemination and engagement among the common people.

7. Cultural References in Art and Media:
Ming literary works, characters, and themes have been a rich source of inspiration for various forms of artistic expression, including traditional Chinese paintings, operas, films, television series, and other media. These references continue to be incorporated into contemporary creative works.

8. Historical Understanding:

Historical novels like "Romance of the Three Kingdoms" and "Water Margin" not only entertained but also educated readers about Chinese history, historical figures, and societal dynamics. They contributed to a deeper understanding of the country's past and cultural heritage.

9. Moral Lessons and Role Models:

Ming literature often presented moral dilemmas and the actions of virtuous characters. These narratives served as educational tools, imparting valuable life lessons and ethical guidance to readers.

10. Scholarly Influence:

Ming essays, encyclopedias, and reference works, such as the "Yongle Encyclopedia," continue to serve as valuable resources for scholars and researchers studying Chinese history, culture, and knowledge.

In summary, Ming literature played a pivotal role in shaping Chinese culture by influencing language, values, cultural identity, and artistic expression. Its enduring legacy can be seen in the continued popularity and reverence for classical Ming-era texts, as well as their ongoing impact on contemporary Chinese culture and society.

Chapter 5: Ming Imperial Gardens and Architecture (1400s)

The Ming Dynasty (1368-1644) was known for its grand imperial gardens, which were meticulously designed and laid out to showcase the emperor's power, love of nature, and appreciation for traditional Chinese aesthetics. These gardens combined natural elements with carefully planned features to create harmonious and visually stunning landscapes. Here are some key aspects of the design and layout of Ming Imperial Gardens:

1. Integration of Nature:
Ming Imperial Gardens were designed to integrate seamlessly with the natural landscape. They often featured natural elements such as hills, rivers, ponds, and forests. These elements were carefully incorporated into the garden's layout, enhancing the sense of harmony with the environment.

2. Symbolism and Meaning:
Ming gardens were rich in symbolism and conveyed deep philosophical and cultural meanings. Elements like rocks, trees, and water bodies were carefully selected for their symbolic significance, often representing elements from Chinese mythology, literature, or Confucian virtues.

3. Central Axis and Symmetry:
Ming gardens typically followed a central axis layout, with the main buildings and features aligned along a central line. This axis emphasized symmetry and balance, creating a sense of order and stability. The central axis often extended from the entrance gate to a central hall or pavilion.

4. Man-Made Structures:
Ming gardens featured an array of man-made structures, including pavilions, halls, bridges, and corridors. These architectural elements were meticulously designed, often incorporating intricate woodwork, colorful tiles, and decorative details.

5. Water Features:
Water played a central role in Ming Imperial Gardens. Ponds, lakes, and streams were strategically placed to reflect the sky and surrounding landscape, creating a sense of expansiveness and

tranquility. Water also symbolized the flow of time and life's journey.

6. Rockeries and Stones:
Ming gardens often included artificial rockeries and carefully arranged stones. These rock formations were designed to mimic the rugged beauty of natural landscapes and were used to create visual interest and a sense of scale within the garden.

7. Plantings and Vegetation:
Carefully selected trees, shrubs, and flowers were planted throughout the gardens to provide color, fragrance, and seasonal variation. Traditional Chinese garden plants like bamboo, plum blossoms, and lotus were commonly featured.

8. Thematic Areas:
Ming gardens were often divided into thematic areas or courtyards, each with its own distinctive design and purpose. These areas might be devoted to different types of plants, architectural styles, or cultural themes.

9. Enclosed Spaces and Privacy:
Ming Imperial Gardens were designed to offer secluded and private spaces for the emperor and his family. High walls, lattice screens, and strategically placed vegetation provided privacy while allowing glimpses of the surrounding beauty.

10. Preservation and Restoration:
Today, many Ming Imperial Gardens have been designated as UNESCO World Heritage Sites and have undergone extensive preservation and restoration efforts. These efforts aim to maintain the gardens' historical authenticity while ensuring their continued enjoyment by visitors.

Ming Imperial Gardens remain important cultural and historical landmarks in China, offering a window into the aesthetics, philosophy, and lifestyle of the Ming Dynasty. Their design principles, rooted in traditional Chinese culture, continue to influence contemporary landscape architecture and garden design. Ming architecture is renowned for its grandeur, sophistication, and adherence to traditional Chinese design principles. During the Ming Dynasty (1368-1644), a wide range of architectural structures were built, including temples, palaces, city walls, and gardens. Here, we explore the architectural features and characteristics of Ming architecture, from temples to palaces:

1. Traditional Chinese Elements:
Ming architecture retained many traditional Chinese architectural elements, including the use of wooden structures, upturned eaves, curved roofs, and intricate wooden brackets known as dougong. These elements contributed to the distinctively Chinese appearance of Ming buildings.

2. Imperial Palaces:
The most famous example of Ming palace architecture is the Forbidden City in Beijing. This vast complex of palaces and halls served as the imperial palace of the Ming and Qing dynasties. It features a symmetrical layout, large courtyards, decorative tile roofs, and numerous halls for official ceremonies and administrative functions.

3. Temple Architecture:
Ming temples were places of worship and meditation. They often featured prominent pagodas, multi-tiered towers with curved roofs. The Hall of Prayer for Good Harvests in the Temple of Heaven, also in Beijing, is a remarkable example of Ming temple architecture.

4. Use of Courtyards:
Ming architecture made extensive use of courtyards, which provided both aesthetic appeal and functional purposes. Courtyards allowed for better ventilation and lighting while creating serene and secluded spaces within larger complexes.

5. Wooden Architecture:
Ming architecture predominantly used wood as the primary building material. Timber-framed structures were common, and the use of mortise and tenon joinery techniques allowed for flexibility and stability in construction.

6. Decorative Features:
Ming architecture was characterized by ornate decorative features. Elaborate carvings, colorful glazed tiles, and intricate lattice work adorned the exteriors and interiors of buildings. Dragon motifs, floral patterns, and historical scenes were commonly depicted in architectural decorations.

7. Roof Styles:
Ming roofs were typically sloped with upturned eaves and colorful glazed tiles. The number of tiers and the curvature of the roof often signified the building's importance. Important structures, such as imperial palaces, would have more tiers and greater curvature.

8. Temple Layout:
Temples in the Ming Dynasty were designed with careful attention to layout and symbolism. The main hall, dedicated to a particular deity, was often situated at the rear of the temple complex, emphasizing the sacred nature of the space. Courtyards, gardens, and secondary halls were used to create a sense of order and tranquility.

9. Use of Gardens:
Gardens were an integral part of Ming architecture, providing a harmonious and natural setting for buildings. Ming gardens featured classical elements like ponds, bridges, rockeries, and meticulously arranged plants, creating serene and picturesque landscapes.

10. City Walls and Gates:
Ming city walls and gates were constructed for defense and security. These massive structures were often made of stone and brick, with imposing gate towers and watchtowers. They were designed to withstand attacks and were equipped with defensive features such as arrow slits.

11. Preservation and Restoration:
Many Ming architectural treasures have been preserved and restored over the centuries. Restoration efforts aim to maintain the historical authenticity of these structures while ensuring their safety and accessibility to visitors. Ming architecture represents a remarkable fusion of traditional Chinese design principles, technical innovation, and artistic expression. Its enduring legacy can be seen in the preservation of iconic Ming-era structures and the influence it continues to exert on contemporary Chinese architectural design.

Chapter 6: Silk, Textiles, and Fashion (1400s - 1500s)

During the Ming Dynasty (1368-1644), silk production in China continued to flourish, building upon centuries of expertise and innovation. Silk was a highly prized commodity both within China and for trade along the Silk Road and with foreign nations. Here is an overview of silk production during the Ming Dynasty:

1. Sericulture:
Sericulture, the cultivation of silkworms (Bombyx mori), remained a vital component of silk production during the Ming Dynasty. Silk farmers carefully tended to the silkworms' life cycle, from hatching to cocoon formation. Mulberry leaves were the primary food source for silkworms, and special attention was paid to their diet and health.

2. Cocoon Harvesting:
When the silkworms completed their cocoon stage, the cocoons were carefully harvested. The cocoons were then boiled or soaked in hot water to soften the sericin, a protein that holds the cocoon threads together.

3. Reeling and Spinning:
After boiling, the softened cocoon threads were unwound, or "reeled," from the cocoons. These long threads of raw silk were then twisted together to create stronger strands. The spinning process produced spools of silk thread ready for weaving.

4. Weaving:
Skilled artisans wove silk threads into various types of fabric, such as satin, brocade, damask, and taffeta. Ming Dynasty silk fabrics were renowned for their quality, sheen, and intricate designs. Weavers often created intricate patterns, floral motifs, and scenes from Chinese folklore and history.

5. Dyeing and Coloration:
Dyeing techniques during the Ming Dynasty were highly advanced. Various natural and plant-based dyes were used to achieve a wide range of colors. Ming silks were known for their vibrant and lasting hues.

6. Embroidery:
The Ming Dynasty was famous for its intricate silk embroidery, which was applied to clothing, accessories, and decorative items. Skilled embroiderers used silk thread to create detailed designs, often depicting nature, animals, and traditional Chinese symbols.

7. Trade and Export:
Silk production during the Ming Dynasty played a significant role in China's trade with other nations. The famous maritime explorer Zheng He, during his voyages in the early 15th century, is believed to have carried silk and other Chinese goods to foreign lands.

8. Imperial Patronage:
The Ming emperors were known for their patronage of the silk industry. They often ordered the production of elaborate silk garments for court officials, and sumptuary laws regulated who could wear certain types of silk fabrics.

9. Quality Control:
Ming authorities established standards and quality control measures to ensure the production of high-quality silk. Silk workshops were monitored, and inspectors would check for the correct weaving techniques and the use of proper dyes.

10. Legacy:
Ming Dynasty silk production left a lasting legacy in the history of Chinese textiles. The tradition of sericulture and silk weaving continued into subsequent dynasties and remains an important part of China's cultural heritage.

Ming Dynasty silk was not only a symbol of luxury and refinement but also a testament to China's expertise in sericulture and textile production. Today, silk from this period is highly prized by collectors and historians, and the techniques developed during the Ming Dynasty continue to influence modern silk production in China and beyond.

During the Ming Dynasty (1368-1644), Chinese fashion and dress codes underwent significant changes and developments that reflected the culture, social structure, and values of the time. Here is an overview of fashion and dress codes in Ming China:

1. Robes and Gowns:

The most common attire for both men and women during the Ming Dynasty was the robe, known as "pao" for men and "ruqun" for women. These robes were typically made of silk, and the quality and color of the silk indicated one's social status. Bright and vibrant colors were popular, and clothing was often adorned with intricate embroidery.

2. Social Hierarchy and Dress:

Ming society had a strict social hierarchy, and dress codes played a role in distinguishing one's social rank. Sumptuary laws regulated what colors and styles of clothing people of different social classes could wear. The emperor and his officials had the privilege of wearing yellow, which was reserved for the highest authority.

3. Hairstyles:

Hairstyles in Ming China were elaborate and often indicated one's marital status and age. For example, married women typically wore their hair in a braided bun, while unmarried women left their hair loose. Men often sported long, coiled hairpieces called "bianfa" as a sign of their status.

4. Accessories:

Accessories were an important part of Ming fashion. Women wore hairpins, combs, and jewelry made of precious metals and gemstones. Men adorned their attire with decorative fasteners and accessories. Both genders used folding fans and carried pouches and handkerchiefs.

5. Footwear:

Foot binding was practiced during the Ming Dynasty, particularly among women of higher social classes. Bound feet required specialized footwear, such as small embroidered shoes. Men typically wore cloth or leather shoes, with different styles for different occasions.

6. Outerwear:

In colder weather, people wore additional layers of clothing, including padded jackets and coats. These outer garments were often lined with silk and elaborately decorated.

7. Imperial Court Dress:

The imperial court had its own set of dress codes and ceremonial attire. Emperors wore dragon robes, which featured intricate dragon motifs and were symbolic of imperial authority. Officials' robes were adorned with rank badges known as "buzi."

8. Regional Variations:
Ming China was vast, and regional variations in clothing existed. Different provinces and ethnic groups had their own traditional clothing styles and designs, influenced by local customs and climate.

9. Changes in Fashion:
Fashion trends evolved during the Ming Dynasty, with changes in clothing styles and accessories reflecting shifts in aesthetics and cultural values. Ming fashion often emphasized modesty and balance in design.

10. Legacy:
The clothing and fashion of the Ming Dynasty continue to influence traditional Chinese attire and cultural celebrations today. Traditional Chinese wedding attire, for example, often draws inspiration from Ming-era styles.

11. Preservation:
Some Ming-era clothing and accessories have been preserved and can be found in museums and private collections. These artifacts provide valuable insights into the fashion of the period.

The clothing and fashion of the Ming Dynasty reflect not only the aesthetic tastes of the time but also the complex social structure and cultural values of Chinese society during this era. Ming fashion continues to be celebrated and appreciated for its beauty and historical significance.

Chapter 7: Ming Artisans and Craftsmanship (1500s)

The late Ming Dynasty (1368-1644) witnessed a remarkable period of artistic flourishing in China. During this time, various forms of art, including painting, ceramics, literature, and decorative arts, experienced significant developments and innovations. Here is an overview of the artistic achievements and cultural trends that defined the late Ming Dynasty:

1. Ming Painting:

Landscape Painting: The late Ming period is often referred to as the "Great Age of Chinese Landscape Painting." Artists like Dong Qichang and Shen Zhou explored new approaches to landscape painting, emphasizing expressive brushwork and the depiction of inner emotions.

Bird-and-Flower Painting: Artists like Xu Wei and Chen Hongshou made significant contributions to bird-and-flower painting during this period. Their works featured vivid depictions of birds, flowers, and insects, often accompanied by poems and calligraphy.

Individualistic Styles: Late Ming painters embraced individualism and self-expression. Artists sought to convey their personal emotions and experiences through their artwork, leading to diverse and innovative painting styles.

2. Porcelain and Ceramics:

The late Ming period is celebrated for its contributions to Chinese porcelain and ceramics. The famous "Ming Blue and White" porcelain, characterized by intricate blue patterns on a white background, reached its peak during this time.

Jingdezhen, known as the "Porcelain Capital" of China, continued to produce high-quality porcelain items, including vases, plates, and bowls, which were sought after both domestically and for export.

3. Literature:

Ming literature witnessed the development of vernacular Chinese as a literary language. The novel "Journey to the West" by Wu

Cheng'en and "The Plum in the Golden Vase" by Lanling Xiaoxiao Sheng are considered masterpieces of Ming fiction.

Poetry remained an integral part of Ming literature, with notable poets like Tao Yuanming and Yuan Hongdao contributing to the literary landscape.

4. Calligraphy:

Calligraphy continued to be a highly regarded art form in the late Ming Dynasty. Calligraphers like Dong Qichang and Zhu Yunming developed distinctive calligraphic styles that are still studied and appreciated today.

5. Furniture and Decorative Arts:

The late Ming period saw the production of exquisite furniture and decorative arts. Ming-style furniture, characterized by its elegant design and craftsmanship, is highly valued by collectors and enthusiasts.

Decorative arts, such as lacquerware, cloisonné, and jade carvings, also thrived during this time, reflecting the Ming Dynasty's appreciation for fine craftsmanship and aesthetics.

6. Cultural Exchange:

The late Ming Dynasty was marked by increased cultural exchange with foreign nations, particularly through maritime exploration and trade. The voyages of Zheng He and diplomatic missions facilitated cross-cultural interactions and the exchange of art, artifacts, and ideas.

7. Influence on Subsequent Dynasties:

The artistic achievements of the late Ming Dynasty had a lasting impact on later Chinese dynasties and artistic traditions. Many Ming artistic styles and techniques continued to be practiced and refined in the Qing Dynasty and beyond.

8. Preservation and Legacy:

Despite the passage of time, many late Ming artworks and artifacts have been preserved and can be found in museums and private collections worldwide. These items provide valuable insights into the artistic and cultural achievements of the period.

The late Ming Dynasty stands as a testament to China's rich artistic heritage and its ability to produce some of the most iconic and enduring artworks in Chinese history. The period's emphasis on individualism, self-expression, and cultural exchange contributed to the diversity and vibrancy of late Ming art.

During the Ming Dynasty (1368-1644), artisans played a crucial role in Chinese society, contributing to various aspects of culture, economy, and daily life. Their craftsmanship and skills were highly valued, and they were an integral part of Ming society. Here is an overview of the role of artisans in Ming society:

1. Craftsmanship and Skill Development:

Artisans in Ming China were highly skilled individuals who had often undergone years of apprenticeship to master their craft. They excelled in various fields, including ceramics, metalwork, woodworking, weaving, embroidery, and more.

2. Artistic Expression:

Artisans were responsible for producing a wide range of artistic and utilitarian items. They created beautiful and functional objects, such as porcelain vases, lacquerware, silk fabrics, carved furniture, and intricate jewelry. These items often featured exquisite designs and craftsmanship, reflecting the Ming Dynasty's appreciation for aesthetics.

3. Ceramics and Porcelain Production:

Artisans working in ceramics and porcelain production were especially renowned during the Ming Dynasty. They created exquisite porcelain items, including vases, bowls, plates, and figurines. The famous "Ming Blue and White" porcelain, characterized by blue patterns on a white background, was highly sought after both domestically and for export.

4. Furniture and Woodworking:

Woodworkers and furniture artisans crafted elegant and functional Ming-style furniture. These items were known for their intricate joinery techniques, design aesthetics, and durability. Ming-style furniture remains highly valued by collectors today.

5. Textile Production:

Artisans involved in textile production, including weavers and embroiderers, produced high-quality silk fabrics and garments. The Ming Dynasty was known for its vibrant silk textiles, often adorned with intricate patterns and designs.

6. Calligraphy and Painting:

Artisans skilled in calligraphy and painting were respected for their ability to create beautiful artworks. Calligraphers used brush and ink to create expressive and artistic characters, while painters produced landscapes, portraits, and other artistic pieces.

7. Preservation of Tradition:
Artisans played a vital role in preserving traditional Chinese craftsmanship and passing it down through generations. They adhered to established techniques and styles while also innovating and experimenting with new designs.

8. Economic Contribution:
Artisans contributed significantly to the Ming Dynasty's economy. The production of fine crafts, ceramics, textiles, and other goods not only provided livelihoods for artisans and their families but also generated income through trade and commerce.

9. Cultural Exchange:
Some artisans, such as those involved in porcelain production, were involved in trade and cultural exchange with foreign nations. Ming artisans' works were highly sought after in international markets, contributing to China's global reputation for craftsmanship.

10. Artisan Guilds: - Artisan guilds and organizations were prevalent during the Ming Dynasty. These guilds provided support, training, and protection for artisans, ensuring the continuation of their craft traditions.

11. Legacy: - The legacy of Ming Dynasty artisans is still evident in the appreciation of Ming-style furniture, porcelain, textiles, and artwork. Their contributions continue to influence Chinese craftsmanship and artistic traditions in modern times.

Artisans in Ming society were not only skilled craftsmen and women but also cultural custodians, preserving and advancing traditional craftsmanship while contributing to the beauty and cultural richness of the era. Their work remains celebrated and cherished for its enduring quality and artistic excellence.

Chapter 8: Cultural Exchanges and Foreign Diplomacy (1500s - 1600s)

During the Ming Dynasty (1368-1644), China engaged in various diplomatic relations and interactions with neighboring states and foreign powers. Ming Dynasty diplomacy was marked by a combination of assertiveness, cultural exchange, and the pursuit of regional stability. Here is an overview of the Ming Dynasty's diplomatic relations:

1. Diplomatic Missions and Envoys:
The Ming Dynasty conducted diplomatic missions and sent envoys to neighboring states and foreign powers to maintain and strengthen diplomatic ties. These missions were often led by high-ranking officials and ambassadors.

2. Tributary System:
The Ming Dynasty continued the practice of the tributary system, in which neighboring states paid tribute to the Ming court in exchange for various privileges, including trade and diplomatic recognition. This system helped maintain regional stability and acknowledged China's superior status as the "Middle Kingdom."

3. Relations with Korea:
China's diplomatic relations with Korea, particularly the Joseon Dynasty, were important during the Ming Dynasty. The two states maintained a close and mutually beneficial relationship, with frequent diplomatic missions and cultural exchanges.

4. Relations with Vietnam:
The Ming Dynasty sought to exert influence in Vietnam, which was divided into multiple regions. Ming China supported various Vietnamese factions in their struggles for power. However, relations were complex due to internal Vietnamese conflicts.

5. Relations with Japan:
The Ming Dynasty had limited diplomatic relations with Japan, but it did send diplomatic missions to the Japanese court. These missions aimed to strengthen trade ties and cultural exchange but were not always successful.

6. Diplomacy with Central Asia:
The Ming Dynasty sought to maintain diplomatic ties and control over the Silk Road trade routes that connected China to Central Asia, the Middle East, and Europe. Diplomatic missions were sent to negotiate with neighboring states and to secure these trade routes.

7. Diplomatic Missions to the West:
Ming Dynasty China sent exploratory missions led by Admiral Zheng He to the Indian Ocean and beyond, reaching as far as East Africa. These missions were intended to establish diplomatic and trade relations with countries in the Indian Ocean region.

8. Relations with Mongolia and the Mongol Yuan Dynasty:
The Ming Dynasty maintained diplomatic relations with the Mongol Yuan Dynasty, which had ruled China before the Ming. While tensions existed, diplomatic efforts were made to secure the northern border and prevent Mongol incursions.

9. Cultural Exchange:
Diplomatic missions often involved the exchange of cultural artifacts, books, and scholars. This cultural exchange contributed to the spread of Chinese culture and knowledge to neighboring regions.

10. Preservation of Borders: - Ming China placed a strong emphasis on defending its borders and maintaining control over its territory. Diplomacy was often used to secure peaceful relations with neighboring states and prevent conflicts.

11. Legacy: - The Ming Dynasty's diplomatic efforts helped maintain regional stability, secure trade routes, and preserve China's cultural influence in neighboring regions. These diplomatic practices and principles would continue to shape Chinese foreign relations in later dynasties.

The diplomatic relations of the Ming Dynasty played a significant role in shaping China's position in East Asia and beyond. While some interactions were marked by conflict and competition, others fostered cultural exchange and cooperation, leaving a lasting legacy on China's foreign policy and regional influence.

The Ming Dynasty (1368-1644) played a crucial role in Asian diplomacy and exerted significant influence over its neighboring countries and regions. Ming China's diplomatic strategies were characterized by a combination of cultural exchange, the use of the tributary system, and the pursuit of regional stability. Here is an overview of the Ming Dynasty's role in Asian diplomacy:

1. Tributary System:

The Ming Dynasty continued the practice of the tributary system, which was a hierarchical diplomatic framework where neighboring states recognized China as the superior power and paid tribute in exchange for various privileges, including trade and diplomatic recognition. This system helped maintain regional stability and acknowledged China's central role in Asia.

2. Relations with Korea (Joseon Dynasty):

China's diplomatic relations with Korea, specifically the Joseon Dynasty, were especially close during the Ming Dynasty. The two nations maintained a mutually beneficial relationship characterized by cultural exchange, trade, and the exchange of envoys. This relationship contributed to stability in East Asia.

3. Relations with Vietnam (Đại Việt):

The Ming Dynasty sought to exert influence in Vietnam, which was divided into several regions at the time. China supported various Vietnamese factions in their power struggles, and Vietnamese rulers often paid tribute to the Ming court. However, relations were complex due to internal Vietnamese conflicts.

4. Relations with Japan (Muromachi Period):

Ming China had diplomatic interactions with Japan, but these relations were not as extensive as those with Korea and Vietnam. Diplomatic missions were sent to Japan to strengthen trade ties and cultural exchange, but they did not always lead to lasting cooperation.

5. Diplomacy with Central Asia and Silk Road States:

The Ming Dynasty aimed to maintain diplomatic ties and control over the Silk Road trade routes that connected China to Central Asia, the Middle East, and Europe. Diplomatic missions were dispatched to negotiate with neighboring states and ensure the security of these trade routes.

6. Diplomatic Missions to the West:

One of the most renowned aspects of Ming Dynasty diplomacy was the series of naval expeditions led by Admiral Zheng He to the Indian Ocean and beyond. These expeditions aimed to establish diplomatic and trade relations with countries in the Indian Ocean region and showcase China's power and influence.

7. Cultural Exchange:

Diplomatic missions often involved the exchange of cultural artifacts, books, and scholars. Ming China's cultural influence extended to neighboring regions, with Confucianism, Chinese language, and Chinese art and literature being disseminated.

8. Defense of Borders:

Ming China placed a strong emphasis on protecting its borders and defending its territory. Diplomacy was frequently used to secure peaceful relations with neighboring states and prevent conflicts that could threaten China's security.

9. Legacy:

The Ming Dynasty's diplomatic strategies and interactions left a lasting legacy on Chinese foreign relations. The principles of the tributary system, cultural exchange, and the pursuit of regional stability continued to shape China's foreign policy in subsequent dynasties.

The Ming Dynasty's diplomatic efforts played a crucial role in shaping the political and cultural landscape of Asia. Through its diplomatic interactions, China was able to establish itself as a dominant regional power and exert a lasting influence on its neighbors.

Chapter 9: Decline and the Arrival of the Qing Dynasty (1600s - 1644)

During the Ming Dynasty (1368-1644), while China experienced periods of stability and cultural flourishing, it also faced significant internal challenges and issues, including corruption. These challenges contributed to both the decline of the dynasty and the Ming's struggle to maintain effective governance. Here are some key aspects of the internal challenges and corruption during the Ming Dynasty:

1. Political Corruption:
Corruption among government officials was a persistent issue during the Ming Dynasty. Bureaucrats and officials at various levels of the government were known to engage in bribery, embezzlement, and nepotism, which undermined the effectiveness of the state.

2. Eunuch Influence:
Eunuchs, who served the imperial family and had significant access to the emperor, often wielded considerable political power. Some eunuchs used their influence for personal gain, engaging in corrupt practices and interfering in government affairs.

3. Taxation and Fiscal Mismanagement:
The Ming Dynasty faced financial difficulties due to the costs associated with maintaining a large bureaucracy and the construction of projects like the Great Wall. Heavy taxation and fiscal mismanagement contributed to social unrest and discontent among the population.

4. Land Distribution Issues:
Unequal land distribution and land-grabbing by the wealthy elite led to land disputes and social unrest. Peasant uprisings, such as the Red Turban Rebellion, were partly fueled by these grievances.

5. Factionalism and Court Intrigue:
Court factions and power struggles among officials and eunuchs were common during the Ming Dynasty. These factions often put

personal interests ahead of the welfare of the state, leading to instability.

6. Loss of the Mandate of Heaven:
The concept of the "Mandate of Heaven" was central to Chinese dynastic rule. When natural disasters, famines, and social unrest occurred, they were sometimes seen as signs that the ruling dynasty had lost the Mandate of Heaven, which eroded the legitimacy of the Ming rulers.

7. The Jiajing Emperor and the "Rule of Terror":
The Jiajing Emperor's reign (1521-1567) was marked by a repressive and authoritarian regime known as the "Rule of Terror." His erratic behavior and persecution of officials contributed to internal turmoil and instability.

8. Peasant Rebellions:
Throughout the Ming Dynasty, there were several major peasant uprisings, including the Red Turban Rebellion (1351-1368) and the later Li Zicheng-led rebellion (1639-1644). These rebellions were fueled by a combination of economic hardship, social inequality, and government corruption.

9. Decline in Military Strength:
While the Ming Dynasty initially maintained a strong military, it faced challenges in maintaining the Great Wall and defending the northern border against the Mongols and Manchu invasions. Corruption and neglect in the military contributed to vulnerability in these areas.

10. Fall of the Ming Dynasty: - Ultimately, the internal challenges, corruption, and external pressures from the Manchu Qing Dynasty led to the fall of the Ming Dynasty in 1644. The Chongzhen Emperor's inability to address these issues effectively played a role in the dynasty's downfall.

Despite its cultural achievements and contributions, the Ming Dynasty struggled with internal challenges that weakened its governance and ultimately led to its decline. These issues serve as a reminder of the complex factors that can influence the rise and fall of dynasties in Chinese history.

The rise of the Manchus and the Qing conquest marked a significant turning point in Chinese history. The Qing Dynasty

(1644-1912) was established by the Manchu people, who originated in the northeastern region of China known as Manchuria. Their conquest of China marked the end of the Ming Dynasty and the beginning of the Qing Dynasty. Here is an overview of the rise of the Manchus and their conquest of China:

1. Emergence of the Manchu People:
The Manchus were originally a semi-nomadic people native to the region of Manchuria, located northeast of the Great Wall of China. They had their own distinct language, culture, and political organization.

2. Ming-Qing Transition:
During the late Ming Dynasty, China faced internal challenges, including political corruption, economic instability, and social unrest. The Ming government's inability to address these issues weakened its rule.

3. Li Zicheng's Rebellion:
The Ming Dynasty faced a serious threat from Li Zicheng, a former Ming official who led a peasant rebellion known as the "Shun Dynasty" (1639-1644). The rebellion contributed to the destabilization of the Ming Dynasty.

4. Manchu Seizure of Beijing:
In 1644, Li Zicheng captured Beijing, the capital of the Ming Dynasty, prompting the Chongzhen Emperor to commit suicide. During this turmoil, the Manchus saw an opportunity to advance southward.

5. Establishment of the Qing Dynasty:
In June 1644, the Manchu leader Nurhaci's son, Dorgon, and his forces captured Beijing and declared the establishment of the Qing Dynasty. They claimed the "Mandate of Heaven" and ruled in the name of the last Ming emperor, who was still alive but had abdicated.

6. Ming Loyalist Resistance:
Despite the Qing conquest, Ming loyalists continued to resist Qing rule in southern China. The Southern Ming Dynasty, led by figures like Zhu Yujian and Zheng Chenggong (Koxinga), resisted Qing rule for several decades.

7. Consolidation of Qing Rule:

The Qing Dynasty implemented policies to consolidate their rule over China, including efforts to win over the Chinese elite and maintain the structure of the imperial bureaucracy. They also expanded their territories, notably into Taiwan, Mongolia, and Tibet.

8. Qing Policies and Society:
The Qing Dynasty implemented a set of policies known as "Manchu Banner System," which integrated Manchu and Chinese societies. They practiced religious tolerance and promoted Confucianism while preserving their own culture and traditions.

9. Kangxi and Qianlong Eras:
The Qing Dynasty experienced its zenith during the Kangxi (1661-1722) and Qianlong (1735-1796) emperors' reigns. These periods saw stability, territorial expansion, and cultural flourishing.

10. Qing Decline: - Over time, the Qing Dynasty faced internal challenges, including corruption, social unrest, and foreign pressures, notably from Western colonial powers. These challenges contributed to its eventual decline.

11. End of the Qing Dynasty: - The Qing Dynasty faced numerous internal and external challenges in the 19th and early 20th centuries, including the Opium Wars, Taiping Rebellion, and Boxer Rebellion. These events led to the Qing Dynasty's eventual downfall, with the abdication of the last Qing emperor, Puyi, in 1912, marking the end of imperial rule in China.

The rise of the Manchus and the establishment of the Qing Dynasty had a profound impact on China's history and culture. The Qing Dynasty would go on to rule China for nearly three centuries, making it one of the longest-reigning dynasties in Chinese history.

Chapter 10: The Ming Dynasty's Enduring Cultural Legacy

The preservation of Ming cultural heritage has been a significant endeavor in China's history, as the Ming Dynasty (1368-1644) left a lasting impact on various aspects of Chinese culture, including art, literature, architecture, and more. Over the centuries, successive dynasties and governments have recognized the value of preserving this heritage. Here are some key aspects of the preservation of Ming cultural heritage:

1. Architectural Legacy:
Many Ming architectural wonders, including the Forbidden City in Beijing and the Temple of Heaven, have been meticulously preserved. These structures showcase Ming-era architectural styles, with their grandeur, symmetry, and intricate details.

2. Restoration Efforts:
The Chinese government and conservation organizations have invested in the restoration and maintenance of Ming-era architectural sites. Skilled craftsmen and preservationists work to ensure that these historical treasures are kept in their original glory.

3. UNESCO World Heritage Sites:
Several Ming-era architectural complexes have been designated as UNESCO World Heritage Sites, such as the Forbidden City, the Ming Tombs, and the Temple of Heaven. This recognition underscores their global cultural significance and the importance of their preservation.

4. Museums and Cultural Institutions:
Museums throughout China house collections of Ming Dynasty art, including ceramics, paintings, calligraphy, and furniture. These institutions play a crucial role in safeguarding and displaying Ming cultural artifacts for the public.

5. Art Conservation:
Ming-era artworks, particularly porcelain and ceramics, are highly regarded for their craftsmanship and aesthetics. Conservation efforts ensure that these delicate pieces are protected from deterioration and damage.

6. Cultural Festivals:
Traditional festivals and events that have their roots in the Ming Dynasty continue to be celebrated. These include the Lantern Festival, Mid-Autumn Festival, and Double Ninth Festival. Preserving these cultural traditions helps maintain a connection to the Ming era.

7. Literature and Scholarship:
Ming-era literature, including classic novels like "Journey to the West" and "Romance of the Three Kingdoms," remains influential. Scholars and researchers continue to study and promote these literary works, ensuring their continued relevance.

8. Calligraphy and Painting:
The Ming Dynasty produced renowned calligraphers and painters. Their works are preserved in museums and collections, and calligraphy and painting techniques from the Ming era continue to be studied and practiced by artists today.

9. Educational Initiatives:
Educational programs and initiatives emphasize the importance of Ming culture in Chinese history. Schools and universities offer courses in Ming history, art, and culture to foster a deeper understanding and appreciation.

10. Cultural Tourism: - Many Ming-era sites have become popular tourist destinations, drawing both domestic and international visitors. Revenue generated from tourism often contributes to the preservation and maintenance of historical sites.

11. Conservation Laws and Regulations: - The Chinese government has implemented laws and regulations to protect cultural heritage sites and artifacts. These legal frameworks help prevent looting, vandalism, and unauthorized alterations to historical sites.

The preservation of Ming cultural heritage reflects China's commitment to its rich history and its recognition of the Ming Dynasty's enduring cultural legacy. These efforts ensure that future generations can appreciate and learn from the achievements of this influential period in Chinese history.

The Ming Dynasty (1368-1644) had a profound and lasting influence on subsequent dynasties in China, as well as on Chinese culture, art, and governance. Its impact extended far beyond its own era, shaping the course of Chinese history in numerous ways. Here are some of the key aspects of the Ming Dynasty's influence on later dynasties and Chinese society:

1. Architectural Legacy:
The Ming Dynasty's architectural achievements, exemplified by the Forbidden City in Beijing, became a model for subsequent dynasties. Its distinctive style, characterized by grand palaces, courtyards, and intricate design, influenced the architecture of the Qing Dynasty and later periods.

2. Imperial Examination System:
The Ming Dynasty reformed and standardized the civil service examination system, which became a cornerstone of Chinese governance. This system was carried forward and refined by the Qing Dynasty and continued to play a crucial role in selecting government officials.

3. Confucianism and Neo-Confucianism:
The Ming Dynasty placed a strong emphasis on Confucian values and the Neo-Confucian philosophy of Zhu Xi. These principles continued to shape Chinese thought and governance in later dynasties, including the Qing Dynasty.

4. Art and Culture:
Ming-era art, including blue and white porcelain, silk textiles, and paintings, left a lasting legacy. The techniques and aesthetics of Ming art continued to be cherished and emulated in the Qing Dynasty and beyond.

5. Maritime Exploration:
The voyages of Admiral Zheng He during the Ming Dynasty established a tradition of maritime exploration and diplomacy. This legacy influenced later maritime endeavors and trade routes, including those of the Qing Dynasty.

6. Confucian Educational Tradition:
The Ming Dynasty's emphasis on Confucian education and the civil service examination system contributed to the enduring importance of Confucianism in Chinese society. Confucian values continued to shape education and social norms in later dynasties.

7. Cultural Festivals:

Traditional Chinese festivals and customs from the Ming Dynasty, such as the Mid-Autumn Festival and the Lantern Festival, remain integral parts of Chinese culture and are celebrated to this day.

8. Administrative Structure:
The Ming Dynasty's administrative structure and local governance systems influenced later dynasties, including the Qing Dynasty, in their approaches to governing a vast empire.

9. Literature and Philosophy:
Ming-era literary classics, such as "Journey to the West" and "Water Margin," continued to be read and studied in subsequent dynasties. The philosophical works of Ming scholars, including Wang Yangming, had a lasting impact on Chinese thought.

10. Confucian Rituals and Ceremonies: - Ming-era Confucian rituals and ceremonies, including those associated with ancestor worship and state ceremonies, set the precedent for similar practices in later dynasties.

11. Legal Reforms: - Legal reforms implemented during the Ming Dynasty, such as the codification of laws, had a long-lasting influence on the legal systems of subsequent dynasties, contributing to the development of Chinese jurisprudence.

The Ming Dynasty's influence on later dynasties was not only cultural but also structural and philosophical. Its legacy shaped the foundations of Chinese governance, education, and society, leaving an indelible mark on the trajectory of Chinese history for centuries to come.

Ming cultural elements continue to hold a significant place in modern China, contributing to the nation's identity and cultural heritage. These elements, rooted in the Ming Dynasty (1368-1644), have persisted and evolved over the centuries, influencing various aspects of modern Chinese society. Here are some ways in which Ming cultural elements remain relevant in contemporary China:

1. Architecture and Heritage Preservation:
Ming-style architecture, characterized by its grandeur, intricate designs, and use of traditional building materials, continues to influence modern Chinese architecture. Historic sites like the

Forbidden City and the Ming Tombs are well-preserved and serve as important cultural landmarks.

2. Confucian Values:

The Ming Dynasty's emphasis on Confucian values and ethics, including filial piety and respect for authority, continues to shape Chinese society and interpersonal relationships. Confucianism remains a fundamental aspect of Chinese culture and philosophy.

3. Art and Craftsmanship:

Ming-era art forms, such as blue and white porcelain, silk production, and traditional painting styles, are celebrated and practiced in modern China. Skilled artisans continue to produce Ming-inspired artworks, ceramics, and textiles.

4. Traditional Festivals:

Festivals and cultural traditions from the Ming Dynasty, including the Mid-Autumn Festival and the Lantern Festival, are still widely celebrated in modern China. These events strengthen cultural bonds and provide opportunities for family gatherings and community engagement.

5. Calligraphy and Literature:

Ming-era calligraphy and literature, such as the works of scholars like Wang Yangming, remain integral to Chinese literary and academic traditions. Calligraphy, in particular, is a respected art form and a popular practice in contemporary China.

6. Martial Arts and Tai Chi:

Traditional Chinese martial arts and Tai Chi, which have roots in Ming-era martial practices, are still practiced for self-defense, physical fitness, and spiritual development. They are an essential part of Chinese culture and wellness.

7. Confucian Rituals and Ceremonies:

Rituals and ceremonies associated with Confucianism, including ancestral worship and traditional weddings, continue to be observed in modern China. These rituals maintain cultural continuity and connect individuals to their heritage.

8. Cultural Heritage Tourism:

Ming-era historical sites, such as the Forbidden City and the Great Wall, attract millions of tourists annually. This tourism not only contributes to the preservation of cultural heritage but also supports the local economy.

9. Language and Literature:

Classical Chinese literature, including Ming-era texts, remains a part of the Chinese literary canon. Ancient texts and idioms from this period are still studied and referenced in modern Chinese literature and language.

10. Philosophy and Scholarly Traditions: - The philosophical ideas of Ming scholars, particularly Neo-Confucianism, continue to inform modern Chinese thought and intellectual discourse. These traditions are studied in universities and philosophical circles.

11. Tea Culture: - The Ming Dynasty played a crucial role in popularizing tea culture in China. Today, tea remains an integral part of Chinese daily life, with various traditional tea ceremonies and practices.

Ming cultural elements provide a sense of continuity, identity, and pride for modern Chinese society. They remind people of the rich history and heritage that has shaped China's cultural landscape and continue to play a vital role in preserving and celebrating the nation's cultural legacy.

Conclusion

In the pages of "Ancient China 221 BCE - 1644 AD: Emperors to Philosophers & Walls to Masterpieces," we embarked on an extraordinary journey through the rich tapestry of China's history and culture. This four-book bundle has illuminated the fascinating chronicles of a civilization that spanned centuries, from the dawn of the Qin Dynasty to the twilight of the Ming Dynasty. Through the exploration of emperors, philosophers, engineering marvels, and artistic treasures, we have unearthed the essence of Ancient China's enduring legacy.

In Book 1, "Emperors of the Silk Road: Ancient China's Dynastic Saga," we traced the rise and fall of dynasties that ruled with imperial might. From the visionary Qin Shi Huang, who united the warring states and constructed the Great Wall, to the golden era of the Han Dynasty, we witnessed the sweeping changes and pivotal moments that shaped the nation.

Book 2, "Confucianism: The Moral Compass of Ancient China," allowed us to delve into the philosophical realm where the sage Confucius imparted his wisdom and moral teachings. This philosophy, emphasizing the importance of ethical conduct and the five fundamental relationships, became a cornerstone of Chinese culture, influencing governance, education, and social harmony.

The journey continued in Book 3, "The Great Wall: Engineering Marvel of Ancient China." We marveled at the incredible engineering feats that led to the creation of the world's most iconic fortification. From its early defensive structures during the Warring States period to its expansion under the Qin and Han Dynasties, the Great Wall stood as a testament to China's resilience and determination.

Finally, in Book 4, "Ming Dynasty Treasures: Art and Culture in Ancient China," we immersed ourselves in the flourishing art, literature, and craftsmanship of the Ming Dynasty. This period saw the creation of exquisite blue and white porcelain, magnificent imperial gardens, and a thriving cultural renaissance that continues to inspire artists and artisans to this day.

As we close the pages of this bundle, we are reminded that the legacy of Ancient China transcends time and continues to shape the world. Its emperors and philosophers, its monumental walls, and its artistic treasures are threads in the tapestry of human history. This comprehensive exploration has provided us with a deeper understanding of China's rich and diverse heritage, inviting us to appreciate the enduring contributions of a civilization that thrived for over two millennia.

The story of Ancient China is a testament to the ingenuity, creativity, and resilience of a people who left an indelible mark on the world. It is a story of emperors who forged mighty dynasties, philosophers who cultivated timeless wisdom, engineers who built monumental wonders, and artists who crafted masterpieces that continue to captivate hearts and minds. It is a story that will continue to be told and cherished for generations to come.

About A. J. Kingston

A. J. Kingston is a writer, historian, and lover of all things historical. Born and raised in a small town in the United States, A. J. developed a deep appreciation for the past from an early age. She studied history at the university, earning her degree with honors, and went on to write a series of acclaimed books about different periods and topics in history.

A. J.'s writing is characterized by its clarity, evocative language, and meticulous research. She has a particular talent for bringing the lives of ordinary people in the past to life, drawing on diaries, letters, and other documents to create rich and nuanced portraits of people from all walks of life. Her work has been praised for its deep empathy, its attention to detail, and its ability to make history come alive for readers.

In addition to her writing, A. J. is a sought-after speaker and commentator on historical topics. She has given talks and presentations at universities, museums, and other venues, sharing her passion for history with audiences around the world. Her ability to connect with people and make history relevant to their lives has earned her a devoted following and a reputation as one of the most engaging and insightful historical writers of her generation.

A. J.'s writing has been recognized with numerous awards and honors. She lives in California with her family, and continues to write and speak on historical topics.